Adapted to the Lake

American University Studies

Series IX
History

Vol. 141

PETER LANG
New York • San Francisco • Bern • Baltimore
Frankfurt am Main • Berlin • Wien • Paris

Adapted to the Lake

Letters by the Brother Founders of Notre Dame, 1841-1849

Edited and Translated by
George Klawitter

PETER LANG
New York • San Francisco • Bern • Baltimore
Frankfurt am Main • Berlin • Wien • Paris

Library of Congress Cataloging-in-Publication Data

Adapted to the lake : letters by brother founders of Notre Dame, 1841-1849 / [compiled by] George Klawitter.
p. cm. — (American university studies. Series IX, History ; vol. 141)
Includes bibliographical references.
1. University of Notre Dame—History—19th century.
2. Congregation of Holy Cross—History—19th century.
I. Klawitter, George. II. Series.
LD4113.A33 1993 378.772'89—dc20 92-3081
ISBN 0-8204-2181-2 CIP
ISSN 0740-0462

The paper in this book meets the guidelines for permanence and durability of the Committee on Production Guidelines for Book Longevity of the Council on Library Resources.

Printed in the United States of America.

Dedication

Brother Bernard Gervais, CSC

TABLE OF CONTENTS

1848

1849

List of Illustrations

INTRODUCTION

In 1820 at Ruillé-sur-Loir in France, Father James Dujarié organized the Brothers of St. Joseph, a religious group of men intended to help educate a generation of French children left unschooled by the Revolution. Fifteen years later, Dujarié, aged and in poor health, entrusted his community of fifty Brothers to Father Basil Moreau, a seminary professor who had himself organized a band of two priests and two seminarians into an auxiliary unit of clerics for the diocese of Le Mans. In 1837 Moreau joined the two groups, Brothers and priests, headquartering them at Sainte-Croix, a Le Mans suburb, thus bringing into existence the Congregation of (from) Holy Cross (Sainte-Croix). Although the Brothers eventually came to be known as Holy Cross Brothers, they were long referred to within the Community as Brothers of St. Joseph or Josephites. As the Community grew, Moreau was pressured to send missionaries out of France, and in 1839, Celestin de la Hailandière, a bishop newly appointed for the Indiana Territory, begged Moreau for help. Already committed to a foundation in Algiers, Moreau delayed a commitment to Hailandière until the summer of 1841, by which time Moreau had readied a number of religious for the American venture.

On September 13, 1841, seven Holy Cross religious arrived in NewYork City to pursue missionary work. After an arduous trip mostly by river and canal, the seven settled in early October at St. Peter's, near Black Oak Ridge, a small settlement twenty-seven miles east of Vincennes. Of the band Brother Vincent at age 44 was the senior member, sent by Moreau to serve as novice master for the new establishment. Brother Joachim, a tailor aged 32, soon weakened with tuberculosis and died within three years. Brother Lawrence, 26, was a farmer, and Brother Marie, 21, a carpenter. The two youngest, Anselm, 16, and Gatian, 15, were both sent because their intelligence marked them as future teachers capable of learning English quickly. The two teenagers did, in fact, master the language beautifully, as their later letters composed in English verify. The six Brothers were accompanied by their religious superior, Edward Sorin, a young priest aged 27.

Although their missionary work thrived at St. Peter's, the group's interest in starting a college brought them into conflict with Bishop de la Hailandière, who feared their plans would jeopardize the future of a Eudist college in Vincennes. Hailandière offered the St. Peter's colony a tract of land in northern Indiana near the St. Joseph River. Charmed by the offer of property as well as by the prospect of being far away from a rather testy prelate, the Brothers decided to accept the offer. Two of them left St. Peter's in November, 1842, with Father Sorin and five new Brother novices to travel 250 miles to the north in a particularly harsh winter. The remainder of the colony joined them the following February. What they discovered near South Bend excited them: their land nestled two lakes joined by marsh and seemed a beautifully remote area on which to build their college. Under snow the lakes seemed one, so despite its previously being called Ste. Marie des Lacs (St. Mary of the Lakes), it was henceforth known as Notre Dame du Lac (Our Lady of the Lake). Not until 1855 would the land be drained sufficiently to discriminate the two lakes, but by then the name "du Lac" was part of history. In the earliest letter we have from the pioneer Brothers, Brother Francis Xavier, the carpenter, remarks how easily he had become "adapted to the woods" of southern Indiana. No less easily did the Brothers become adapted to the lake[s] at Notre Dame.

Francis Xavier was born at Clermont (Sarthe) in 1820, entered the Community September 5, 1840, became a novice February 2, 1841, and was professed July 25, 1841. The name he first took in the Community was Marie, but he changed it to Francis Xavier in September, 1848, at Notre Dame where he died November 12, 1896, having served the area as undertaker for fifty years. Two days before Francis Xavier died, Brother Bernard Gervais arrived as a postulant at Notre Dame and was sent by the assistant novice master to help dig the grave for the pioneer, who is remembered as "the last survivor of that little band of heroes who changed the bleak forest into a bright fairy-land, and reared on stones cemented with their blood the domes and turrets of our noble college home" (Trahey 83). Bernard Gervais, who would one day compile the general matricule for the Congregation of Holy Cross, thus becomes an important link between the pioneer Brothers and the Congregation in the twentieth-century. Bernard died in 1963.

Readers of these letters may wonder why the title of this collection of letters refers to the Brothers as "founders of Notre Dame" since most of the letters were written far from the campus, written from Vincennes, from Brooklyn, from New Orleans, but anyone who reads the letters carefully will discover that wherever a pioneer Brother was, he longed to be with the Community at Notre Dame, a place formed by the dreams and hard work of more than one man. Thus we must come to understand "founder" in a wide sense of the word. Sorin himself, traditionally considered the "founder" of Notre Dame, realized that he could not have succeeded in his efforts without, for example, Brother Vincent. In his 1861 chronicle, Sorin notes that he had dug a burial vault for Vincent and himself under the nave of the campus church where they are "both to rest in the expectation of a blessed resurrection" (Sorin 274). He refers to Vincent as the "pious patriarch of the Brothers of St. Joseph." Vincent was revered with good cause. Born at Courbeville in 1797, he had entered the Josephites November 1, 1821, and became a novice in August, 1822, under Father Dujarié, the eighteenth novice to receive the habit from the hands of Father Dujarié himself. In his first year in America, he directed a dozen candidates and started a novitiate in which nine novices made their year of probation. Three of these nine died at Notre Dame. He was a member of the Provincial Council almost without interruption until his death, and he was the man usually sent to oversee new foundations. Directing schools in St. Peter's, Brooklyn, and New Orleans, he also served as a baker and commissioner. In 1858 he was named procurator of the American houses. He died at age 93 on July 23, 1890.

No less important to the "founding" of Notre Dame was Brother Lawrence. A farmer and steward, he was sent by Sorin to look for gold in California with Brothers Placidus, Justin, and Gatian in February, 1850. He returned to Notre Dame a year later. At his death in 1873, the Superior General noted, "If anyone is to be named as having contributed more than others by earnest and persevering exertions, both of mind and body, to the development and prosperity of Notre Dame, if I did not do it here, the public voice would declare it, and name Brother Lawrence" (Trahey 72). He was highly popular with the farmers and businessmen in the South Bend area.

The brightest of the early pioneer Brothers is Gatian who was born at Chéméré-le-roi (Mayenne) in 1826, became a novice August 23, 1840, and came to America with the first colony in 1841 at the age of 15. At Notre Dame he taught mathematics and appointed himself watchdog on Sorin. After being sent west by Sorin to look for gold with Brothers Lawrence, Placidus and Justin, he left the Community in 1850. Remaining in California for about two years, he returned to France on hearing that his father was seriously ill. He is the only one of the original six pioneer Brothers who did not persevere in the Community. His letters are vibrant, sometimes harsh, and some are very long. His mind is agile and sharp, and he knows the Constitutions well as evidenced in letter #2. He organizes his attacks like a fine lawyer (e.g., letter #4), but the letters also give evidence of a troubled mind, one possibly plagued by delusions and suspicions. Although he made a proposal of marriage to a young lady after he left the Community, there is evidence in his letters (#5 and #20) that he had a strong emotional attachment to one of his students (John Hays) at Notre Dame. He died in France July 29, 1860. His is a restless soul: in his earliest letters he wonders if his vocation is to priesthood rather than not. He is one of the few letter writers to show interest in American politics (the Mexican war in letter #3, mayoral elections in letter #21), and his insight into Community politics, e.g. the separation of provinces (letter #4), seems prophetic. We sympathize with Gatian when Sorin sends him to New York in the middle of the winter: he loses much of his hearing (letter #18) as a result of harsh travel conditions. Outspoken, brash, he shows throughout his correspondence a youthful zest for power. It is difficult not to like him.

The most touching of the early Brothers associated with Notre Dame is Anselm who lived but a few months at the northern Indiana location. He yet deserves a niche in its founding no less than the other members of the Community since his heart was ever there. Born March 19, 1825, in Gennes (Mayenne), he became a novice August 23, 1840, at Le Mans and went to America with the first colony in 1841 at the age of 16. He taught school with Brother Vincent in Vincennes in 1842, but by the time of Anselm's June 18 letter (letter #1), Brother Vincent had already been assigned to Notre Dame, and Anselm at age eighteen was left to run the school alone. He suffered miserably under Bishop de la Hailandière, begged to go to Notre Dame, and angled to study painting in France, torn by his love for the Community and the miseries he experienced in Vincennes. His pitiful letter of August 4, 1844, must have moved Sorin to effect a change. After a serious illness of two months, in which he was delirious (see his letter #14), he was sent alone on November 17, 1844, from Notre Dame to teach a school of sixty students in Madison, Indiana. We must question Sorin's judgement in sending this young man off alone when Anselm's schooling was minimal and his need for Community was so obvious. By February, he was homesick for Notre Dame. His final letter is full of plans for the annual summer retreat, and details show he has had a successful year teaching. Unfortunately, he did not get back to Notre Dame. He drowned in the Ohio River at Madison, July 12, 1845, and is buried in the town. The details of his death were reported to Father Moreau in a letter which Moreau circulated to the Community. The writer was the pastor at Anselm's school:

My dear friend:

I have sad news for you. Sudden death has taken Brother Anselm away from us. He came to see me Saturday afternoon, July 12, to tell me he was going swimming. After hesitating a bit, I agreed to accompany him. He went into the water about seven or eight hundred feet away from me, in a place which did not seem the least bit dangerous. He went out more than five hundred feet without finding water deep enough for swimming. I was in water about three or four feet deep, a little distance off the bank. All of a sudden, while he was swimming, I noticed an expression of suffering on his face. He went down, but I thought he was doing it on purpose. He came up, then went down again, while uttering a cry for help. What a moment for me! I was more than three hundred feet away from him and did not know how to swim. We were two miles from the city, with no houses nearby. He came up again and then sank. A moment later he lifted his arms and I saw him no more.

All aghast, I hastened to give him absolution. He had probably received it that morning for, as usual, he had gone to confession, and he went to Communion at least every Sunday. I ran to a cabin. A child told me that there was an old man not far away. I ran to him and brought him with me and pointed out from afar the place where the Brother disappeared. "He is lost for good," he told me. "Right there is a drop-off at least twenty feet deep, and the current all around is very swift. Anything I could do would be useless." I went home, got some good swimmers together, and procured boats and nets.

All our efforts proved useless. It was ten o'clock in the evening before he was found, five hours after he had drowned. An inquest was held by the civil authorities, and then we brought him back to the church at one-thirty yesterday morning. He was laid out in the basement chapel. Some of the Irish settlers watched beside the coffin until daybreak. I clothed him in his religious habit and he remained exposed in the Chapel until yesterday afternoon at four. Everyone was dismayed by the event. Thank God for having borne me up throughout this trial and its accompanying fatigue. Sleepless, and almost without having tasted food, broken-hearted and yet forced to stifle my grief in order to look after all the details, I suffered more yesterday than I ever thought I could.

At four in the afternoon we brought him to the church. The coffin was uncovered, and the calmness of his features made him look as though he were only asleep. Protestants and Catholics alike gathered to the number of more than a thousand. The choir sang the Vespers of the Dead. With painful effort I preached on Chapter Four of the Book of Wisdom, beginning with verse seven. ["But the just man, if he be overtaken by death, shall be in rest. For venerable old age is not that of long time, nor counted by the number of years...He was taken away lest wickedness should alter his understanding, or deceit beguile his soul."]

I had the thirteenth verse written in English on a black banner: "Being made perfect in a short space, he fulfilled a long time." After the *Libera*, the children from his school kissed his forehead; then the coffin was closed and covered with the funeral drape. The two schools led the funeral procession with the banner and the cross. The hearse followed, and then the people, two by two. I marched between the school children and the carriages. We crossed the city to the cemetery, which is a mile from here.

Your friend, J. Delaune

The Brother founders of Notre Dame are forgotten on campus today. Their names are found on a plaque behind the architecture building, but the names listed are incorrect as the plaque lists the names of the Brothers who landed as a band in New York in 1841, not the names of the Brothers who arrived at Notre Dame in November, 1842. The credit for founding the university has settled on one man, Edward Sorin, whose statue stands on the Main Quad. A dormitory bears his name and another the name of his patron. He is honored in stained glass and scholarships. He is at the heart of any history of the early Notre Dame and is the subject of biography. Part of this skewed heritage derives from his position as superior of the group, a position which afforded him a natural deference that surfaces in letter after letter written to him by the Brothers, and part derives from the fact that he kept the Notre Dame *Chronicles* so any official spin on events revolves around his persona, but readers today will find in the Brothers' letters characters as fascinating as the established character of Edward Sorin. Vincent, the patriarch, reminds Sorin of his religious obligations, and Joseph manipulates Sorin's favors; Anselm begs for a new assignment, and Gatian lashes out at Sorin's imprudence and stupidity. Sorin the compassionate priest emerges from these letters as well as Sorin the politician: when Sorin sees a pet project meeting with opposition, he wins enough votes in the Council to have the project approved, but he then casts his vote against it so later he cannot be accused of officially favoring the project. Sorin is never far from these letters: the bulk of them are addressed to him, and his personality emerges in ways that it cannot emerge in his own chronicle and letters.

Readers who expect pious letters from pioneer missionaries are going to be disappointed by these letters, very few of which are "religious" letters. These men reacted to practical matters like floods (Brother Vincent), epidemics (Brother Théodule), persecution by Bishop de la Hailandière (Brother Anselm), and lack of supplies (Brother Gatian). The young men seem particularly frank with Sorin, and one of them (Gatian) appoints himself to spy for the Le Mans motherhouse, reporting on Sorin's maneuverings and indiscretions, even the matter of Sorin's rendezvous with the local mother superior of the Sisters. The drama of ordinary life is heightened, of course, by the pioneer need to adjust to new surroundings and new ideas, but the letters also reveal a drama particular to an all-male world where survival regulates all details of daily living. Pettiness turns Théodule against Vincent on mission in New Orleans, and cruel nastiness turns Gatian against Basil the bed-wetter.

The poverty of the early Brothers is everywhere evident. Brother Francis de Sales abbreviates his name on a letter to Sorin (9-26-47) because he cannot afford the postage and presumes the letter cannot be returned to him postage-due because no one in Vincennes will recognize the name behind "B.F.deS." This seems a naive trust on his part. Everyone begs for money: Brother Anselm loses socks in the wash, and Vincent asks for money to send a Brother back to Notre Dame from New Orleans.

Some of the Brothers were poor writers. Transcribing a letter written in poor English (e.g., from Brother John of the Cross) is difficult, but to wrestle with a letter written in poor French can be exasperating. For example, Brother Théodule spells as he wishes and ignores tense endings ("je ne croit pas"). If this were not enough, a translator has to fight Théodule's idiosyncratic handwriting: he crosses his f's. New words appear not found in Boyer's nineteenth-century dictionary (a dictionary the missionaries knew because Anselm mentions it): words for New World pests like ticks and mosquitoes appear (Vincent #4).

For Brothers who were native speakers of French, the transition to an English speaking frontier was not always smooth, but their facility in the new language is often amazing. In fact, they sometimes thought in two languages at once. In the middle of a parenthetical aside, Gatian (3-29-49) slips into English: "et alors vous n'auriez à lui fournir neither board, nor lodging nor anything whatever." Then he goes back into French. Gatian has a rich vocabulary, but even he, the most brilliant of the letter writers, occasionally slips through haste. In a letter to Sorin (8-20-48), he writes that he thought it impossible to become a priest after having been a priest, but he means he thought it impossible to become a priest after having been a Brother, because in the first half of the sentence he strikes through the word "Brother" and corrects it to "priest," but he does not correct the final word ("priest") to "Brother."

The Josephite Brothers thrived in America. By spring of 1843 the Community at Notre Dame had grown to twenty (see Brother

John letter #3), the Brothers all recruited in America except for the six who had come from France in the first colony of 1841. To help them in their work were three of Basil Moreau's Auxiliary Priests and five Marianite Sisters who left France for Notre Dame in June and September of 1843.

That the letters of these pioneer Brothers survive we owe to the admirable organization of their religious superiors, Edward Sorin and Basil Moreau, who had the sense of history to realize the importance of the Brothers' work in the New World. Would we had the correspondence the Brothers exchanged among themselves and with their confreres in France, but scores of such letters have probably disappeared, gone because their authors considered their work unexceptional and because they had been trained to consider worldly attachments and friendships impediments to spiritual perfection. A simple life meant few possessions and an ability to move hundreds of miles with little baggage. Letters were things that administrators, not lay Brothers, kept and filed. Fortunately the correspondence we do have can give us an appreciation of pioneer Brothers who would be otherwise lost to the dust of history.

In a first draft of this book, the letters were arranged by author so that a reader could experience all of Vincent or all of Benedict at one clip, but on the advice of historians, I rearranged the letters into a strict chronology so that a picture of the Community developing out of Notre Dame would emerge, rather than a series of individuals. The present arrangement has the advantage of reading like an epistolary novel or an epic: the various voices of the Brothers intermingle, and a reader has to drop temporarily one story line to pursue another in the best tradition of Boiardo and Ariosto. The Joseph saga of the depot, for example, is particularly compelling, but we keep getting interrupted by other Brothers and their troubles: Théodule's college woes in Kentucky and Bernard's vocation crisis in Madison. The chronological arrangement of the letters also gives us some very jangling juxtapositions of tone. For example, in letter #134 Brother Gatian opens his soul rather dramatically, dragging us through a very dark confession, only to be followed by six Joseph letters full of the sputter and schemes of that man's whimsical dreams in Indianapolis. The chronological arrangement of letters makes the Community of Notre Dame come alive as letter writers wind in and out of each other's sorrows and joys. Moreover, we can appreciate several views on one event when the letters are arranged in a time sequence: e.g., Anselm's comments juxtaposed with Vincent's on the fate of Father Weinzoepfel, a priest accused of rape by an Evansville woman. For readers interested in reading the letters by only a single Brother, a second table of contents has been included at the back of this book.

When a manuscript is torn or illegible, possible missing words are suggested and enclosed in brackets. If the missing element is anybody's guess, brackets without a suggested word are used. Where words are misspelled in the letters, I have left them misspelled. Nineteenth-century ecclesiastical titling is retained in the translations: priests are referred to as "Mister." Terms specific to the governing of a religious community are generally understandable in context: Reverend Father Rector is Moreau in France; Father Superior is Sorin at Notre Dame; the Minor Chapter is that small group of religious delegated to meet at Notre Dame as a council to the superior; the Major Chapter meets only at the motherhouse in France under the direction of Moreau. Place names in the letters are generally self-explanatory. The one exception might be the two Notre Dame foundations: one in France called Notre Dame de Sainte Croix (Our Lady of Holy Cross) and one in Indiana called Notre Dame du Lac (Our Lady of the Lake). The titles are often shortened to "Holy Cross" and "du Lac."

I wish to thank the many people who have helped in this project, particularly Father James Connelly, CSC, the archivist of the Indiana Province of the Congregation of Holy Cross, and Mrs. Jackie Daughertie, assistant in the archives. Father Jacques Grisé, CSC, at the Holy Cross Generalate in Rome graciously provided typescript copies of the letters held in Rome. Thanks are also due the archivists at the University of Notre Dame for assistance and the University for granting permission to reproduce the photos found in this book. Since photography was in its infancy in the 1840's, we have photos of only three of the six original pioneer Brothers, those who survived into old age: Vincent, Francis Xavier, and Lawrence. I thank the Sisters of Providence at St. Mary-of-the-Woods for providing access to the letter they hold in their archives. Brother John Stout, CSC, assisted with research in Evansville, Indiana. Sister Bernyne Stark, FSPA, of Viterbo College helped with the translation of various problem phrases in the French letters. Brian Bridgeforth solved computer problems, Carolyn Hanoski assisted with the final manuscript, and Brenda Peterson helped with typing. The book was typeset at the Dahl School of Business at Viterbo College. I thank also Brother Thomas Moser, CSC, provincial of the Brothers of Holy Cross, Midwest Province, for his encouragement. My hope is that readers will experience first-hand in these letters the hopes and sorrows of the early pioneer Brothers, whose work endures long after they themselves have become the forgotten founders of Notre Dame.

BIBLIOGRAPHY

Archives

Generalate of the Congregation of Holy Cross, Rome, Italy.
Generalate of the Sisters of Providence, St. Mary-of-the-Woods, Indiana.
Indiana Province of Priests of Holy Cross, Notre Dame, Indiana.
Midwest Province of Brothers of Holy Cross, Notre Dame, Indiana.

Published Sources

Alerding, Herman J. *A History of the Catholic Church in the Diocese of Vincennes.* Indianapolis: Carlon and Hollenbeck, 1883.
Beirne, Killian. *From Sea to Shining Sea: A History of the Holy Cross Brothers.* Notre Dame: Holy Cross Press, 1966.
Catta, Etienne, and Catta, Tony. *Basil Anthony Mary Moreau.* 2 vols. Milwaukee: The Bruce Company, 1955.
Connelly, James T. *Holy Cross in New Orleans: The Crisis of 1850-54.* Notre Dame: Indiana Province Archives Center, 1988.
Cullen, Franklin. *Holy Cross on the Gold Dust Trail.* Notre Dame, Indiana Province Archives Center, 1989.
Hope, Arthur. *Notre Dame: One Hundred Years.* Notre Dame: University of Notre Dame, Press, 1943.
MacEoin, Gary. *Father Moreau, Founder of Holy Cross.* Milwaukee: The Bruce Publishing Company, 1962.
Morin, Garnier. *Holy Cross Brothers: From France to Notre Dame.* Notre Dame: Dujarie Press, 1952.
Schlereth, Thomas J. *The University of Notre Dame: A Portrait of its History and Campus.* Notre Dame: University of Notre Dame Press, 1976.
Sorin, Edward. *The Chronicles of Notre Dame du Lac.* Trans. John M. Toohey, C.S.C. Ed. James T. Connelly, C.S.C. Notre Dame: University of Notre Dame Press, 1992.
Trahey, James. *The Brothers of Holy Cross.* Notre Dame: The University Press, 1901.

Chapter One

1841 and 1842

1. Brother Francis Xavier (1) to Father Moreau

[Translated from French]

St. Peter [Indiana] October 1, 1841

My reverend Father,

I am happy at having made the sacrifice of leaving and am very well adapted to the atmosphere of the woods. It's rather natural because I am in my element: we don't lack lumber, and we don't even have to leave the woods to return home. I'm sure that not one of the three Brother carpenters would want to return to Sainte Croix. We've measured oaks 20 feet around, straight as candles, and as high in proportion. These poor oaks die standing. You can't take a step without encountering a rotting tree. If they fall in the road, instead of removing them, people make a new road.

I'm working at things for the house. I have a carpenter with whom I wouldn't know how to chat because we don't understand each other, and all I can say is, "Yes, very well."

I beg Brother John Mary not to forget me in paradise as soon as he gets there.

Tell Mr. Philbert that if he doesn't have wood to make trunks, he can come to America. His trunks fell apart in New York, and thus Mr. Bayerly was forced to do an act of charity because he repaired them for us for free.

We're building an oven at our place, and we'll soon do as the French, because we have to accommodate the taste of the people who came from there. The Americans, when they have someone over, go to the hen-house to kill a chicken, put it on a plate, make corn bread, and put their coffee on the fire. And in half an hour or an hour, dinner is on the table. With this note, my promise to Brother John of the Cross is accomplished. They make nothing with yeast, and they put bread to bake in kettles after having mixed the dough in these same kettles.

I beg Brother John of the Cross not to forget me in his visits to the Blessed Sacrament. I am your very humble and very obedient son,

Brother Marie

2. Brother Vincent (1) to Mother Theodore
[Translated from French]

[St. Peter] January 1, 1842

My dear Sister,

I'm glad to have the chance to be able to write you a few words. For a long time I wanted to do so, and passing by Terre Haute, I had wanted to stop for a chat, but we paused only long enough to feed our horses.

When I left my establishment near Graville, good Sister St. Bernard d'Argentre gave me a little package for your address. I gave it to Monsignor as soon as I got to Vincennes. I hope you got it. When we left Le Mans, Father Tulau or Brother Bonaventure suggested we tell you a thousand things. He's good for his age. He's as happy as a 20 year old. He's more respected by the entire community for his virtues than for his 73 years. You know that his son, Brother Alphonse, is in Africa where he gives great service by his good example. In sending us this family, you have rendered service to our congregation. God will reward you.

We have to thank you, my dear Sister, for your carriage and the two fine oxen. They have worked well recently, and the Brother farmer has looked for a board carriage at Washington with which he can test their strength a bit. What is better yet, they are very good natured. For all of that we thank you and offer you our wishes for a happy New Year and a big share of our prayers, as feeble as they are, on condition that you give us a share of yours and those in your house. Please remember me to Sister St. Francis Xavier. Mrs. Desgemetez and Brother Leonard ask for your prayers. Goodby. Please pray for he who is with gratitude, my dear Sister, your very humble servant,

Brother Vincent

3. Brother Vincent (2) to Father Sorin
[Translated from French]

Vincennes March 2, 1842

My very dear Father,

Here's what's going on: Monsignor told me that if I had an opportunity to go to St. Peter's, he would send you a sack of coffee and a biscuit boric compound. We will add three turkeys to that. After thinking a bit, I proposed to him that you'd send someone on the 17th of the present month with a fourth part [of the transaction], and on Friday the 18th I'd go by carriage, like a priest. His Grace found this'd be fine. Now I'm happier to have permission to be celebrating the feast of St. Joseph with all of you than I am with anything else.

Brother Anselm asks in his letter for a pronunciation dictionary. Should I buy it for him?

The rascal cobbler has not yet made our wooden shoes. You could send me some quires of paper and two or three packets of quill pens. I'll sell what I can.

Please say an Ave Maria and an invocation to St. Joseph for me and my students.

Please believe that I am with the greatest respect, my very dear Father, your very humble and obedient son in our Saviour Jesus Christ,

Brother Vincent

4. Brother Vincent (3) to Father Sorin
[Translated from French]

Vincennes March 8, 1842

My very dear Father,

Monsignor just told me to write to you again to send someone here right away to carry away the items I spoke to you about in my letter of the 2nd or 3rd of the present month. Some excellent shrubs for your garden are already too mature. If the present letter gets to you in time, come then this week, or rather please send [for them]. My plan to go away by carriage has fallen through. God be praised I still have the legs of a fifteen year old. If the weather isn't too bad, I'll put them into gear the 18th at 7 AM.

Your letter of the 3rd just got to me. I'm very glad that the good God put so much charity in your heart for me who merits it so little. I promise you that I do not grieve for France, but not to be able to respond to the views that you had of me in the beginning! I believe that the good God permits it to confuse my pride and my self-respect. May He always be blessed.

I had never assembled so many children as this evening. Almost every day I have new ones. If they stayed in class as in France, I'd have almost 80. His Grace gave me pictures and medals. You need not send me any, thank you.

I'm going to take your message to the post office. May your name be written in the sacred hearts of Jesus and Mary and mine also. It's what he desires who is with all the submission possible, my very dear and worthy Father, your very humble and respectful son in Jesus Christ,

Brother Vincent

PS Good wishes to all my Brothers. If you have circular weights [?], please send some here. The girls told me that they don't have any at all.

5. Brother Vincent (4) to Father Moreau

[Translated from French]

Vincennes April 10, 1842

My very reverend Father,

I haven't been able to hear your letter read without shedding many tears, it is so paternal. At Easter I had this consolation, because you know that I've been at Vincennes since December 15 or 16. Our good Father Superior asked Monsignor if I might go to St. Peter's for the feast of St. Joseph and spend my Easter vacation with them, which I did with great pleasure. We had prepared ourselves at our best for the feast of our holy patron. We had three Masses that day, which is not easy in our forested area. There was an instruction at the 10 o'clock Mass. A rather good number of faithful attended, and the entire Community had the benefit of taking Communion. On Palm Sunday and all Holy Week we did the entire office, which our Americans had never seen. We also had people there out of curiosity perhaps as much as devotion. On Holy Saturday our superior baptized a mother and a baby, and another woman was to share their good fortune, but she was held back by her lying in [for child birth]. In a neighboring congregation three Protestants had the same good fortune the same day. This is what rejoices the heart of the missionary and makes him forget his weariness and troubles; it's the result of prayers and alms from our good friends in France.

I must cite to you here, very reverend Father, some zealous traits of our dear Father. On Easter Monday at 6 pm after Benediction of the Blessed Sacrament, he made an excursion. Here's an abridged version: first he went to an old fox who hadn't made his [Easter] duty for a long time. "Come with me," said the missionary, "to such a place." Not suspecting any mystery, he mounted a horse and led Father there. After the ordinary greeting, which consists of giving each other reciprocally a hand, the missionary says to the master of the house, "I come to hear your confession, Let's get going! Get out of here, the rest of you." The poor man, seeing himself grabbed by fate, falls to his knees, makes his confession, and admires the priest's charity. "We haven't finished," says the missionary to his guide, "Let's go to a certain man's house." When they got there, everyone was sleeping because it was 8 o'clock. Nevertheless, the head of the house gets up, seemed surprised to receive a visit at that hour. "But I'm going to hear your confession," said the priest. "Wait, let's go into the little bedroom so as not to disturb your family." Without more explanation, he goes with the priest, made his confession and admired, like the first man, the charity of the priest missionary. But let's come now to the guide who found himself in the same case. He saw that he was going to have his turn, but coming in front of the priest, he asks him for three or four days to prepare himself.

On Tuesday, the priest visited a family of ten people, none of them baptized. He found them generally well disposed. Our good Father is well liked in his congregation. He'll do there, with the help of God, great good.

Our novitiate is going well. During the twelve days that I spent there, I was happy to find a good spirit among all. Our superior waits for postulants. We don't lack for establishments. I rather fear we won't find enough recruits.

These are the tiresome details for you, very reverend Father, who have so many things to do, but they'll make you see how Christian schools are doing so well among people yet half savage. If you could see these little Creoles with naked feet running in the water half way up their legs! That's their pleasure. They also like running races. Little children aged seven could outrun children aged ten in France.

Now let's talk a bit about my school. When I was put in charge of it, it had 25 to 30 students. Thanks be to God, the number has doubled, and I know they're happy with it in town since they talk positively about it. I'm not surprised since they'd never seen a school capably run, and seeing the children go two by two to church on Sunday and return there the same way each school day, without noise or racket, touches the heart. One no longer sees them fighting nor swearing, especially in the last month. They pray to God and help at services as much as, and I can say with more, peacefulness than the children in our schools in France. They're susceptible to rewards; they learn a catechism lesson although they still read very badly. I had a little distribution of crosses and medals for them. The next day they came back to school carrying their cross or their medal hanging around their neck without my telling them to. What I haven't yet been able to get from them is real silence during classes. Nevertheless, I hope that God, who has already given so many graces to these children, will put His greatest hand to it.

Vincennes is a town of two to three thousand souls, scarcely half of them Catholic and the rest divided into various sects. The entire lower city is French, which is why I can teach there, because two-thirds of my children speak French, and a seminarian comes twice a day to give reading and arithmetic lessons. There's also a school for girls run by Sisters named the Sisters of St. Vincent de Paul. There's only one house for the bishop and the seminary. We all eat at Monsignor's table and as well as he does. There are ten students in all, of which only three are in theology, and the others in different courses. The high school of the Eudists is bigger. They have just under twenty boarders. Our cathedral is rather nice. It's the most beautiful I've seen in the United States. Only the Wabash River separates us from Illinois, formerly very barbarous and wild. Our house is situated in a vast plain. One quarter hour by road finds marshes on almost every side covered with woods. Snakes, turtles of all kinds abound there. There's especially a kind of small beast they call wood ticks (resembling our bed bugs) which pierce the skin in such a way that, pulling them out, they sooner leave their head than let go, and after having pulled them out, there remains a swelling and itching which lasts three to four weeks. Mosquitos are also beginning to buzz loudly in our ears. They're enemies of another kind, more bothersome than the first. Enough said about this.

I still have to tell you I've been very happy in America. I have only one trouble: here it is, good Father. You know that Father Superior Sorin earnestly begged you to send me with him to help in his labors in the novitiate, and I find myself incapable of giving him any help, seeing as I can't learn the language. Before I was settled in [at Vincennes], I was scarcely more useful at the novitiate than a zero in arithmetic since I could neither understand nor make myself understood by the postulants nor by other people with whom I had to have contact. The intention of our good Father is nevertheless to call me back to the novitiate. He told me that formally at Easter. If I can't be useful in the novitiate on account of my language, I'll try to make up for it with my arms. In Holy Week I was there and washed the laundry. I baked once also, and my bread was not bad. My talent isn't to teach, very reverend Father, but to obey. I made war on my will as much as I could, but I've got much more yet to do. My soul is in peace almost as much as when you directed me. I haven't forgotten your advice, and I'm very glad to remember it in time of need. Good grief, my good Father, how happy one is when one looks only for God! One finds Him everywhere, and He consoles us in any situation. My good fortune here is to go find our Lord who's in a chapel which is separated from my bedroom by only a wall. At the feet of our Lord I make all my exercises of piety, except my spiritual reading which I do in my bedroom.

Good-by, very reverend Father. I am your very respectful son in our Lord Jesus Christ.

Brother Vincent

P.S. We can't get either collar or cords for our crucifixes. My brother has to send a small package to Brother Leopold for me, which I beg you to send me when you send us someone here.

A thousand respects to the priests; good wishes to all my dear Brothers; my remembrances to the good Sisters. In the prayers of everybody and to the religious of the good pastor. Also union through prayers. Oh, pray for us and for the conversion of our Protestants.

Brother Gatian's health has come back.

6. Brother Vincent (5) to Father Sorin

[Translated from French]

Vincennes April 21, 1842

My very dear Father,

On the 7th of the current month, a letter passed through here for you from France. It was first at the college, came back to the bishop, and left finally for St. Peter's.

Although the labors of the season take me away often from the pupils, my class is always crowded. I've been terribly distressed this past week. A bad boy threw a big stone at another boy's head and gave him a rather bad cut. The wounded one took his revenge yesterday. He waited for his enemy on his way home from school, stretched out in the street with a brick. At the cry of this child, I ran and picked him up. He went off with his brother. I don't know where he is today. I asked not to see these two culprits at school again. That's not Monsignor's opinion nor Mr. Shaw's. Although these things took place outside of school, it could be thought of as typical of the class.

The good Mother of Terre Haute is laid low by a putrid fever, to the point of complete despair for her recovery. Monday Monsignor sent there Mr. Corbet and Mr. Ducouril who experienced an unfortunate accident. Their carriage broke; they both lost consciousness. Some people carried them to the nearest house. The man who brought the news here yesterday evening believes they are not as badly hurt as was thought, but we have nothing certain on their state. His Grace [will come] to the aid of his children.

Yesterday evening a letter from Charleston announced the death of the bishop of that town. It was one of the principal colonies of the American church.

Mr. Happuman's health is deteriorating more and more. He doesn't know when he'll get it back. He thinks about France. If he makes this trip, I'll tell you ahead of time. He would gladly do your errands or at least carry your letters and the Brothers', if they wish to write.

You have great work especially in this season, but I encourage you, very reverend Father, to take care of your health for the good of your students and of your dear congregation. Neither trunk nor package has yet come to the bishop for St. Peter's. Meanwhile the steamboats go up the Wabash at their convenience.

Please—my good wishes to the entire little family and prayers from everyone. Goodby, very dear Father. Lunch is going to be served pronto. I am and wish to be always your very humble and obedient son in our Lord Jesus Christ,

Brother Vincent

7. Brother Vincent (6) to Father Sorin
[Translated from French]

Vincennes May 4, 1842

My very dear Father,

The letter carrier I welcomed Saturday evening must have carried off to you one of them I had entrusted to Mr. Lalumière in which I gave you news about the good Mother of Terre Haute and about our priests. Monsignor has come back and is now gone for a fortnight.

Let's talk now about the letter of April 7. It was of course addressed to you. It came from France. It was delivered to Mr. Shaw who, instead of directing it to you, put it in the letter packet for Monsignor who was on the circuit and only returned on the 15th. At his arrival, did he have time to see to everything? I know nothing about it because he kept himself busy in Terre Haute.

I thought the letter from Brother Eugene could well be the one in question—it must have the seal from Le Harve for February 5. That rather agrees with his Grace's return and the period when you received it. The postmaster says that if somebody delivered it to him, it must have reached its destination.

What you tell me about Brother Gatian and the entire little family rejoices my soul. Likewise the good he does in your chapter. I believe that the prayers of our dear ones at sea from France help much. I read not long ago that the prayers of St. Theresa obtained the conversion of a thousand Indians.

Sunday we had a very sad spectacle. Twelve unfortunate blacks were made Methodists. You undoubtedly know they go into the Wabash River with their minister to be plunged three times in the water.

You bathe the earth with your sweat while I am here as fresh as a roach [fish]. You'd be surprised that the American air has done nothing to me, but I'm not surprised, because I'm not yet worthy to suffer. I recommend more than ever my poor students to your prayers. The devil wishes to mingle with them. I have to watch more closely than ever although the exterior of the school may be rather good. I have grounds to fear the corruption of morals. I hope that the Very Holy Virgin and St. Joseph will not allow it in children whom I dedicate to them. Often they become the slaves of sin.

Goodby, very dear Father. Please believe me, I'm happy to be your son in Our Savior Jesus Christ,

Brother Vincent

8. Brother Vincent (7) to Father Moreau
[Translated from French]

St. Peter [Indiana] June 6, 1842

Very reverend Father,

Father Superior charges me to write you how our processions of the very Blessed Sacrament took place, not being able to do it himself, seeing that he leaves this morning for Louisville, thirty leagues from here. He offers you his very humble respect, and his best wishes to all his confreres.

I'll try to relate nothing here except what I saw and witnessed. On Trinity Sunday our good Father asked some men of the congregation to help him make a repository, an astonishing thing. On Saturday of the feast, more than forty came to offer help. Women didn't show themselves less generous in doing what is their art and readying what they could.

Across from the church, they opened a passage in the forest belonging to a pagan who permitted everything we wanted for the beauty of the ceremony. At the end of this avenue was built a beautiful repository. On two sides was a large alcove where the men had to stand on one side and women on the other. Along the avenue from space to space were arches, some of leaves and others covered with white, which offered the most beautiful sight possible.

Order of the Procession

Following the cross marched the little boys; then came the banner of the Blessed Virgin, followed by girls and then women. Finally following the banner of St. Joseph were all the Catholic gentlemen, Protestants, pagans, etc., etc. The Brothers ended the procession. A rather pretty canopy was carried by four good Catholics and surrounded by six men carrying a sash and weapons. The chant was done by two choirs of lady singers, and we ourselves formed a third. The procession was large. They came here from more than thirteen miles away which equals at least five French leagues. Although our processions were composed of people from all different religions, everything nevertheless took place with the greatest order.

Arriving at the repository, a missionary from a neighboring congregation preached for two hours, and with the book of the holy evangelists in his hand, he showed his audience all the possible proofs for the real presence of Jesus Christ in the Blessed Sacrament of the altar. A sermon so long would have bored our Catholics in Europe, and here those who couldn't keep standing sat down or lay down on the ground, but their attention seemed sustained to the end.

Procession on the octave. It took place only at vespers. The same order was followed as on the feast day, the same devotion manifested by the congregations and the same abundance of people. One of the nearest neighboring missionaries, who on the day before made bricks like a true laborer, carried the Blessed Sacrament. Arriving at the first station, our good priest preached almost an hour. He was heard with all the attention possible. I don't doubt, very reverend Father, that the divine word which was carried to so many ears for the first and second times under these antique oaks of our forests will one day bear fruit. After the first station, the procession moved by a route we had prepared toward a little hermitage we had made in honor of St. Joseph. This humble repository was placed among four superb oaks where we had made a little altar, but only from what the forest was able to furnish us, so that it took neither nails nor wire nor cloth except at the exposition spot which had three nails and a little wire.

From there the procession returned to our court where there was a third repository, and finally to the church. After the last benediction, our Americans remounted their horses or got in the carts and returned home, with joy painted on their faces.

There's no need to say that our good Father was, after God, the principal wheel which made everything move, and if he gets no help, I fear for his health. God blesses his labors. The small community of Brothers is doing well. We've received an excellent postulant for manual labor. Two from New York are en route and should arrive here next.

All the Brothers offer you their regards and their most sincere thanks for having given them such a good priest. They wrote you occasionally. I don't know when their letters will reach you.

I'll return to my establishment at Vincennes at the return of our good Father. Brother Anselm has been there with me for some weeks. Brother Gatian's restored health has effected a great change in him. All the Brothers and our Father himself are astonished at how good a religious he is. Brother Lawrence earns the admiration equally of our congregation by his work. Brother Mary [Francis Xavier] has become a butcher, carpenter, etc. In a word everything is going well, thanks be to God. No one seems to miss France.

The newspapers have no doubt informed you of the terrible calumny which weighs on the person of one of our missionaries in the diocese of Vincennes. A conspiracy had been made against him by a Catholic woman, married to a Lutheran husband. Happily the conduct and virtue of this worthy priest are so well established that the Protestants who have a little good faith have believed none of it. Meanwhile his case is in process and should be judged in September. The Catholics here pray to God to keep in His chruch so good a minister. He's now in the seminary at Vincennes. I know him in a special way. He's 29 years old, Alsatian by nationality, ordained a priest by Monsignor de la Helandière. He told me himself that the conspirators wanted to put him in a wooden prison so they could burn it down at night. The Catholics got him with their own hands and hid him in a chest while the people looked for him in the house where he was. After this racket, they led him out of town in secular clothes. Then he went into the woods, hid there one night, and finally he came to us, heavy with fatigue.

Goodby, very reverend Father. The commissioner is leaving for the post-office. Please believe that in America, as in France, I'm your very humble and obedient son in our Lord Jesus Christ,

Brother Vincent

Regards to all your good priests. Please give my prayers and good wishes to all the Brothers

9. Brother John (1) to Father Moreau

St. Peter's, Indiana September 23, 1842

Reverend Father,

Although a distance of over two thousand leagues lies between us, yet I assure you that you are ever present in my mind, and I hope that the moment when I shall be able to introduce myself personally to you will not be long delayed. I have the happiness of being among the first who spoke to good Father Sorin on his arrival in New York, with the intention of joining his little Community; but I put off entering it until I had fully reflected on what I was about to undertake, and until I was sure of my vocation. I joined this holy colony in the month of June last. My dear Father, you cannot form an idea of our delightful little Community: we now number fifteen, all very happy, and indeed it could not be otherwise under the direction of a man so eminently suited to the duties of his office, as is our good and lovable Superior. Our retreat was all too short for me, and you may believe that we were all sorry to see it end. As you watch constantly over us, we have united our prayers to those of the Community in France. It is superfluous to say more on this score, and so I pass on to something more interesting, by telling you that many conversions occur here daily, thanks to the efforts of our dear Superior. I was present the other day with him at the baptism of a father and his children; it was, I assure you, a charming spectacle: several Protestants were present. It was then, my dear Father, that the poor Missionary come from the far West, gathered the fruits of his harvest and was recompensed at the hands of God Almighty, for all his trials and crosses. It is at such times that the soul realizes what it owes for the good wrought by the Missionary, and prays fervently to Him Who sent him, with sentiments that can be fully appreciated only by those who share a similar happiness.

Dear Father, you know that here we are obliged to speak English, and you can hardly realize what progress the Brothers have made since their arrival. As for me, I am of English origin, and I speak very little French. Brother Gatien speaks English very well, and has a very fine school at the distance of about four miles from Saint Peter's. I doubt that you can correctly visualize a school house in America; I do not believe you can, and I shall try to depict one for you. Imagine a huge pile of logs lying one above the other, with the openings necessary to let in the air and light of day, for there are no windows. From this, you can easily conclude that it is very comfortable in summer, and also that it is very cold in winter.

As I have nothing else to write about, you will kindly pardon the brevity of this letter, and I hope that the next one will be more agreeable.

I am forever, my dear Father, your devoted son in Jesus Christ,

Brother John

10. Brother Vincent (8) to Father Sorin
[Translated from French]

Vincennes October 9, 1842

Very dear Father,

His Grace is letting me write in his letter. I'm taking advantage of it to save you the postage for mine.

We arrived at Vincennes yesterday at 6 PM, very wet after the trip on the White River. A cart that we were following made us go at least three or four miles too much. On the other hand, the stagecoach was so late that it met up with us not very far from our destination. We let it also pass, and we saved two dollars. Monsignor received us rather well, telling us, however, that if we weren't so wet, he would grumble that the vacation had been too long and that he had said something to you about it. Today I'll ask him for books for Brother Anselm. He gave Mr. Corbé orders to take an arithmetic book and a geography book to the college. I spoke to him about several things necessary for the school. He didn't say anything to me in response.

The frontpiece of the altar in question stayed at Monsignor's. Mr. Man was absent when the matter came up for St. Peter's. That's the major reason why it hasn't reached you. Tomorrow at 8:30, holy Mass will be said for our children. I greatly desire that God will bless our school more. Several students came to see us this morning.

I was profoundly afflicted this morning in seeing only a handful of people at High Mass. How great is the indifference here! Mr. Lefrance will certainly not find Monsignor here: he has to be away at least three days this week.

Goodby, very dear Father. Please pray for us and our poor children.

Brother Vincent

11. Brother Vincent (9) to Brother Augustine
[Translated from French]

Vincennes October 9, 1842

My dear Brother,

You thought you put stockings in Mr. Chartier's trunk, but you didn't. There wasn't a pair of them in our two trunks. Mr. Chartier was kind enough last night to loan us two pair, because we were soaked at last half way up the leg. Ask our good Father when Mr. Lefranc is coming to Vincennes. I think he'll gladly take charge of your little package, or have it put on the stagecoach. We'll go look for it Friday or Saturday. Thanks to all the Brothers, if you said your rosary for us yesterday.

Brother Vincent

Chapter Two

1843

12. Brother Vincent (10) to Father Sorin
[Translated from French]

Vincennes February 2, 1843

My very dear Father,

God be praised, I'm very consoled since I received your letter of January 31 which tells me that the good God restores our little Brother to us. May He be ever praised as well as our good Mother whose feast we celebrate today.

Don't expect me on Saturday. Monsignor has been at Terre Haute since last week. I don't know when he'll return. I have to tell you this. I'm not leaving my school before Easter vacation. God again be praised. If it's necessary to make sacrifices, it must be done with the best heart possible. You've told me only a few thing about Holy Cross. You imagined you didn't have to tell me any more about it. May God also be praised. I'm troubled by the rotten work at St. Peter's and how you can kill yourself from everything. But I think all of that can work to your benefit. God again be praised. Finally, may He be praised in everything and everywhere. Our labors grow constantly. Thank God my health doesn't fail.

I think you have more time to take things to Washington than to send for them from here, especially as I still don't have wooden shoes. It seems that the cobbler is always sick.

There are two beautiful turkeys here that his Grace wants to send you, but I don't know how, and then I asked the servants to buy a male so that we can have chicks.

I think that Father Rector could now be told that I've been settled in for several months. If I find an opportunity to write to France, will you permit me to say a word to him about it?

Lent will soon be here. Father Rector doesn't allow the teaching Brothers to have lunch without his permission. He usually left me free. I have to tell you the young man [Anselm] has never been contrary, and I think that I could please the Seminary with further help. Please try to tell me what you'll let me do.

I want to have with you the same frankness that I had with Father Rector. I experience many consolations in my little cell which is separated from the chapel only by a wall. My first visit is to Our Lord, and in the evening I sleep nicely after having visited. Before and after my classes I can also make a little visit.

Although my students don't know all I'd like them to know, I nevertheless see goodness among them, above all on Sunday when I can lead them to our Good Lord. I always have some deserters who believe, I think, that the church will fall on them!

I just saw the doctor. He told me I have to carry on, that everything is fine. He prescribed nothing new. When this thing coming from death's gates be cured, he'll have to pray to the good God for us and for the students in my class.

I think that Brother Marie [Francis Xavier] is going to do all kinds of good things to your little church. How difficult it will be for me to recognize it when I see it again! As for Brother Lawrence—he can no longer wear out either shoes or wooden shoes—he's always on horseback or in a carriage. He takes care of himself! The Apostles were not so comfortable. Oops! Brother Lawrence, forgive me! As for Brother "baker"—he tries to learn how to make good bread, good soup. The last soup was good. Brother Anselm caught a dozen rabbits. I'm asking him for one of them for Easter, an orange colored one, if I can keep it. I wish Brother Joseph's teeth would let him sleep.

I have much pleasure in talking freely to you, my dear Brothers, but I fear missing the mail. My best to the postulants, for their prayers and to the boarders.

All the priests bid you a thousand kind wishes, my very dear Father, and I believe myself capable of saying I love you and that I am your very humble and obedient son in Jesus Christ.

Brother Vincent

13. Brother John (2) to Father Moreau

Notre Dame du Lac February, 1843

My Reverend Father,

Everything being in readiness for our departure from St. Peter's to Notre Dame du Lac, we commenced our journey at a period when all nature seemed combined against us, but notwithstanding the severity of the weather, our little troop, consisting of eleven persons, viz. Brothers Vincent, Laurence, Joachim, Thomas, Ignatius, Paul, Joseph, two postulants, one boarder and myself, proceeded on our journey as unconcerned about its distance as if we were only to go two or three leagues. Our mode of conveyance was a large wagon made under the direction of Brother Laurence, contained our beds, provisions and four trunks well filled with kitchen apparatus, our load in all amounting to near three thousand pounds weight. The wagon was drawn by four large horses. Besides that we drove on foot eight head of large working cattle.

Our dear congregation assembled and assisted with us at parting in singing Ave Sanctissima in honor of the blessed Virgin, then recited the Litany of the Blessed Virgin, bid adieu to our dear little chapel and the congregation who with tears in their eyes begged of God to bless us; never in my life had I witnessed such a scene (no never) nor ever did I witness such a time. It had rained the night previous, and from the door of the house to the gate was one clear sheet of ice, and our horses being but imperfectly shod could scarcely stand on their feet, and it was laughable to see the poor oxen sliding from one side of the road to the other, and at one place between St. Peter's and Washington, about two leagues distant, we had to ascend a steep hill; our poor horses tried their utmost to arrive at the top and had nearly reached [it] when the wagon slipped backwards and dragged horses and all to bottom again. We then had to call to our aid some of the neighbors to assist us for we could hardly do anything our fingers were so much benumbed, and it was not until a great deal of exertion we reached the top, and [after] a toilsome route of two leagues we arrived at Washington where I had all the horses shod properly.

We remained that night at the house of a good, pious soul named W. Gallagher who entertained us with great hospitality and would not allow us to proceed until we had all our horses properly fixed for such a journey, and which [when] I look back sometimes and consider what we then undertook, I am really surprised to see how well we got through with everything. The Americans themselves who were accustomed to travel told us at the time we started that they would not undertake such a journey under any conditions, and the good Mr. Gallagher would not on any account receive remuneration.

We departed the next morning and in crossing a river seven miles from Washington were nearly precipitated into the water (which was not too warm) by our cattle becoming restive, and at last they all jumped into the water and swam back. It was rather difficult for us to return back to the shore as the river being frozen over, there was only a small passage cut through the ice for our flat boat; after some delay we succeeded in getting our cattle, and then we crossed to the opposite shore. No accident happened, and we proceeded on our journey, the ground being covered with frozen snow, and the more we advanced, the deeper it became, and to the latter part of our journey we found five feet of snow and the weather extremely cold.

At four o'clock every afternoon I mounted on horseback and proceeded in advance of our little troop in search of a lodging for the night, and having succeeded in finding one, I remained until the company came up, and as soon as they had arranged every thing for the night, we commenced our prayers, recited our beads and performed our devotion as if we were at St. Peter's, but the inmates of the houses where we stopped were generally surprised to see such a body of Baptists [Papists] or pagans, and during the time which we occupied for our prayers, they would sit or stand in the corner and regard us with an air of superstitious awe. After we had partaken of our frugal repast, we stretched ourselves on the floor in front of a large fire, and one or two Brothers covered us with blankets, sometimes one blanket serving for three persons. There was also one Brother obliged to remain by the fire to replenish it with wood as often as was required during the night.

We arose at half past five, prepared our breakfast, and continued on our route. Every one of our dear little troop was as happy as could be, not a word of complaint from anyone, and during the day when we commenced to feel hungry, we would ask the good Brother Vincent, who had the care of our stores, for some bread. He would take a loaf, place it on the trunk of a fallen tree, and with an axe give three or four heavy blows before he succeeded in cutting a piece, and then we ate that as savory as if it was as good as the bread which I have since tasted in France. We were obliged to walk the greater part of the time, our wagon being so loaded as to allow of only three or four to ride at a time, and we were glad to walk to keep ourselves warm.

But I must not forget our good dog Azore. Every day he came with me as far as the house we were to lodge at, and as soon as he saw me place my horse in the stable, he would scamper away to meet the rest as if to say he would show them the way, and then he jumped and fawned until he came up to me when, after receiving his supper, he mounted up into the wagon and slept there more comfortable than we who were near a fire. Many a time have I envied him his bed.

We met with an accident one day when near the end of our journey which, if it had happened a few miles farther back, might have caused us a great deal of trouble. One of our wagon wheels gave way and could do us no farther service, but as kind Providence had directed, there was a large sled at the house we slept at last, so I immediately bought it, placed our wagon as it was on the sled, and away we went with more speed than ever as the sled would slip with more ease on the snow than the wheels which used to turn heavily and sink deep in the snow. We made our journey in fourteen days without any accident except that Brother Laurence had two or three of his toes frozen, and Brothers Joseph and Paul their faces. It [is] very painful to have the face or hands frozen. You cannot enter a warm room without suffering a great deal, but thanks be to God we are all safe and happy, and in a short time I hope to write you a more interesting account.

I remain, my dear Father Rector, your obedient son in Christ,

Brother John

[The following paragraphs were written by Brother John but not as part of his February (?), 1843, letter. They are printed in the *Etrennes Spirituelles* for 1843 (pp. 113, 114) and are attributed to him.]

On arriving at Notre Dame du Lac, I was agreeably surprised at the beauty of the place. I already knew its location, but when I now saw the numerous advantages it presented, it was impossible for me to doubt that God had destined it for the Community of Saint Joseph. Our house is built with large trunks of trees of equal length and placed end to end. The chimney is also made of wood plastered with glazed clay to prevent danger of fire.

Within half an hour's walk is the village of South Bend which contains about five thousand souls. It is agreeably situated on the banks of Saint Joseph River. The Protestants have several churches in the village. Over the river there is a bridge high enough to let pass steamboats of about 120 feet in length. These come from Lake Michigan and the village of Saint Joseph situated at the mouth of the river.

Our holdings in land comprise more than six hundred acres at an elevation of ten or twelve feet above the river. Beyond the house are two beautiful lakes partially connected around a little island crowned with a cluster of trees, making a charming view. The larger lake is about thirty-six acres and the smaller one about twenty-six. The lakes discharge into the Saint Joseph River by a little waterfall of seven or eight feet in height which is useful for mill purposes. The land, already cleared for cultivation, consists of about ninety acres; the rest being covered with forest. Our livestock consists of fourteen head of cattle and six horses.

14. Brother John (3) to [Ignatius F. Norsman ?]

Notre Dame du Lac March 10, 1843

Dear Sir,

I am directed by the Reverend E. Sorin to address you concerning an order sent by him to you for payment of three hundred dollars, two hundred and fifty of which was to have been paid to Mrs. Parmentier of Brooklyn and the other fifty to be remitted to him, but not having heard from you, he is fearful it might have miscarried or that our Right Reverend Bishop of Vincennes had not given him the right direction to you, in case of which Mr. Sorin begs that you will be so kind as to pay Mrs. Parmentier the amount stated until he can receive from the bishop another order for the same. The reason for wishing you to do this is that we are at such a distance from Vincennes that too much delay would intervene between return of letters and Mrs. Parmentier's bill which ought to have been paid two months back. It is now six weeks since Mr. Sorin sent you the bishop's order, and he expects shortly to draw on you for the sum of five hundred dollars, but if you do not wish to pay the amount to Mrs. Parmentier without the bishop's order, you will be pleased to write immediately so that we may procure it. But by paying Mrs. Parmentier and sending the balance to us by post would greatly oblige your most humble and obedient servant,

P. Steber
Secretary, Mr. E. Sorin

P.S. Mr. Sorin would also wish to know when you could send the children you spoke of to Mr. Delaune and if you think they are well disposed and any young men you may know of as desirous of joining our Society. You would confer a great favor by letting him know. We are now twenty in number.

P. Steber
Secretary

15. Brother Vincent (11) to Father Sorin
[Translated from French]

Vincennes May 14, 1843

My very dear Father,

You have undoubtedly already learned about the persecution which just broke out in Evansville against the missionary whose name doesn't come to me. Brother John will tell you. What I'm going to write I got almost entirely from the missionary, because yesterday I had a rather long conversation with him.

An unhappy Catholic woman, wife of a Protestant, said that the missionary had raped her while in confession. A faction made a lawsuit for her of 4000 dollars to which four principal Catholics were required to respond under penalty of seeing fire on their property. On the 6th, the missionary sent a courier to Vincennes. Mr. Shaw and Mr. Thomas, a lawyer in our town, went to the rescue on the 8th. It seems that the gathering was large on the 9th or the 10th when Mr. Shaw and our lawyer appeared at the public square. The woman was called and to the first question our men made to her, she contradicted herself, but her husband, who was present and who saw what was happening, started to stamp his feet in the room or the square, saying that they were abusing his wife's patience and ridiculing her. At once the faction started to move to arrest the missionary and our men, but the Catholics threw themselves in a circle and encouraged the escape of our supposed culprits. At least 500 cutthroats searched all the Catholic houses. They came right to the one where the missionary was—he had only time to get himself in a well while somebody bunged the top. Finally, night having come, the Catholics took him out of town in lay clothes without mishap, thank God.

It was the 9th of the current month that these things happened and not the 10th. The poor missionary finally came to us on the 11th after sleeping one night on the run, worn out and anxious.

He thinks that his church is going to be burned. It was very dear to him, even though he abstained more than once from necessities for it. Up till now there's been no blood shed. Only the doctor was beaten when the mob formed at his house. God knows how this lawsuit will end and if we'll not yet see this holy priest taken.

Recommend this business to your prayers and to those of the little community. Monsignor is not back yet. I hope for that next week.

When you write to me, please tell me if the letter in question came to you. I could at least speak to his Grace about it.

If Brother Marie has not yet confessed to you, I think nothing more is to be gained since our Protestants have such evil intentions.

Fortunately I didn't post my letter yesterday because here's more news to give you. Monsignor arrived yesterday evening. Today after dinner his Grace made us read a letter from Mr. Martin who announced the death of Mr. Zamion, pastor of Fort Wayne. Monsignor wept and all the priests took part in his grief. He died at Logansport, at the home of his friend Mr. Abartin. He died holy because he led the life of the just. I don't think I can talk to his Grace today. He is overwhelmed with business, hard work, and troubles. [Mr.] Thomas, our dear missionary's lawyer, is at home. Almost every day he comes to me about new [schools]. [Un]fortunately the season's labors don't allow punctuality in everything.

Father Rector is going to be in serious anxiety on learning about the persecution of the missionary at Evansville, because the newspapers are going to publish it all over the world. If you write to him, please offer him my very humble respects.

Haven't you yet received anything from France? I don't doubt that the little family hears everything with holy joy. I've prayed with all my energy to the Holy Spirit to renew our hearts. I think that I haven't forgotten a single one of us. I have more need of grace than anyone else because without grace, how could I work in the midst of these young people on whom is all the hope of religion for the future?

When will you come to Vincennes since I can't go to St. Peter's?

Goodby, very dear Father. Please believe that I'm happy to be able to call myself your son in Jesus Christ,

Brother Vincent

16. Brother Anselm (1) to Father Sorin

[Translated from French]

Vincennes June 18, 1843

My dear Father,

Last night I received your kind letter, and with Mr. Barret leaving for South Bend tonight or more probably tomorrow morning, I'm taking this opportunity to thank you for your letter and to offer my humble regards to you as well as to all my Brothers, especially to good Brother Vincent (whom you have forgotten to mention in your letter) because he is my old and eternal friend and I often deplore losing him. Truly, my [Father], I'd good reason to feel bad when you told me about his departure.

I intend to answer all the things you have asked me about after conferring with Mr. Martin, and I would have you aware of all the setbacks I've had in administering my poor establishment and of those I have undergone in my post as principal regarding Brother Celestine.

We had a beautiful procession today.

Tomorrow our bishop and the bishop of New Orleans will come and examine our class. We expect that Bishop Henrick will be here in a few days.

Goodby...it is 10 o'clock, and I'm going to bed—Good night.

17. Brother Anselm (2) to Father Sorin

Vincennes July 9, 1843

Dear Father,

It is to comply with your wishes that I will in this day [MS torn] conscience before you, but I shall be brief for I have [another] letter to wrap up in this one, and if this were too big you [would] pay double the price.

Relative to my religious duties or Exercises I can [say] that I have always been faithful to do them [in the] same way as I did them when Brother Vincent was [here]. Only I have sometimes taken 2 or 3 minutes on my [morning] prayer, either to light the fire, or to finish dressing my[self.] I was surprized by the bell and though I have had always a multitude of distractions in my exercises, I have never omitted any one, ex[cept] the particular examination, and that for punishing some boys after school and once the spiritual reading, knowing not w[hat] time it was.

I have not room enough to tell you in what manner I spent my recreations, but I will tell you [abou]t the retreat, and a great many other things too. Have the goodness in your next letter to tell me when I must give vacation, and go to South Bend, and if I must go post or on horse back for Mother Theodore told me that she would lend me her horse. Indeed, Father, you murder me in giving me so much work for the number of my boys is daily increasing: 4 or 5 new scholars have come since the Brother's departure, and instead of 5 seminarians I had before the Brother's departure, I have now 8, and however nobody helps me. I am so much fatigued after teaching, that, notwithstanding the affection I have for study, I will fall asleep, and I lose all my time. I have 6 different kinds of tortoises and snakes and some insects, which I will bring to South Bend if you juge it proper. I am studying natural history under Mr. Martin. If you want the tortoises I will be obliged to buy some poison to stuff them up. If I am obliged to go to South Bend by myself I beseech you to let me take a coat at the Bishop's. I also want a hat. Tell [me] if I must bring all my things with me for if I am to come back here [I will] take none but the most necessary.

[Forgive] my poor English style; and be assured that [I] always have the feelings of a son for you, my [Fa]ther.

[Give] my respects to all the Brothers.

Anselm

18. Brother Anselm (3) to Father Sorin

Vincennes July [16?], 1843

Dear Father,

I received your last letter Thursday last, and if I am not mistaken, you have already received the answer I had promised you, for I put it to the post office last Sunday. I have nothing new to tell you, except that I have changed of room, and that I am in a great deal worse one, so very damp that if I leave my shoes 4 or 5 days without brushing them, they will be very mouldy, and my books suffer the same inconvenient. My old room has been converted into a Sacristy, and the Bishop has given me his domestic's, which is indeed larger, but much more damp too.

I am longing for your answer every day, and I pray you to answer to all the things I have asked you. Don't omit anything. Give my love to all the Brothers and tell them that I rejoice to see them in a very short time.

Brother Anselm

I am very sincerely your very affectionate and devoted servant, Brother Anselm.

19. Brother Anselm (4) to Father Sorin
[Translated from French]

Vincennes July 26, 1843

My dear Father,

I'm waiting for your letter day by day, and as nothing comes, I need to know when retreat will begin and if it's necessary to bring my things to South Bend or leave them here. Monsignor just asked if it will be 4 or 5 days before retreat begins. I told him that I knew nothing about it because you told Mr. Martin that you yourself didn't know. Then he asked me if you knew if Mr. Shaw would preach the retreat. I said no, and that I thought that you hoped Mr. Martin would, on which point he replied that that was "nonsense" on your part and that you ought to understand that the pastor of the parish could not leave his flock to go preach a retreat to Brothers 300 miles away. Mr. Shaw had asked me one or two days before when the retreat would be. I told him that I knew nothing about it. He told me then that he would preach the retreat, but that he could not leave here before August 12 and many other things that are too long to enumerate. Relative to the retreat the bishop told me last Monday that I would make my retreat here and that you had told him that I would not go to South Bend to which I replied in a slightly angry tone that that didn't matter as long as I had a Brother to help me next year and that I certainly wouldn't be able to do everything all alone. To that he said that Sister did the free school well by herself but unfortunately I forgot to tell him that she didn't have to teach French. Then I went to Mr. Martin's house to bring him an insect, and I told him what the bishop just said to me, and he was really surprised because he had always said to me I would go to the retreat. He told me to write you a letter of complaint. Two days later the bishop told me that you had given him the freedom to send me to South Bend or to keep me here and that if I could find a horse to borrow, he'd let me go. That consoled me a little because I was really sad about not going to the retreat.

My Father, I can't fool you that in learning all this news, I had some resentment against you as well as the Community, because after wearing myself out teaching for a year and having the Community's interests in everything I did, it seemed to me that you'd not hold back six or seven dollars to let me enjoy the benefit of the retreat with my confreres.

I don't yet know if I'll go because I don't yet have a horse to borrow and the bishop probably won't let me go by stagecoach. Be assured that I'll do everything possible to go, and if I do go, I'd leave from here probably on the tenth.

Please answer my first letter and this one because I await your response day by day.

I suppose that the new colony has arrived at South Bend, and the bishop's of my opinion because yesterday he received a letter from New York which announced their landing—on the sixth of this month.

Brother Anselm

20. Brother Mary Joseph (1) to Father Sorin

Madison October 13, 1843

My dear Father,

I take the opportunity of writing to you by Father Delaune's letter. I am sure you will be glad to get this little help from Father Delaune. He wants it very bad himself, but I told him you was more in need of it than he was, so he concluded to send it. It seems as if Providence rewards your labors for we have seen many instances of it in our little community. I hope you are getting along with our college. I pray for your success. I should be glad to know of the safe arrival of our dear Brother John. I hope you are all well. I am teaching in the church. Our basement is not yet finished. It will be a fine schoolroom. Besides, Father is getting a room dug out next to the schoolroom for me to sleep in. I have 38 scholars, some of them very bad ones. I tried to get along without whipping them, but I tried all to no purpose. Father Delaune told me it would not do so I keep a little cane which keeps them in order better than all the other punishments. Dear Father, tell me what you think about it. My school has not been kept very regular yet. I have no clock or timepiece. Father says he will buy one when the school is finished. Besides, I work when I am not teaching. I have not kept silence for Father leaves me sometimes to direct the men. Dear Father, pray for me and my school that I may succeed to your best wishes. I pray for you all. Father Delaune is very kind to me. No more at present but remain your obedient son in Christ,

Brother Mary Joseph

21. Brother Anselm (5) to Father Sorin
[Translated from French]

Vincennes October 26, 1843

My dear Father,

I promised you in my last letter it would not be long before I'd write to you, and this is really recreation for me because I'm upset here.

First, I suppose I have to complete for you the beautiful reception the bishop gave me.

After having told me that I'd taken a brush from the kitchen, he told me class was not conducted as it was supposed to be, and that I'd given almost 4 months of vacation whereas I'd given only 3, and yet it was he who told me to give them 8 days at Christmas and 15 days at Easter, because otherwise I would not have done it. Then he told me ["] I know what some priests told me about the Brothers.["] I didn't understand very well what he meant by that except that some priests had told him bad things about us. When I saw that he'd finished and had stopped talking, I was confused, had nothing to say, although I still had many things to ask him, among other things permission to eat something after my classes, as you told me to, but I was afraid that he would ask me, "Do the seminarians eat anything?"

Please, Father, speak to him yourself because Mr. Martin doesn't like to; he knows him too well.

I told you, I believe, that he finally told me I would not have a bedroom and that he could not conveniently give me one, and that if I were cold it'd be necessary to light the stove in the corridor; well, Father, do you think that a little stove, such as it is, can warm my bedroom through a wall almost two feet thick? It is true that I can open my door, but if I do it, very probably something would be taken, because last year Brother Celestine's flannel jacket was taken while he and I were in class, and furthermore that [stove] scarcely warms the place. If I had yet what I had last year, it wouldn't worry me to spend my winter here, because the room was rather nice, but they made it into a sacristy, and I now have what the servant had which is very damp, and so dark that I have trouble drawing there at noon (because of the trees which are in front of the window); moreover if I open my window to see more clearly to draw, the wind blows dust on my painting or on my paper, so that I can no longer work, and my room is always untidy. Truthfully, Father, it is like that, and I don't exaggerate at all, and I'm telling you definitely that if I don't have another room or at least a stove in my room, I will not stay here, because the vow of obedience that I made does not oblige me to kill myself, or to make myself sick to obey the bishop who has at least more than ten rooms standing empty, because last week he bought a beautiful house for the Sisters on Market Street, and he is going to have the one they had previously, which is certainly very beautiful; but perhaps he didn't find it beautiful enough to receive the Sisters from Terre Haute because the Sisters of Charity who were here have left.

The Sisters are fine; they have good rooms, a nicely furnished classroom whereas the Brothers have one [ ] for their schoolroom and nothing else in it but three tables and one stove. Last year Brother Vincent had put two small picture frames there; well, somebody took them while I was gone, so there is no longer crucifix, no bulletin board, nor anything at all there; so the children don't know what side to turn to for prayers.

Father, if you'd been present when I arrived here, you'd have seen the state in which everything was in my room. And the books that I'd left there were so mildewed that if I wished to sell them now, I'd lose more than 0.25 on some of them. The velvet itself of my math box was mildewed, even though it was firmly closed; even the wood of my bed was almost green with mildew.

In the classroom it was even worse. There I found toads, caterpillars, spiders as big as your pinkie, a notebook fallen on the floor and almost entirely reduced to mud, two picture frames had disappeared; someone had drawn figures [graffiti] on the walls, on the door, on the blackboard, etc., etc. The girls had bunked there for 8 days, and the day I began school, there were still six mattresses on one table, and all that had been done by the seminarians. Of three chairs that I had in my bedroom, I found only one. My mirror and my brushes had been taken. No one had the heart to refill my mattress nor to clean my bed whereas everything was done nicely for the seminarians.

In a word, Father, I have to saw and chop my own wood if I want to make a fire in the small stove in the corridor, mend my clothes because the girls don't like to mend them, and do all sorts of things that have nothing to do with my contract, and I tell you truthfully that I'd prefer to be worse off in another place and to see zeal for schoolwork, than to be here and to see the negligence which Monsignor has for the school boys, and I beg you in the name of Mary to get me out of here soon, but meanwhile your will be done.

Mr. Galagher has not yet written to me.

Yesterday I spoke to the bishop and he told me honestly perhaps that he regrets what he said to me. I began my class last Monday and I have about 20 students now. I am teaching only one language as you told me to.

It continues to be cold here, and right now it's snowing. You have told me to apply myself to drawing, but you know that if I don't have a fire, I won't be able to do it. I have spent only $2.75 to come here from South Bend, although from that I took one dollar to shoe my horse, and I am going to tell you how I did it: one day I ate lunch, and the next day in the evening I ate supper, and I did that for 4 days. I think that another time you'll let me go to South Bend without the bishop's permission.

Brother Anselm

Give my respects to all the good priests, Brothers, Sisters, and tell them to pray for me and also for my children.

22. Brother Anselm (6) to Father Sorin
[Translated from French]

Vincennes November 7, 1843 JMJ

My Reverend Father,

Finally the postulant you are waiting for decided to go to South Bend. He stayed at the college 15 days with the intention of becoming a priest, but he's disgusted and wishes now to become a Brother.

They finally gave me my brushes, and I found my mirror in the verger's bedroom. He left the bishop's house during the last vacation for the sole reason that his bedroom was unhealthy and his wife and children were always sick, but I can assure you this bedroom is better than mine.

The seminarians' vacation, which began on August 15, ended last Monday.

I'd like a clock or a watch to time my Exercises because the church clock doesn't always chime.

Everything is extremely beautiful here; we have a magnificent dining room. The seminarians have splendid and comfortable rooms and dorms, etc. It's only I who am miserable, without a fire inside.

Has Brother John arrived? Is good Father Gouesse better?

Please tell Mr. Marsille that there is a paper mill at La Fayette and that if he wants to buy some drawing paper for his maps, he'd find some inexpensive there. Tell Brother Vincent to send me everything I had left at the office and at the Sisters' house, and not to forget above all my glazed paper for cut-outs. If you can send me one of the large Murray grammar books as well as an algebra book, you'll do me a big favor, or let me buy one. I won't be able to take math lessons at the college this year because there's no one to replace me here. I'm really upset, but I will study them a little myself. I'm very successful doing oriental painting, and I'm sure that if I had a teacher I would learn to do it perfectly with a few lessons. But as a good teacher of this kind of painting can't be found in America, I'm going to propose to Father Rector to return to spend a year in France to learn all of it, which is hard because it includes landscape and portraiture. I would learn at the same time linear and academic drawing, etc.

Don't believe, Father, that I wish to defrock. No, truthfully, but as Father Rector promised I could return sometime to France, I prefer to go there now while I am yet young because I would have much more facility in learning drawing, and I'd be more able to give service to the Community. Otherwise I'd prefer to go only after a long stay in this country—or not to go at all. I won't nag. (But you know the usefulness of drawing and painting in a college [secondary school]).

A thousand greetings to our good priests, Brothers, and Sisters. Your Reverence's obedient and respectful servant,

Brother Anselm

PS I beg you to excuse my scribbling because the postulant's in a hurry and waiting for me.

23. Brother Anselm (7) to Father Sorin
[Translated from French]

Vincennes December 17, 1843

My dear Father,

For three weeks Brother John has been at St. Peter's, and I don't know when he will come back. While waiting for him, I've decided to write you this short letter to beg you once more to kindly send me all my things by way of Mr. J. Marsille and to forget nothing. I'm waiting for my drawing patterns, my tracing paper, my cap, my hat, etc., etc. with the greatest impatience because my head is very cold, and I have nothing to cover my head other than my straw hat, my other hat being infinitely too small.

Send me also a pair of shoes, two boxes of coral to clean my teeth, tooth medicine that Brother Augustine had given me and that I put in my box at the Sisters' house. Arrange the medicine in such a way that it won't spill because it would stain all my drawing patterns, my levite, etc., etc., and if you find it impossible to send it to me, keep your eye on it, and tell Brother Augustine to write me about its composition and I'll make it myself.

If you've received some beautiful drawing patterns from Brother John, send me some of them because Brother John brought me only four of them. Did Brother John bring an accordion from France? Because Brother Donatien told me in his last letter that he sent me one.

The bishop has finally had a small quilt made for me, and I sleep much better. He also offered via Mr. Martin a new bedroom on the fourth floor. It is much healthier, but also much colder and darker than what I now have. I asked him if it would be possible to put a stove in there. He said no. Well, in light of that, I resolved to talk to you about it before taking possession of it. Tell me what I should do. Truthfully, it's the worst of all the rooms that the bishop has. Mr. Martin no longer wants to ask the bishop for anything for me, and he told me that he'd given up entirely.

Mr. Courgean begs you to send him his English Imitation as well as his Bible, or to send him his Hebrew grammar book. He also told me that he'd done your business the best he could. Send us these things by way of Mr. Marsille at Vincennes.

My dear Father, as a member of the Community, I am obliged to tell you that Brother John behaves very badly or at least very frivolously at St. Peter's and at Washington. A priest told me that, and he told me that probably Mr. Parray or some people from Davies's County would write to you to recall him. I know why and if you want the reason, I'd write to you about it in my next letter. He had the craziness to say here that he studied philosophy—to people who knew very well that he didn't even know his grammar very well. He also is spreading around all over that he's no longer a Brother.

Have you asked the bishop to give me permission to eat a piece of bread in the evening after my class? The seminary is now at the Sisters' place, and I am obliged to go there to get my meals. The bishop and his priests have a dining room for themselves at the bishop's house. I would prefer to take my meals in the bishop's kitchen with his servants than to go to the seminary everyday. Tell me what to do!

I now have 40 students, and I'd have more if I dismissed two blacks that the bishop told me to take. There are several of them who want to learn French, but I don't teach it as you have told me [not to]. Mr. Martin no longer visits my class. I don't know why.

Happy New Year to all,

Brother Anselm

I'll write when Brother John comes back. If I had a half ream of ruled paper, I could make a good sale here. Answer me as soon as possible, and tell me if I can have the books that I asked for in my last letter. I don't need a large English grammar book. Does Father Rector want me to return to France? I told him I'd gladly go for two years to learn drawing, but not to stay forever.

Chapter Three

1844

24. Brother Mary Joseph (2) to Father Sorin

Madison January 22, 1844

Reverend Father,

I received your kind letter last Wednesday. We are all well at present. Mr. Delaune has been very sick in bed for two weeks of inflammation of the bowels and bilious fever. We had no Mass on one Sunday. The next Sunday Reverend Mr. Weinzlophen said Mass. Madison is improving daily. Mr. Delaune is speaking of getting Sisters. The Presbyterians have moved their college to Madison. It is called the Hanover College. They have published a violent book on the Inquisition speaking of the Catholics in the most wicked manner. They are about to build a splendid college. The citizens of all denominations have contributed several thousand dollars. Reverend Mr. Delaune wishes to know what grammar, geography, and catechism we shall use in the school. Mr. Delaune thinks the Douay Catechism would be the best for those to study who have finished the small catechism. I am glad to hear that you are so soon to enter the college. I hope that God will look kindly on your efforts. Mr. Delaune held a meeting for the purpose of collecting money for the purpose of defraying the expenses of the Brother. They have collected $10 at the first meeting besides fifty have agreed to pay 10 cents a month. There are collectors for the different wards of the city.

Dear Father, pray for me, your obedient son in Jesus Christ,

Brother Mary Joseph

25. Brother Anselm (8) to Father Sorin
[Translated from French]

Vincennes February 8, 1844

My Reverend Father,

For a long time I hoped to receive a letter from you, and I really didn't know if you had not forgotten me, but now I've received one which, although short and devoid of the information I asked for, consoles me very much.

Reverend Father, I'm not at all unaware of the name of the man who told you that the Brothers and I especially are proud; I know very well that it is Mr. Martin, who 3 or 4 months ago seemed to be my best friend as well as that of the Brothers generally, but who for some time has shown himself to be my greatest enemy.

1. No longer coming to visit my class.
2. No longer speaking to me.
3. Refusing to ask for anything from the bishop for me.

(Because he told me some time after I'd arrived here that he had stopped that practice totally.)

4. Depriving me sometimes of my meals, etc., etc., etc. because, as I told you in my last letter, he told me that when I'd arrive at the dining room after the others, I'd have nothing to eat, and that I could go eat wherever I wanted, that I'd have no privilege here. On that point, having told him that I had rules to follow, he replied that that meant nothing to him, but that it was necessary to follow the rule he gave me, and if I weren't happy, I could go elsewhere. He told me also I shouldn't hold students after class, although Brother Vincent had told me to because it follows our rules.

In that regard I have not obeyed him, and that's partly why he called me proud. When I come 4 or 5 minutes to the dining room after the others, he would like me to tell him why. I think that it's for all these things that he calls me proud.

I've always had all the respect and devotion for him that I could have. I lost a rather considerable portion of my time last year getting him insects, snakes, etc., etc. He promised to give me some but no, he paid me in stupid answers, if I may so express myself. I know, Reverend Father, that you believe Mr. Martin more than I, while what I tell you is in fact true and I take God as witness.

I just received your letter dated January 30, and I'm going to send you by way of dear Brother Lawrence the note you asked from Mr. Marsille. Having almost no room, I can't impart to you all the feelings that your long awaited letter suggested to me. You tell me, Father, that Mr. Martin still likes me; I don't think so, at least he doesn't act that way. I promise to offer him your greetings, but I don't know if I will ask him to give me his goodwill; I don't think so because I never offended him, and I was not at all wrong to tell him what I told him. Reverend Father, once more, please call me away from here for my own good, because I'll perhaps lose my vocation here. I don't doubt but that Mr. Martin seeks to prejudice you against me, but, if you still have confidence in me, be assured that I will do all in my power to remove the bad opinion they have about the Brothers.

Do you think, Reverend Father, that it's not hard to teach sometimes while fasting, or to go from 8 AM to 8 PM without eating a single mouthful of bread or to go to bed without supper? Nevertheless since he made the case, that has happened to me several times, because I didn't hear the bell ring and much less the clock because it doesn't run regularly. How can you expect me to like Mr. Martin who is the cause of all that?

If you were here, you'd see how everything is, how they talk about the Sisters and the Brothers. Somebody here told me that the Sisters and Brothers slept in the same dormitory, and it was a clergyman who said that to me.

I am for life your very humble and devoted servant,

Brother Anselm

Write to me more often than you've done so far because I'm suffering here all alone and I don't have anyone to console me.

I still have many things to tell you but as Brother Vincent told me to write to him and as Brother Lawrence is in such a hurry, I'll tell you those things in another letter which will be clearer than this one because people come in very often to talk to me. Write me soon and please tell me to come back to South Bend.

26. Brother Mary Joseph (3) to Father Sorin

Madison, Jefferson County March 16, 1844

Reverend and dear Father,

I have been unwell for some time in consequence of being confined to the schoolroom and not taking enough of exercise. My lungs were affected. I began to spit blood. I went to the doctor. He gave me some medicine and told me I must take more exercise. Also the schoolroom being very damp I must be careful as I had the first stages of consumption. The water runs in the back room and under the schoolroom. I am better at present, thank God. My school is in the same situation. We have a society for paying all expenses. The people pay very well. Mr. Delaune has had a meeting of the congregation in order to petition the common council for a share in the taxes appropriated for the use of the Protestant seminaries. Mr. Delaune said he had been speaking to the mayor, and he said he had told "the mayor that if they sent Protestant scholars to our school he would pledge to have no religion taught during school hours." He then said to the meeting that the Protestants would not be present during every class and the Brother might teach what he pleased. He said the Brother could have a time after the school was over to teach religion. After the meeting I told Mr. Delaune that could not be, as we had religious exercises in the conduit for our school. I have 60 day scholars, more than I can well manage. I expect about 30 more when the weather gets fine. I have 36 girls attending Sunday school and as many more are of age to attend. Mr. Delaune is erecting [a] gallery 18 feet by 45. It will be ready for Easter. He had some thoughts of getting an organ, but he has given up the idea at present.

Madison is improving rapidly. The railroad will soon be finished to Indianapolis. They have removed the students here from Hanover College and the college will be put up in summer. The Methodists will erect a church in summer. This the third in this town for that sect. There will be a great many dwelling houses erected this summer. The people are rather bigoted here, writing and preaching against the Catholics.

Mr. Dalaune has just come home from Louisville. He saw Reverend Mr. Weinzlophen in the penitentiary. He has to work at the wheelwright's trade. Mr. Weinzloephen is [a] very pious man. Every person that knew him feels sorry for him. Mr. Delaune saw him last Tuesday. When he saw Mr. Delaune, he began to shed tears for the first time. Reverend Mr. Durbin from Kentucky was with Mr. Delaune. Mr. Weinzloephen said he was sentenced last Saturday to five years in the penitentiary. The witnesses were proved to have contradicted themselves seven times. The jury were asked if they had prejudged the case and would not answer. One was a Methodist preacher. Mr. Weinzloephen slept at Princeton jail that night on a bed of ropes with a buffalo skin. He was manacled to a man who was sentenced for stealing. The sheriff took them to the blacksmith's shop, riveted the manacles, and hurried them to the boat. The day was Sunday in Evansville. He had to pass through two rows of persons. Some laughed and mocked. Some pitied him. What surprised him most was that none of his congregation came to see him with the exception of a few Irishmen who shook hands with him. The sheriff then hired a stage. They came to a town line. The sheriff got out and staid about one half an hour. He told the people he had the Catholic priest so they came to insult him. On board the steamboat to Louisville the sheriff ordered him some coffee without milk or sugar and a piece of dry bread for breakfast. Soon after the passengers waited on the sheriff and begged he would allow them to come in the cabin. The sheriff consented, and the passengers treated him kindly and said he was innocent. All the money he had was $1.62. Mr. Delaune gave him some money, bought a bed for him, agreed with an Irishman to bring his dinner every day as the prison fare was very coarse being bacon and cornbread. He seemed to be resigned to the will of God. He will not have time to say his office. The priests of Louisville will bring him the Holy Communion once a week. They have only to cross the river. It is two miles from Reverend Mr. Heyxon of New Albany. The prison is let out by contract like a farm so they make them work very hard.

I hope you are all well and remember me in your very pious prayers for I need them very much. Believe me your obedient son in Christ,

Brother Mary Joseph

Mr. Delaune wishes me to ask you what grammar you use in the schools. They use Smith in all the schools in this place. It said to be very good for learners.

Pray for me, dear Father.

27. Brother Anselm (9) to Father Sorin
[Translated from French]

Vincennes April 9, 1844

My Reverend Father,

I received your kind letter of February 22 last Saturday, and I would have responded immediately, but Mr. Marsille had gone to Terre Haute and was supposed to return from there the next day. So it was absolutely necessary to wait for him if I were to see him, and he told me that he no longer had those two bills, but that he'd given them to Mr. Bagerlay before leaving, and that of all the bills which he still had, he had only one (a bill for wood) which I'll send to you if you judge it appropriate.

I haven't received yet the 50 dollars you told me about, and I don't know when I'll receive it.

Finally, thank you for the advice you gave me, and although it will be hard, I'll try to put it in practice.

I see rather clearly, because you tell me in your letter, that you think that I have exaggerated the things that Mr. Martin and Monsignor have made me suffer. But, Father, think as you wish! The truth is on my side, I am sure and certain.

You tell me to give you good news, but I don't have any except good Mother Theodore came about 15 days ago. She brought a small trunk for us and gave me eighty medals for my students. As bad news offends your good heart, I won't tell you any.

Please put on letters you address to me "Care of the Right Reverend Bishop" because there's a new postmaster here, and he kept the last letter you sent me at least a fortnight.

Some Catholics, especially those who have children in my school, wish that I'd go see them some time. May I go? Some here have also invited me several times to dinner, etc., and I admit to you I'm afraid that they're angry.

Please tell me what to do.

Good wishes to all the good priests, to dear Brother Vincent, and in general to all my dear confreres. I'm losing my English now, having no one to speak to. The students speak it very badly because I no longer go to the seminary to take recreation, Mr. Martin wishing that the seminarians no longer have contact with anybody from the outside. I was there only very rarely before, and sometimes 1, 2, 3 or 4 weeks passed without my going there a single time; I haven't gone walking a single time with them this year at all, except perhaps once when I first came here. Please send me my Constitutions.

Brother Anselm

28. Brother Vincent (12) to Father Moreau
[Translated from French]

Notre Dame April 11, 1844

My reverend Father,

Father Superior just received your letter with the two checks enclosed. Thanks to you and our two benefactresses. The evening it arrived we said our rosary as a way of showing thanks for such good help that came in due time. Thus Providence treats us since we've been in America, or rather it always has treated us so. May we be able to recognize it and see it in everything.

I'm taking advantage of a free moment that Brother Joachim leaves me to write you these lines. This poor Brother draws to his end, and I believe in a few days you'll have one child fewer. It's been almost eighteen months that he's suffered, but with an admirable patience. We hope you'll replace him if Providence doesn't do it directly, because it'd be extremely expensive to have our levites and the soutanes of the priests made by strange hands.

Brother John began an establishment in a small city named Fort Wayne. He has almost 80 students. His class is doing as well as possible. The bishop of Philadelphia wrote recently to Father Superior that he wanted at least eight Brothers immediately. He would entrust the schools of the city to them, then some principal places of his diocese. I'm not speaking here of the numerous requests made to us by other dioceses. I think you've been informed by letters from Father Superior. We groan at not being able to satisfy these venerable bishops who'd make all the sacrifices possible to have schools run by Brothers. I believe that one can say what our Divine Master said: the harvest is great, but the laborers are few.

Fathers Cointet and Marivault are on mission for Easter with our Indians and others. If Father Superior were sufficient almost fifteen months ago, presently three priests are not enough, because there are still certain congregations which haven't been visited. Likewise a year ago, our chapel was more than sufficient. We made an addition to it of a big tier and it's still too small. We had such a mob of people on Easter Sunday that the like had never been seen in this part of the country. The chapel, the sacristy, the choir, etc., everything was so full that it was impossible to get around. You understand that all were not Catholics. But there was no trouble. Before the High Mass, two Indian ladies received baptism with a child. On Holy Saturday likewise there was the baptism of a Lutheran, the head of a family. He edified us greatly the day of his baptism and on Easter Sunday. He made his first communion with his eldest son. The goodness he felt in his soul was painted on his face and that of his poor wife who rejoiced because she's a good Catholic. Those of his sect said to him before his baptism, "If you turn Catholic, we'll burn your house, ruin your farm, etc." "Oh well, I'll turn Catholic all the same."

I'm not going into detail about the mission. Our priests are making it undoubtedly, and they're giving you an exact account of it, one more interesting than I'd be able to do.

In the midst of so many consolations, we are nevertheless in pain with all the clergy and religious souls in the matter of that good and virtuous priest I told you about more than eighteen months ago. I'll take up the story in a shortened form. In case you've forgotten, this priest, Alsatian by nationality, about 30 years old, was sent to Evansville by Monsignor, our bishop, to direct that congregation. An unfortunate woman accuses him of having done violence to her in the confessional. It'll be two years ago on the eve of the Ascension. The case was begun immediately and lasted until last March when the priest was given five years of forced labor. Here's the response a judge made in the penultimate examination: "It's sufficient that he's a Catholic priest. He must be condemned."

The little family of Notre Dame du Lac is growing more and more. Three years ago we left with seven, as you know. Now we have at least sixty. This is a great increase in three years. Divine Providence has been taking care of everything for three years. We're in its care, and we've suffered; nevertheless, we have never lacked food, clothing, and other things necessary to life. Oh, what a good mother Providence is. I'll go into detail a bit on these things. Imagine seven poor strangers arriving 1800 leagues from their country with almost nothing; nevertheless, they had to live, had to make themselves a little furniture, buy animals, carts, and all the utensils necessary to make a large farm worthwhile. Soon the personnel increase. Expenses increase in proportion so that after having cleared and enclosed 70 to 80 acres of land at great expense, it fails. I can say purposely by Providence. All leave to go 100 leagues to start over again at even greater expense. We find in this new habitat only old log buildings open to all the winds of a winter that lasts nearly six months. In spite of the hardships of the weather, we had to build a chapel which cost plenty although it was only wooden. We had to clear 40 acres of land as soon as spring came, make bricks, a large building amounting to 4000 francs, if we hadn't put it up by hand,

and with that the personnel increased. Consequently, we have to keep increasing the furniture. We have to clear another 100 acres of woods, enclose them, increase the livestock, and for the entire crop we had only potatoes. We had to buy bread, meat, etc., etc. Oh, my reverend Father, Providence is a good mother!

After having spoken to you in the heart of my letter about Brother Joachim's sickness, now I have to tell you that God called him to Himself on the 13th at 9 PM. His death was, we hope, that of the just. He had the good fortune to receive all the helps of religion and to give up his soul to his Creator under the eyes of Father Superior and other priests. Although he was conscious up to the hour of his death, he wasn't terrified. He spoke of it, on the contrary, as a thing he desired. He asked me often in his last days, "Do you think I have a deadly fever?" "I don't know," I replied, "but I know that you can't go far now." As much as his energy permitted him, he wouldn't miss hearing holy Mass for all the goods in the world. He charged me also to say to Brother Leopaul that he should write about his death to his brother from Evron. He's a shoe-maker and lives in the town. Our St. Mary Island is now dearer to us than ever. It's there the future life lives for the children of Notre Dame of the Lake. We hope, my reverend Father, that you'll come some day to say a "de profundis" on the graves of your dead children. The shape of the cemetery is a triangle. The priests, the Brothers, and the Sisters will each have their angle, and a Calvary scene will be placed in the middle. A little more to the East will be a little chapel in the shape of an octagon dedicated to Our Lady of the Lake. We'll begin it as soon as we have bricks. Later the Brothers' novitiate will be likewise on the island and attached to the little chapel in question.

I regret that paper and time doesn't let me say more about it, but what consoles me is that Father Superior is thinking about sending you someone to get you up to date about everything, and if obedience wants it to be me, the 1800 leagues separating us will seem but one day of fatigue and danger. All your American children offer you their homage, but no one does it more sincerely than he who is your Reverence's respectful servant,

Brother Vincent

29. Brother Anselm (10) to Father Sorin
[Translated from French]

Vincennes May 10, 1844

My Reverend Father,

Since you weren't able to come here for the retreat, on account of your health and work commitments, I think that you'll be happy to know how everything went.

The retreat was conducted by Rev. Mr. Timon, superior of all the United States Lazarists, and Italian by birth, I'm told.

This venerable priest is perhaps 50 or 55 years old and is extraordinarily remarkable for his fluency and his eloquence in the pulpit, and although English isn't his native language, he speaks it with ease, and I believe even more clearly than Mr. Shaw. There were in all 21 priests here for the retreat. I think that it'd be useless of me to give you their names as you don't know all of them.

From the north there were only Mr. Rodolphe from Fort Wayne and Mr. Clarke from Peru, who's going to live now in La Fayette.

Sunday, which was the last day of the retreat, all the priests received Holy Communion from the bishop's hand. Last Monday there was a solemn service for Monsignor Bruté as well as for all the deceased priests of the diocese. Tuesday there was a High Mass of thanksgiving.

Mr. Shaw, who'd been at St. Louis during Holy Week, came here last Friday, and consequently didn't attend the retreat; to me he seemed very devoted to the Brothers. At least he showed me many signs of friendship.

I received a letter from Brother Mary Joseph by way of Mr. Auroock [O'Rourke] who arrived here a little before Mr. Delaune. He told me that he had been sick, but that now he's better.

One of the seminarians, about 20 years old, defrocked secretly during Easter vacation. He was Irish. I have no more than 30 or 40 students now, many absent to plant corn. They're well behaved and as remarkable now for their obedience as they were before for their disobedience.

Almost a month and a half ago I had a cough which settled in my stomach and made me suffer a lot. I consulted Mr. Heron (a priest) and without prescribing any remedy for me, he said he'd speak to the bishop. I don't know why he didn't wish to prescribe any remedy for me. I also have an extremely weak stomach, which probably comes from my not taking enough nourishment, but that's not my fault because ever since Mr. Martin became superior of the Seminary, the portions are really too skimpy, above all at supper because there is never more than a very weak dish without soup, nor anything else except a cup of tea, whereas last year there was butter and much bigger portions. I have not yet asked the bishop for the snack you spoke to me about, but I think that fatigue will soon make me ask him [although] that displeases me a lot.

I need socks, not having but a single pair. The three that I had are successively found [and] lost in the laundry. They weren't very good, it's true. I also need a pair of shoes because mine while yet good won't take me up to retreat time. I wish that you'd make arrangements with the bishop to give me the things indicated above, because having asked him once for two dollars, he told me that he didn't want to give it to me because you had not made arrangements with him to give me anything.

I said to Brother Mary Joseph that if he could find a good horse and a good cart to borrow or even to rent, it would be good to take advantage of it because then we could take our trunks with us, and moreover during the trip we'd have to pay for only a horse, whereas if we each had a horse, we would have to pay almost as much for the rental and half as much more for the trip, and furthermore, we would have to pay for the transporting of our things (as we aren't sure of coming back to our respective establishments, but you, Father, know that, and consequently you can tell us what to do): because, as you know, we can take only a few things with us if we go by horse. However, I think the best way for us, if we can't find a cart, will be to borrow horses and to send our most necessary items by the stagecoach or by some other means.

In your next letter tell me if I should rent a cart (if we can find one), or get some horses. It's all the same to me: the only thing I want is to save money.

I told Brother Mary Joseph to answer me in about a month and to tell me if he found a cart to borrow or not. As soon as he's responded, I'll let you know.

Give my greetings to all the good priests, to Brother Vincent as well as all the Brothers in general.

I am your Reverence's very humble and obedient servant,

Brother Anselm

Send me my Constitutions if you find an opportunity because I no longer remember the prayers I'm supposed to say for the deceased Brothers.

30. Brother Augustine (1) to Father Sorin

Detroit May 27, 1844

My dear Father,

As I presume Brother Vincent has given all the particulars of our journey thus far, which has been very prosperous, I need not say anything concerning it. Since I left South Bend my health has been good notwithstanding the bad roads over which we had to ride all night in a miserable stage. *Opposition* which in America is called the life of *trade* has given us an opportunity to go to Buffalo for nearly one fourth the usual charge. As I will write lengthily from New York, I will say no more but recommend myself to your pious solicitude and the prayers of the Community.

Your affectionate son forever in Jesus Christ,

Brother Augustine

31. Brother Vincent (13) to Father Sorin
[Translated from French]

Detroit May 27, 1844

My very dear Father,

We arrived at Detroit on Saturday at 2 o'clock in the evening without any accident. We went straight to Mrs. Beaubien's where we were accommodated in the most kindly manner. She would gladly have acted in our behalf, but she wants you to see and tell him yourself the way you want it. While waiting for you to be able to come to make the acquaintance of this respectable family, have no fear. Mr. & Mrs. Beaubien's word is trustworthy. I saw the lots in question. They are situated in a very beautiful position very near the [cathedral ?] for which they just dug the foundations. Instead of ten lots, one could make twelve out of them. Mr. Beaubien already [ ] 800 for two of these lots. Mr. & Mrs. Beaubien require your presence, and really being at the places, you could better judge what there is to do and empower someone to sell or not.

After dinner we're going to get the $100 for the clock. I haven't found Monsignor. He's at Philadelphia or at Pittsburgh, they say, to look for some Sisters. I spoke to the Vicar General. He told me that his Grace will be satisfied, but for him he believes that St. Joseph would be a better place because he believes that it will grow more than [ ]. As you see, it's necessary, in my opinion, for you to sacrifice four or five days to settle all these things, and if I knew the day of Monsignor's arrival, I would beg you to come at that time. I have reasons for that, but I don't think that he'll come for a fortnight since he has not written. We slept at the bishop's. They received us with much kindness. You see that I'm writing my letter on parting from Mr. & Mrs. Beaubien.

This is how we spent our Pentecost Sunday. In the morning we saw the Vicar General before Holy [Mass], and we all had Holy Communion at the 7 o'clock Mass. We heard High Mass and in the evening we were in Canada to hear Vespers at the Jesuits' place. We had to stay two days. This evening at 6:30 we board a steamboat for Buffalo. Never has one seen places so inexpensively!

We pay five dollars for both of us, and we are in beautiful cabins. I didn't want to take a cabin, but good Brother Augustine didn't want to leave me. I preferred to follow him to the cabin rather than be separated or be sick for so little because five dollars for two persons to go 300 miles fed and bedded is really inexpensive.

When you come here, you can take your horse as far as Jackson because the roads by stagecoach are really rough. At Jackson you take the railroad at 8 AM and you arrive at 2 PM. You pay $2.50 for 70 miles.

I can be no happier with Brother Augustine. He is like my good angel as he takes care of me.

I saw Mr. Le Tourneau's parents. They're fine. Mr. & Mrs. Le Tourneau have been in Buffalo since Saturday evening.

Goodby, good and dear Father. God knows when we'll see each other again. Good wishes to all and a share in everyone's prayers.

Brother Vincent

You have not yet given me the letter of recommendation to present to people I collect from. Mr. & Mrs. Beaubien offer you their respect. Miss Emilie is fine. She is going to try to make a trunk for our orphans and apprentices. There is a young orphan at Mrs. Beaubien's. They'll offer him to you. Mr. Le Tourneau's brother can also go to join his brother.

32. Brother Anselm (11) to Father Sorin

[Translated from French]

Vincennes June 2, 1844

My Reverend,

I received a letter from Reverend Father Rector on the 23rd of last month. He said several things to me which made me happy, but he also said one thing that pained me a lot. Here it is (word for word):

"As for your return to France, I await word from Father Sorin to know if he can consent to it and replace you. Write him about this, and tell me then what he thinks about it because he has not responded to me on this question. I would be happy furthermore if he agreed with me to see you back at Holy Cross, and I love you too much not to desire that fervently."

In my last letter to him last February, I said (knowing well that he wished to recall me to France) that if he wished to let me go spend a fortnight or more with a good master of oriental painting, I'd consent to go teach English at Notre Dame of Holy Cross for one or two years on condition that he would not give me any other job than that and that he would let me spend my free time with dear Brother Hilarion who would show me linear drawing and ornamental drawing. However, at the end of my letter I told him that if he ordered me to return to France, I would do it although it would be hard for me. I begged him (in case he wouldn't approve the proposition I made to him to return to France to study drawing and painting) to let me spend the rest of my days in America near you, my dear Father, and among my dear confreres.

I beg you then, Reverend Father, to ask Reverend Father Rector to accept the proposal that I made to him to return to France for a year or two to study oriental painting and design, but not that he would keep me there forever, because in that case it would be very painful to return there.

If I had never offended and disobeyed you, dear Father, I would have a claim to your assistance now; but as I have had the unhappiness to do so, I have none except by my repentance.

I think that you understand too well how much a good teacher of drawing and painting is necessary at the College of Notre Dame du Lac for you to oppose the proposal I made to Reverend Father Rector. I'm certain that if there were a good draftsman at Notre Dame du Lac, many students would come there just to learn these two fine arts for which I have so much talent, and which I think I could easily teach.

Since I've been here, I've sold almost all the flowers that I did, and the men and women who bought them have framed them as masterpieces. Although I've had only a single painting lesson, which Brother Vincent gave me, I have gained a reputation as a painter here.

I have no response yet from Brother Mary Joseph; in case he doesn't find a cart to borrow, would you prefer that we go on horses (because neither of us, I believe, knows how to handle a cart)? Will you let me buy a saddle, a bridle, in a word what is necessary to go on horseback?

Mr. Bellier's servant, Tourneux, who is my close friend, told me that if you let me buy all that, he'll see to it that I get it inexpensively and of top quality. He was a blacksmith in France for several years, and he knows everything about horses; he also told me that if you want to buy a horse, he'd find one for you better than the one I had last year for 18 to 20 piastres, but if I have to return here, I'd prefer to rent one. As for a saddle, I wouldn't find any to borrow for less than 2 or 3 dollars, whereas I can have a brand new outfit for $12. That's the price Tourneux paid for a priest's who leaves tomorrow for New Albany. Anyway, if I don't return here, you'll keep the saddle that I'd buy if you wish, and if I do return here, it'll help me to come back this year and return the next year and so on.

Goodby, my good Father. I am really in a hurry. Reply to all this as soon as possible because I'm waiting for your letter in order to reply to Father Rector, who told me to ask him for things I needed for painting so that he can send them by way of Monsignor's cousin who is supposed to leave France next September.

Brother Anselm

33. Brother John (4) to Father Sorin

Fort Wayne June 5, 1844

My dear, dear Father,

How are you by this time and all the dear community? Have you recovered from your sickness? I heard you was sick and was surprised not to hear from you by Mr. D. Comparet, but perhaps you have been too much occupied to attend as yet to anything beyond the house. The time is drawing nearer and nearer to my return. Oh, if you knew how I feel with regard to coming back you would wish the time shorter too. I am perfectly happy in mind and still continue ever true to my vocation and I hope that your prayers and the prayers of the good Brothers will enable me to succeed in my expectations. I have merely written these few lines until I can find a more favorable time to lengthen my epistle. Give my love to all. I hope they are all well and accept the fervent love of your,

Ever truly,

F. Steber

34. Brother Vincent (14) to Father Sorin
[Translated from French]

Brooklyn June 6, 1844

My very dear Father,

Before leaving Detroit, I wrote to you about the first part of our trip. I learned at New York that Monsignor had taken some Sisters away and that he is now at home.

Monday, May 26, 7 o'clock PM. We left for Buffalo by steamboat that charged us only five dollars for both of us, and we were in a cabin and well fed. Lake Erie did not trouble us like the first time. We arrived at Buffalo on Wednesday morning.

6 o'clock. We went to good Mr. Whileme who received us well. We stayed there until 6 PM when we took the boat for Connecticut. Then we had to [MS torn] furnished with everything. While we were in Buffalo the good Mr. Whileme was very good to us. He offered us money, which we didn't take. I had to take a half glass of wine with dinner. It was repugnant, but I had already refused him many things before. I shouldn't be so singular.

He told us about Mr. Clark who several days before had asked him for ten dollars which he gave him. It seemed that he left a ribbon and the cross that you had given him. He finally made a kind of search which in the eyes of Mr. Whileme must have produced a bad effect.

I take my itinerary up again. I said that Wednesday at 6 PM we left for Connecticut. We arrived on Sunday morning at 5 o'clock where we soon took the railroad. There Father Gray had the two trunks and the [MS torn] for us. We returned to Albany where we only changed steamboat. We had time to buy our provisions for supper.

At midnight we came to the village of Brother Augustine's relatives, but unfortunately we were put on the other riverbank. I stayed to guard the baggage one hour while Brother Augustine went to find a canal. Finally he found one, and we paid a man four [ ]. We crossed the river, and when we arrived at La Pointe (the name of the village) it was 2 o'clock. There [rested] a little because we were tired. My intention was to stay there only one day, but Brother Augustine was disposed to stay two days and was not too tired to please his good family.

Finally on June 6 we arrived at New York at 10 o'clock. Brother Augustine [ ] in a private house, and I stayed on the steamboat until morning when we returned to the Permentier family's home where we were embarrassed by the solicitude they had for us. I'm not able to give you an idea of this goodness, of this amiability, of this unexpected service. Finally having put us in [MS torn] to pay them. Mrs. Bayer gave us four [MS torn]. [ ] collection. Mr. Bayer himself wrote to some lady about the captain of the Duchess of Orleans. He didn't have for us [ ] $20 [ ]. I believe that you know this ship. It is perhaps the best [ ]. What pleases me is that we embark on Saturday, the day consecrated to our so good and so worthy Mother.

I don't regret the three days that I've spent in New York. I've seen the greatest parts of it. I recommended them to Brother Augustine. Monsignor seemed to receive us rather indifferently. I don't know if it's his way because I had never seen him before.

Good Father Audomet at St. Paul offered us his house. Brother Augustine and I went to confession. Peace between Brother Augustine and me thanks to God alone [ ] He tormented me to make me change habits.

Many respectable people [ ] but thanks be to God. But I anticipate that it will be necessary when we come back. It will be necessary [ ] in coming there; because the spirits are very [ ] because it suffices that we [ ] many in a house [ ] there perhaps great trouble [ ]. We had to spend $43 to get to New York by stage, rail, and steamboat. $4.50 to [ ] and to have our trunks transported. I paid $40 for the trip. I can't finish the tally until Brother Augustine gives me the bill tonight for the cook who wants four dollars for our meals.

As you can see it's costing us plenty. We tried the Liverpool railroad, but the expense would have been still greater. Your letter that [ ] Mrs. Bayer made [ ] tears. The time of our reunion seemed to me very uncertain. I would not want [MS torn]. I'm sorry that you [ ] to present not one part.

I forgot to tell you that I was at Sacred Heart. I didn't find all the Sisters who crossed the sea with us, except Sister Elizabeth who is English. Mother Superior whom we thought dead was to arrive today in New York because she is now in Canada. It was for her that I had gone so far because Mrs. Bayer thought she arrived yesterday.

Goodby. My very dear Father, tomorrow [MS blurred] put to sea. I no longer expect Mr. Bayerley. Good wishes to all my good Brothers of Notre Dame du Lac. Respect to the priests and remembrance to the dear Sisters. In everyone's prayers,

Brother Vincent

35. Brother Mary Joseph (4) to Father Sorin

Madison June 13, 1844

Reverend Father,

I have been very sick for two weeks of bilious fever. I am now getting better, thank God. I was very sorry to hear of the death of our two good Brothers, but I hope they are better off than we are. I am sure you will miss them both, but God knows what is best both for them and us. May they rest in peace.

I have some good boys here. If you think you would want postulants, John Laverny, the oldest, is the son of good parents. He is about the age of 17 years. He is strong and able to work. He would also be able to teach with a little tuition. He is pious and innocent, not as yet having mixed with the world. He attends Sunday school, works during the week. If you think he would be of service to you, you will please to let me know. Reverend Mr. Delaune recommends him to you.

Dear Father, will you please to tell me in your next [letter] at what time the retreat will commence? I long for the time as I am much backward in piety—having much dissipation.

Your obedient son in Christ,

Brother Mary Joseph

36. Brother Augustine (2) to Father Sorin

Havre de Grace July 4, 1844

My Reverend and dear Father Superior,

The anxiety which I know you experience to hear of our safe arrival prompts me not to wait until we get to the Mother House to write to you. As I mentioned in my letter from New York we sailed on the 8th of June at 12 o'clock PM in the ship Duchess D'Orleans with Captain Richardson and we arrived here this morning making our passage 26 days. For the first five days of our sailing we had fine wind, but on the afternoon of the 5th evening a strong north wind set in which continued with increasing vigour for four days during which time we suffered not only from the rolling of the ship which was so severe that it was with difficulty we could keep possession of our beds, but also from large bodies of water that came down like a second Niagarra in force into our miserable steerage. Our clothes and trunks got wet and some of our provisions. The sea was angry and swollen, its waves forming themselves into high mountains creating deep valeys between them. Our ship was one moment over a hundred feet above the usual surface of the sea, and in the next it was ingulphed between immense mountains a corresponding distance in depth. Our danger was not a *little*, especially as we were on the Banks of Newfoundland during this time, which is considered dangerous in the finest weather in consequence of the heavy fogs which darken its atmosphere and of its numerous sand banks. Those mammoth waves threatened destruction every moment to our noble Duchess, but the power which saved St. Peter in his frail bark did not desert us. No, the God of Mercy was not deaf to the fervent prayers offered by you in the loneliness of your closet for the safety of your spiritual children on the dreary ocean. In the midst of our greatest danger, Brother Vincent with his characteristic solid faith made a remark similar to this, "I have one hope and that is in the prayers of so many holy persons which are offered for us daily."

On Sunday 16th when the storm was at its hight, we went on deck to say our Vespers for we had not sufficient light in the steerage, and took our seats where we least expected a wetting, but ere long we were honored by a showerbath for a large wave fell on our heads and wet us thoroughly. Unlike me, Brother Vincent received it with his usual smile of good humor. Our steerage passengers were twenty in number, most of whom are French. One of them, a French lady from Philadelphia, urged me strongly to go there on my return and make her house my home while I would be collecting for our institution. We presented a petition for our orphans to the cabin passengers through the Captain who behaved kindly towards us. A lady, an acquaintance of Mrs. Byerly and Mrs. Waddworth, took charge of it and collected $7.83 cents. She desired to be particularly remembered to the above ladies. Her name is Mrs. Francis of New York.

Our passage was lengthened from 18 to 26 days in consequence of a dead calm we met with in the channel which continued seven days. If possible we will take passage this evening for Mans in order to arrive there for Sunday. I desire to be remembered in the prayers of the community and feel satisfied, my dear Father Superior, you will not forget in yours your affectionate son in Jesus Christ,

Brother Augustine

N.B. I will not write again until I have spent some time at Mans in order to be able to give some information. Brother Vincent says he will write immediately from Mans after seeing Father Rector.

37. Brother Anselm (12) to Father Sorin
[Translated from French]

Vincennes July 13, 1844

My Reverend Father,

Last Saturday I was, as you told me to be, at Washington and at St. Peter's to find out if Mr. Campell and the St. Peter's farmer had the money you spoke to me about. The first had paid Mr. Galaghar close to a fortnight before, but the second told me that he had no money to give me right now but that in 2 or 3 weeks he'd receive some money from New York, and would pay me then. He asked me if I had the bill that he had given to Brother John. I replied no, and that I didn't even know where it was. Please tell me what Brother John did with it.

Mr. Galaghar told me in a letter that he wrote some time before I went to Washington that you owe him $13.50 for various things:

$9.00 for fruit trees
6.00 for sprouting wheat
2.00 for repairing the fence
.50 for burning the chaff out of the wheat
2.00 for hands boarding at Montgomery

But he subtracted from that $6.00 for 12 bushels of wheat that he had taken. When I was at Washington, he gave me only $35.50 and thus he kept $14.50 instead of $13.50, the reason being that the wheat was very bad, and perhaps also because neither he nor I remembered the sum that he had indicated on the letter he sent to me. If I had been informed about your current business affairs, I would perhaps have done better, but as I knew nothing about them, I told him to do as he wished. He told me that he wanted to hear from you; write him then and thank him for me, because he was very kind to me and seemed to me to do his best, only because you have let him alone. He's always afraid you found that he pays too much—that's what he told me.

I asked Monsignor some time ago what would be the most economical way for me to go to the retreat. As the expenses of the trip would be his, I wanted to do as he would tell me. He replied that you haven't yet settled with him as to who would pay for the trips. Furthermore, I could do as I wished. I don't know if he'll pay for my trip or not. He hasn't spoken to me about it at all.

I found a rather good mare to rent rather cheaply, but I have not yet found a saddle, and I don't even know if I'd find a good one to rent, even with lots of money. I really fancy having one made by the father of one of my students. I am sure he would make it for me inexpensively if I spoke to him about it. What I know is that one can get an excellent saddle here for 9 or 10 dollars, but as you didn't tell me specifically what I had to buy in your last letter (because you told me only to buy the most "indispensable" things without telling me what things), I don't know what to do; only I think that you included a saddle in your word "indispensable," but I'm not sure about that. I end this subject assuring you, and this is the truth, that I'll do the best I can and that I'll consider the Community's well-being in everything.

I'm really irritated, Reverend Father, that you didn't let me know about dear Brother Vincent's departure, because a long time before he left, I wanted to send letters to France, and I'd have gotten great pleasure for this opportunity to send them. But as that's passed, and since you can no longer remedy it, please beg Reverend Father Rector when you write to him, to send me a new supply of paints, especially those that are necessary for landscapes and portraits because I don't have a single one of them; those I received last year are beginning to be used up, and if he'd kindly replenish them with others even more beautiful, I would pray to God for him. Then as much paper made expressly for oriental painting as he can send me. I'd like it to be of all sizes and of the finest quality. If he could get me some one and a half feet or two feet wide or wider, two or three feet long, I'd be able to do pictures on it which I'd very easily sell for 10 to 15 francs or even more. Yesterday I sold three small ones that I had done yesterday in about 8 hours for one dollar and 5 cents, and yet people said this was inexpensive, while my paper and paints are very far from being of the best quality.

As soon as he supplies me with patterns of flowers, fruit, landscape, etc., etc., well executed and of all sizes, the price won't scare him because I can very easily sell the pictures that I would make on them for five times more than they cost him, although they'd probably be done more poorly, as fast as I do them.

Since I've given some flowers I made to my students, many persons have come to beg me to do some for them, offering me up to 50 cents and even 75 to make them a small rose, but as I had many other things to do, I could satisfy only a few of them. I feared also that wouldn't please you.

Please tell Reverend Father Rector to send me a new supply of brushes because some of mine begin to wear out.

I wouldn't know how to tell you how happy I am to see this year end and the retreat begin, but this joy turns to pain when I think that I'll probably have to come back here next year and begin again my distressing work which hasn't ended well (and Father, it's so difficult to please everybody here.)

However, I'll do what you say. I don't know when I'd leave here. Please let me know when retreat begins so that I can get there on time. The students' communion is over August 4. Perhaps I'll have to stay here until then.

Please write to me as soon as possible.

I bought a black redingote because the one I had this year became too small for me and because it is too faded. I'd go with my levite, but since the weather will be so hot, and the levite is so hot, I think that you'd not disapprove of what I did. Then I'd have spoiled it with the sweat of the horse, and it would probably make me sick because so hot an outfit is really unbearable right now, especially on horseback and riding as far as I will.

I received a letter from Brother Mary Joseph last Friday. He asks me to go through Madison telling me that as it's been 4 years since he's been on a horse, he's not a very good rider now. I'd go there fearing that something bad is happening to him because the mare he'll take is very frisky. I know that horse. It's Mr. Weincopln's. Being together, we'll spend much less.

Brother Anselm

I don't know if you'll be able to read this. I'm in a hurry, and the weather is so very hot that I can't write in a legible and intelligible manner.

38. Brother Vincent (15) to Father Sorin
[Translated from French]

St. Berthevin July 14, 1844

Very dear Father,

I've been a Normand Brother. I haven't written to you since my arrival at Le Mans as I had promised you. I had to talk to Father Rector and settle the accounts before telling you something certain. The error of 8000 francs in question, I believe, prejudiced Father Rector from authorizing the signature of 400 dollars, and he had called back 2000 on the 4000 francs of Father Zupier. There are also deductions which, with expenses, add up to almost the 8000 above.

Meanwhile, he promised me that he would hold us accountable now for the 2000 that he had withdrawn after I explained to him that he himself had promised us via a letter the sum of 4000 francs. Meanwhile, take care to draw on it before we have finalized everything.

If you have not taken up the matter again of Father Marivault, I advise you strongly to entrust it to Father Rector. He knows the family, and he will arrange everything better than anyone. Father Rector told me that there were precautions to take and that we were late in writing without being accused of avoiding the trouble of a returned bill.

Father Rector won't be able to leave with the small colony. He has to go with the African foundation at the same time. I don't know yet which subjects we'll be given. I've seen neither tailor, nor cobbler, nor cook to be disposed of. Meanwhile we'll have a priest, a Brother, and a Sister superior. I've already asked for Father Verité and Brother Hilarion, but I fear getting neither. The selection for

Africa as well as for us will take place only after the retreat—then the old grey head will return to you.

I arrived at Le Mans on Saturday at noon. The rest of the day I spent in part with Father Rector, Sunday with various people, particularly Father Chappé whom I had found at Charbornière. He devoured your letter, and then we talked about our mission which he has helped by his devotedness and above all by his prayers. All these good Brothers and novices and priests of Le Mans love you and reproach you for having written too briefly.

Monday I made my visit to Le Mans, and the same day at 8 PM I received my obedience to visit the different establishments of our congregation. Friday evening I arrived at La Brulcatte after having supper. The curé came with me to visit your kind family. Your father, who was in bed, jumped up when he saw me. We chatted, but he stopped so that he'd get to morning Mass. Following that, we had lunch together at his place. I stayed there until 10 o'clock, and before leaving I received 20 francs from your brother (he's generous in the same way). Your father gave me 10 also, and the curé of La Brulcatte 5. I went back to Ruillé.

I spent Sunday the 7th there following the schedule. The collection isn't worth anything. In some places I get nothing, in others they refuse me, but good of me to ask, they say. After eight days I don't yet have 100. Everything is also inconvenient. The priests are on retreat this morning. Here I am at St. Berthevin where I'm profitting from a short pause to write to you in haste. Tomorrow I'll go to Laval; perhaps I'll be happier. I received money for Masses, knowing that you'll receive some. I forgot to tell you that I hope to have a St. Joseph from the boarders at Holy Cross. Please tell Father Cointi the abbé of St. Peter La Cour is now curé at Arubrière. I don't stop thinking about and reflecting on the needs of Notre Dame du Lac. I forget no one of its members (although everywhere I'm welcomed a thousand times better than I deserve) because America never lets go of me. I think especially about you, good Father, to whom I am so much attached. You'll not have me back too soon.

We hope, Father Rector and I, that God will help you do your work which is already so well advanced. I tell everyone that you'll come in two years and that perhaps you'll make me come back with you. I know the route now quite well. I don't know what you have determined on the subject of the Sisters, and I'm not able to know [MS covered by seal] to see Notre Dame du Lac again. Respect and good wishes [MS covered by seal] Mrs. Coquil [MS ripped] almost promised me the clock from Holy Cross of Le Mans if Mr. N. hasn't time to make another before our departure.

Goodby. I have to take advantage of the mail. Believe that I want, my very good Father, to join you as soon as possible.

Brother Vincent

39. Brother Anselm (13) to Father Sorin
[Translated from French]

Vincennes August 4, 1844

My Reverend Father,

I'm happily taking advantage of a better moment to answer the two letters that you kindly sent me. I'd have responded sooner, especially to the first which led me to believe you hadn't received the one I sent you July 13, but fever along with a terrible headache forced me to wait until today.

Up till now, Reverend Father, I've had only short sicknesses here which, although sometimes very severe, never prevented me from going to class, etc. But since last Wednesday I've been so sick that I was forced to stop teaching. The fever hit me on Monday, but as I wished to prepare the children for their first communion, I continued to teach until Wednesday. That day I was so sick during the morning class that I told the students there'd be no school in the afternoon, but there'd be school the next day (because I thought that I'd be better).

After morning class, which ends at 10:30, I notified the "girls" or servants that I had a very bad fever, and soon after I threw myself on my bed worn out and very sick. I slept almost five hours without waking up. But, my God, on waking I felt sicker than ever; I had a burning fever, a headache so violent that I was dizzy, a burning thirst and no water. I stayed in bed 3 to 4 hours (incapable of getting up), in this state without a single person coming to ask me, "Do you want something to drink?" At 7 o'clock in the evening Tourneux had the courtesy to come ask if I wished to drink something. I told him "Yes, certainly," and that if he had the kindness to give me something to drink, it would please me very much (it wasn't his job to take care of sick people, and he did it secretly, for love of me).

Father, I can no longer continue the subject. I'm too weak to tell you more. What I can tell you in truth is that they don't take as much care of me here as a human being would of a sick dog. I can't stop crying in telling you this, my well loved Father, but it's the truth. I take God as witness: during the two and a half days I was so sick, no one came to ask "Do you want anything" except Tourneux who came three times after work, etc.

I still have many things to tell you, but as I find myself much better now, I hope I'll have the good fortune to see you again and to tell you all my troubles. In any case, I don't know if I'll be at South Bend for the beginning of the retreat because if I don't wish to fall sick again, I'll have to take things easier. The doctor told me that it would be imprudent of me to leave this week, but I'd rather die on the road of fatigue or something than die of thirst and hunger here.

Father, I bought what was essential, and when you see the things, you'll be happy, I think, with my purchases.

Goodby, Reverend Father. I ask your prayers as well as those of my Brothers at South Bend.

I'm extremely weak now but I'm better.

Brother Anselm

40. Brother Vincent (16) to Father Sorin
[Translated from French]

Notre Dame of Holy Cross August 15, 1844

My very dear Father,

I begin writing to you at 10 PM. Because time is so short, days are like hours.

I'm leaving the retreat. We made it at the Solitude, not all but about fifty.

Here is the staff I'll bring to you. Mr. Granger whom you know. He made his vows today. Two or three veterans. A cobbler. I don't know if it will be Brother Justin or one younger. A tailor and perhaps a cook.

We'll leave the 8th of September, the day of our good Patroness and on the same boat which brought us all together.

Father Rector can't come this winter. All his council oppose it because his absence would be too long, but he is hopeful for spring. Brother Augustine is fine. He is going to begin his medical studies. I report tomorrow morning with Mr. Granger. He is going with his family, and I will continue my search which isn't going well. I'm collecting Masses although I find almost nothing.

Here are the intentions.

30 low Masses for the Desceur family for 30 francs from which
10 for a sister who had [ ]
8 for Mr. and Mrs. Desceur
4 for the husband of her who gives these Masses. He was called Joseph.
4 others for brothers and sisters and
4 others, some living and the others dead
Here is 30 for 30 francs
20 low Masses for a deceased lady. They have to be discharged at Easter.
20 low Masses for [Ambrosian] dead
25 low Masses for the intention of the one who gave them. They have to be said at Easter.

3 low Masses for the relative of James Cireau, father, mother, brothers and sisters
10 low Masses for Miss Garreau's relatives
15 low Masses for Abbé de Basauge's intentions
10 low Masses to unite his intentions with a priest who [ ]
10 low Masses for the sister [ ]
2 Masses for the conversion of a soul
10 other low Masses for a deceased man
100 low Masses for Dubrail and his wife, dead at Paris
30 Masses for the intention of the donor
36 low Masses of foundation
4 low Masses for Mr. Truaume and his relatives
20 low Masses for Mr. Julien Giraud and his relatives. He is named Joseph. All dead.
10 low Masses for Marie Aubut
26 low Masses for the intentions of donors
10 Masses for the intentions of persons who gave them
The intentions of Reverend Father Rector and of his council are such that we won't undertake Baptisms nor found establishments now without his permission.

Mr. Marivault's parents have [ ] if he wants his father to sell out for six thousand francs. He can write at once to Father Rector who will make him draw out his money.

I'll have no time to go to Paris.

Mr. Gourden de Majet is making us a clock that we'll pay 500 for. It'll be good they say.

Father Rector has not yet replied to the Propagation of the Faith. He doesn't know exactly when we'll have it. I won't be able to make big purchases in New York because we'll have little money. Meanwhile write to Mrs. Permentier about what you need most.

I'll be afraid to start the long trip again if I don't have full and complete confidence in the Lord's grace and the protection of the Holy Virgin and St. Joseph for which we will get you relics, and then you will pray for everyone, for us as well as for the good Sisters. I don't know those who are going to join them. I know that she who is destined for superior is at least 30 and the other 40, who will be the nurse at the Sisters' place, and if [MS blurred] Sister of Providence gave you too much work to do, she would take her place. How good it would be to see you all again, the priests and my dear Brothers and the good Sisters. May Sister Mary of Bethlehem pray to God for her cousin Bouvier. He died at Paris.

Six Brothers will leave on the 24th of the present month to found three schools in Africa, no priest with them. I think that you may be starting your retreat at Notre Dame du Lac. I'm going to pray for you all.

Goodby, goodby, good Father,

Brother Vincent

I have to tell you again that many people ask for your prayers and those of your small community. I have matters of the soul to tell you.

41. Brother Augustine (3) to Father Sorin

Notre Dame de Ste. Croix September 4, 1844

My Dear Father Superior,

I delayed writing these three weeks first in order to inform you with certainty of the result of our visit to this place and of the exact time of the departure of Brother Vincent for America, which was not definitely decided until now. He leaves here on the 6th of this month in order to arrive in Harve for the packet of the 8th. He is accompanied by three Sisters, two Brothers, a shoemaker and a tailor (Brothers Justine, August, and by a priest Father Granger, who made his profession this last retreat and whom you knew at college as he informs me). Brother Vincent has bought a splendid clock, a cross for processions and many other things. He has received a good many articles from charitable persons such as clothing, linen for the altar and also some money. He takes with him a beautiful statue of the Blessed Virgin for the Sisters and a small one of St. Joseph for the Brothers.

The Brothers, six in number, left for Africa at the end of the retreat. Brother Hilarion is the director. We endeavored to get him for America, but Rev. Father Rector decided he would go to Africa.

With relation to my studies, it seems the facilities for my studying medicine are not so favorable as you anticipated. Rev. Father Rector has made some efforts to enable me to attend the hospital in this town, but the administration in consequence of enmity towards him have refused me the permission. What his views are in regard to sending me elsewhere, he has not informed me. As for myself, I am unchanged in the desire for the eclesiastical state and would study medicine only through obedience. With permission I have been studying Latin nearly since my arrival, it being necessary for me for medicine if I should study it. I do not see any chance of my going elsewhere to study medicine because I will be employed in teaching English after the vacation and consequently cannot leave here, to judge from Father Rector's sentiments on the matter. It would appear he does not appreciate the importance a knowledge of medicine would afford to our institution at Notre Dame du Lac. On this subject, if it is your desire I should pursue my studies in medicine, you should represent to him the advantages it would afford even to the cause of religion, but in order to be successful in this science and in order to have the weight of character so necessary in America, I should spend some months in Paris which is not very expensive as I could get five months board and tuition for 100 dollars. However I submit myself to your advice as to my future course during my stay here and feel anxious you would write me on this subject.

I made my retreat with Brother Vincent and about fifty Brothers at the Solitude, a charming place which has an appropriate name, where I had been staying since my arrival. Since the retreat, I have been here where I expect to continue during the winter. I go every day to Bon Pasteur to give lessons in English to the Sisters who are going to America. Father Granger took some lessons but not sufficient to make progress because he spent his vacation with his family.

I often feel lonesome for St. Mary's and pray I may see it once more. I can now have true charity for a French person in America beginning to speak English for he must truly suffer Purgatory, as I experience the greatest difficulty in speaking the French here. I am already two months without speaking the language I had been in the habit of speaking since my childhood excepting one day I spoke to an English Sister of the Carmelite Community along with Father Druelle who is my teacher and who has expressed a desire to receive a letter from you.

I am not yet long enough here to be able to give you an account of the changes which have taken place since your departure. All the Brothers inquire about you in the most affectionate manner. I asked permission of Rev. Father Rector to go to England to see my uncles and make a collection for a chapel, but he refused it to me. They have been priests in England many years, and I feel confident they would enable me to make a greater sum than would pay me for my trouble. I feel very desirous to receive a letter from you before long. I wish my love to the Priests and Brothers and recommend myself to their prayers.

I remain, my dear Father Superior, your affectionate son in Jesus, Mary and Joseph,

Brother Augustine

The name of the ship in which Brother Vincent goes is the Zurich. Inform me of the progress of the chapel on the island.

42. Brother Mary Joseph (5) to Father Sorin

Vincennes December 13, 1844

Reverend and dear Father,

I take this opportunity of writing a few lines and sending you the books received from the bishop. There are six books. The young man with whom I have entrusted them is a Belgian. He came to this country with Bishop Lefevre of Detroit. He has been studying here since September, but the bishop of Detroit has sent for him. He told me he would go and see the community. His name is Mr. Foullon. I am troubled with a weakness of the lungs which arises from my having to speak so much in teaching the scholars. Sometimes I can scarcely speak and sometimes I spit small pieces of corruption. I went to Dr. Beattie. He gave me some medicine for it. He said I must not talk much. I have 78 scholars, 18 Protestants. I get along pretty well so far. The bishop has gone to Europe. He will not be back till July next. Mr. Martin says the bishop was speaking to him about the boys having Mass. He told me they could not as he had no priest. Mr. Martin is kind to me. I attend French class every evening from 7:15 till 8:30. Mr. Martin teaches. He told me the bishop would be very glad if you would have a novitiate in Indianapolis. He said the bishop would assist you, but I suppose you know this already. After Christmas I expect to go to Washington for that money. Mr. Gallagher was here to see you on the Sunday after you had left. I received a letter from Brother Anselm. He says he began school on the first December. He has 36 scholars. He complains of having no room except the schoolroom. He wants me to send a box and a large trunk. I think it wrong to be carrying a large trunk from place to place. I suppose it would cost 3 or 4 dollars to take it by stage. There is no other conveyance. I can send all he wants in a box. Brother Anselm said in his letter that the colony had arrived, but he did not say how many there were.

I go to confession every week to Mr. Martin.

Mr. Shaw and Mr. Thomas are at Indianapolis trying to get Mr. Weinzloepflen from prison. Reverend Mr. Bellier is about to leave this diocese for Mobile. Reverend Mr. Beauteaus is going home to France to stay there. No more at present. Your affectionate son in Jesus Christ,

Brother Mary Joseph

N.B. Please, dear Father, to pray for me and remember me to all my dear Brothers, hoping they will pray for the success of my labors, also our dear little colony with Brother Vincent at the head. Yours,

B.M.J.

Chapter Four

1845

43. Brother Anselm (14) to Father Moreau
[Translated from French]

Madison [Indiana] January 14, 1845

My Reverend Father,

I received your letter of August 29, 1844, on the arrival of Brother Vincent, that is to say towards the end of last October. I also received four patterns of oriental painting and the twelve pencils you had the goodness to send me. But having left South Bend before the trunks arrived containing the colors you destined for me, I consequently haven't received them, but I hope to receive them in a short time.

I think that Father Superior already told you that I experienced a great sickness during last vacation. If he didn't tell you, I can tell you that I was dangerously sick almost two months. During the height of the sickness, Father Superior came to hear my confession, but as I couldn't hear or speak or see, I said nothing at all to him, although he used his power to pull something out of me.

The following morning, he came to see me and ask me if I knew that I had made my confession the night before. I told him no. [MS torn] nothing any longer. Then he told me the story, and moreover he told me that I escaped dying the night before, and that I had to prepare for death by confession. I replied that I wanted to confess when he'd like. He came toward evening, and I confessed. After my confession, I got better and better until I was perfectly restored to health.

Last November 17, I left South Bend to go teach classes in Madison, where I am presently. I have 60 students, and I think that with the grace of God the establishment will succeed. However, the parents are very exacting and very difficult to satisfy as regards English instruction.

I imagine, reverend Father, that you'll come see us next summer in our beautiful America. They waited for you last year at Notre Dame du Lac, then up until the arrival of dear Brother Vincent, but unfortunately you didn't come although your presence was really needed. Dear Brother Vincent told me all he saw at Notre Dame de Saint Croix, and his account really surprised me: reverend Father, Divine Providence must help you much to achieve so perfectly everything you begin. Please have the kindness to tell dear Brother Robert that I thank him much for lines he addressed to me, and tell him that if he could (with your permission) get me some paper of different sizes adapted for oriental painting, as well as some painting patterns for flowers (particulaly roses), for fruits, etc., etc., I'll be very grateful to him. To work well, these patterns would have to be of different sizes like the paper and in proportion with the latter. I don't have any more graph paper, and I'll be very grateful to you, reverend Father, if you'd permit Brother Robert to send me some as well as two or three cut patterns because mine are almost used up.

I'm asking you incessantly, reverend Father, and each time I ask you, I have earnest hope of receiving, because I know your heart so well. Moreover, I'm asking for nothing for myself, because as soon as I have something I don't absolutely need, I share it with my dear Brothers. In a word, it's for my own instruction and for that of my Brothers who have a taste for painting that I'm asking you for these objects.

I end, reverend Father, in wishing you with all my heart, a good and happy year, the accomplishment of all your good desires, and Paradise at the end of your days. I hope you'll not forget to give my wishes for a happy new year to good Mr. Fillion, to Fathers Chappé, Hupier, Hiron, etc., etc., and to all my Brothers, particularly to dear Brother Donatien and Hilarion when you write to them.

When you write to me, address your letters as follows: Brother Anselm, teacher at Madison, Jefferson County (Care of Reverend J. Delaune) Indiana, United States, America.

I would have written you sooner, but as one of the Vincennes priests is leaving for France on the 20th of this month, I preferred to wait.

I am with the most profound respect, your Reverence's respectful and obedient servant,

Brother Anselm

44. Brother Anselm (15) to Father Sorin

[First half of letter in English; second half translated from French.]

Madison, Indiana February 7, 1845

Reverend Father,

I do not know indeed what can be the reason you neither write to me, nor even tell Brother Vincent to answer the letter I wrote to him more than a month ago. You have seen that letter I think, and though you know very well that I am very much in need of the objects I mentioned therein, however you do not send me any of them, no, not even a letter.

You called me "Cher Enfant" in the letter you wrote to Mr. Delaune sometime ago, but that (permit to say) just to pay me a little compliment for indeed if I were "Cher" to you (as you say) you would not let me be in want of everything. I wish you would write to Brother Mary Joseph and tell him to send me the books, copy-books, glazed tracing paper etc., etc. in a word everything I told him to, in the three letters I wrote to him, two of which he never answered. Most of the books, copy-books, etc., etc., are of no use to him as they are French but would be of the greatest utility to me, such would be my French and English dictionary of Boyer, my following of Christ, my treatise on line drawing, with the drawing models accompanying it, my geometry book, my French calligraphy book, my bird notebook, etc., etc.—in a word everything I asked him for would be extremely useful to me here, whereas all that stuff won't do him any good. Moreover I did not ask him [for] more than two thirds of the standard furnishings I left in Vincennes; whilst he did not leave anything here, no, not even a *prayer book.*

I think it is useless for me to write to him anymore for he does not even answer my letters.

Have the kindness to send me the things which Brother Vincent took note of before I left Notre Dame du Lac and which I reminded him of in my last letter as soon as possible; for I am very much in need of some of them, particularly of a Levite; for mine is tore in several places, and I am sure that if you saw it you would not let me wear it on Sunday in such a town as Madison. However I have no other one. If you don't send me one soon, I will be obliged to wear my coat for Mr. Delaune cannot buy me one for the present. He has got too many debts to pay. I am also very much in need of a toke or toque [cap] for I have nothing but my straw hat to wear.

Here is a list of the objects I am very much in need of: First, a levite. Second, a cap. Third, a pair of shoes. Fourth, a pair of pants. Fifth, a flat ruler at least two feet long for drawing. Sixth, a square ruler. Seventh, a French grammar and dictionary. Eighth, my accordion, my paints. In a word, everything sent to me from France by the last colony. Ninth, a collar. Tenth, a quire of drawing paper.

If you'd send me some patterns, you'd do me a service because Brother Mary Joseph gave away all those I had left in Vincennes, and moreover, he hasn't sent me my painting tools.

As far as the other things I asked for from Brother Vincent and are not included in this list, you can send them to me or keep them as you wish.

I had a fever for three or four days since I've been here, but now I'm fine, and I hope you are the same.

Lots of love from me to all the priests and to Brother Vincent as well as all the other Brothers.

In my next letter I'll tell you how I'm adjusting here and how delighted I am. You will address my mail the following way: Brother Anselm, Madison, Jefferson County, Indiana (care of W. Griffin, esq.). You have received or will soon receive a letter from here which will, I think, please you. The individual who will write to you is well known to me and is one of Madison's best Catholics, W. Griffin.

With much respect, I am your humble and obedient servant,

Brother Anselm

Answer me as soon as you can because I'm impatient waiting for a letter from you and because this impatience made me talk to you with a little curtness in the course of my letter, but don't get angry.

Please also write immediately to Brother Mary Joseph. It is said that maybe our bishop will not come back on account of his administration.

45. Brother Mary Joseph (6) to Father Sorin

Vincennes February 18, 1845

My Reverend Father,

I received your kind letter three weeks ago. I should have answered it sooner, but I had not received any money from Mr. Robinson. Mr. Ducoudray came here a week ago and asked me if I had received any money from Mr. Robinson. I answered no. I asked him if Mr. Robinson had received money from Europe. He told me that he had. Mr. D. said he went to him when he heard he had received money to ask some for the new church which he is about to build at St. Peter's. Mr. Robinson replied that he would not give him a cent, that he was going to leave St. Peter's.

I immediately told Reverend Mr. Martin. He said I had better go to St. Peter's and enquire about it. I started on Friday at noon, stayed in Washington that night and left early the next morning for St. Peter's. When I got there, I went to Mr. Robinson's, hearing that he was going to Washington. I saw him. He told me that he was about to go to Washington to see if any letter had arrived. He said he had been expecting one ever since I had been there on New Year's Day. He said he was very sorry, etc. I went back to Washington. Mr. Robinson also sent his boy in to see if there was a letter, but there was none. I waited till Monday to see if there was a letter but there was none.

There is a young lawyer in Washington. I asked him if he would find out the transaction in the recorder's office. He went and made the following memorandum. $100 was due June 1844, 100 in 1845, 150 in 1846, and 200 in 1847. This young lawyer is a Catholic. I have been expecting a letter every day from Mr. Robinson, but I have got none. He owes Mr. Gallagher $20. Besides he had a lawsuit with the carpenter who was to finish his house and he has to pay $35.

Reverend Mr. Martin told me about the two shares in the bank. I got Judge Moore, a Catholic, to go to the bank and see about them. He went and gave me the following information. He it was who bought the shares with Illinois money which was not very good. At the time he bought 2 shares in the bishop's name, but the bishop has transferred them to you so they stand in your name at the present time. Judge Moore told me there has been dividend due about every six months which the bishop must have drawn. There are two dividends due now, one of $3 dollars and the other of $2.29. This one of 3 dollars is in the bishop's name, but it can be drawn by Reverend Mr. [MS torn] The shares are going down. I went to the bank with Mr. Heayes. He asked the clerk if he knew of anyone wanting to buy shares and how much were shares. He said he knew of no one wanting to buy, but plenty wanting to sell. He said the shares had been valued a year ago at 45 dollars each share, but they would not fetch that now. It was impossible to sell. Mr. Heayes told me he had taken some shares in trade some time ago, but had got rid of them. He said he would not give 50 dollars for the two for his own use. I asked others, but it will be impossible to do anything but trade and not more than half their value then.

There was a meeting in the schoolroom about choosing this as the district school. The[y] chose this and agreed to pay what the bishop should charge for the rent of the basement. I do not know how much it will come to, but Judge Moore, I believe, has paid Reverend Mr. Martin 10 dollars. I have had 108 scholars, but a few of them have gone to work now. I have sometimes also difficulties with the rowdys of Vincennes. They come amongst my school boys wanting to play with them, and they curse, swear, etc. I tell them I cannot allow them to play with my boys. They curse me, etc.

I hope you are all very well. Please to pray for me and remember me to all my dear Brothers. Your obedient son in Christ,

Brother Mary Joseph

N.B. I would have written more but I was afraid to miss the mail. Mother Theodore is very sick. I shall have vacation at Easter. I think it would do me good to go out some. Would you give permission to go to Madison or some other place?

46. Brother Anselm (16) to Father Sorin

Madison, Indiana, Jefferson County. March 26, 1845

Reverend Father,

At last you have written, and in return for your so long-delayed letter I thank you a thousand times and earnestly entreat you not to be so long without writing in the future.

You ask me how many scholars I have? I have 60 presently on my list, but if I counted all those who have come since the first of December and who have left about the beginning of spring, I would have very near 100. On an average 50 scholars attend the Male Catholick School in winter, and about 40 in summer. They are all Catholick.

There are in Madison 8 *écoles Primaires* [grade schools], two high schools or seminaries wherein are taught Latin, Greek, etc., etc., and the other high branches of education, and also 5 or 6 little schools for children under the age of 7. On an average each of the Primary schools is attended by about 40 pupils throughout the year, but the two catholick (with the exception of one of the seminaries) are more numerously attended than any other school in town.

The exact population of this town (already surnamed city) will be known only in 1850. It is supposed now-a-day to be of about 6000 inhabitants, 900 of whom are Catholick.

There are in this city 12 Protestant churches among which 5 or 6 are pretty buildings, but however none of them vie with the fine Catholick church either in style or in architecture.

Last Wednesday (St. Joseph's day) I went up to Cincinnati to get the holy-oil. I was very well received by the bishop and all the priests. The bishop asked me several questions about our institution such as the number of Brothers, the conditions required to have a Brother, the name of the superior of the institution, etc., etc., all of which I answered as correctly as I could.

During my stay at the bishop's (which was but of 2 days), I was greatly edified by the good and pious priests, and still more by the humble, good and amiable Bishop Purcel.

On Holy Thursday and Good Friday the Catholick churches of the city were crowded by good and pious Catholicks who nearly all went to receive Communion on Holy Thursday. Such an edifying spectacle is not to be seen in Vincennes certainly. *Aussi* [also] what difference is there between some of the priests of Vincennes and those of Cincinnati chiefly between the grand vicars of the two places? A striking one indeed.

Since I am here I have seen persons from Vincennes, and as you had told me that I had a bad reputation around and in that town, I felt some desire to know if it was true for I had some doubt respecting the truth of the charge as I was conscious that I had done nothing that could anyway give the least cause to the loss of my reputation in that place. Therefore, I inquired and found out by what credible persons told me what Very Reverend Mr. Martin had told you was nothing else than a *base slander*.

He charged me, if I rightly understood you, to have had bad intercourse with a woman but that as falsely as 2 and 2 are 10. Indeed I don't know how a priest like Mr. Martin who pretends to be good can fabricate such stories. I would have justified myself sooner, but before, I wanted to know if it were true that some designing men had started stories or *lies* on me in that place.

Brother Anselm

47. Brother Mary Joseph (7) to Father Sorin

Vincennes April 15, 1845

My Reverend Father,

I received the enclosed draft for $50 yesterday by post. I showed it to Judge Moore and asked him what was the best to do with it. He said I could not get it cashed here without a good endorser. All that I could do would be to put it in the bank for collection. I went to the bank to see if they would cash it, as they had received one of the same kind last December from him, but they said [they] could not.

You can put it in the bank at South Bend, and you will receive an answer in about 18 days. This is what Judge Moore says.

I went to St. Peter's at Easter. I do not know what to do with Mr. Robinson. I believe you will not get the money for many years. He was not at home when I called. I spoke to Mrs. Robinson. She said he was squandering the money. He might have paid you $100 easily enough if he wished, but she says you are too easy with him. He has received $250 in 18 months. He has bought but one old horse worth $10, two steers, and an old waggon. They have bought no clothes since they came here, having provided themselves in New York. He is in debt in several stores, and the carpenter work of the house is not paid for. Besides he is continually running about, seldom at home. I told Mrs. Robinson I expected a letter every day from you, which would be severe. She said that would be the best way, for if you [do] not push him, he will use the money.

In the letter he sent with the draft, he says he expects to give you $50 soon and for the other note due he wishes you to give him more time.

I hope you are all well. I had forgotten to tell you that James Marsdon, the young man I sent you, had been a play actor and very wild. I have seen another young Irishman who teaches school seven miles from Vincennes. He speaks of going to the Brothers. He was to have been here last Sunday but did not come.

I was sick in Washington, spitting blood, and Dr. Anderson gave me some medicine and a plaster for my breast. If I speak more than five minutes at a time, I am sick. The doctor says it is want of exercise and speaking much.

Dear Father, I should be very happy to hear from you. It is a long time since you wrote to me. I wish to know how your health is and all my dear Brothers. Please remember me to their pious prayers.

We expect Reverend Mr. Weinsloepflen here next Tuesday. There will be about fourteen priests here to receive him. Reverend Mr. Martin and all here are well. Reverend Mr. Shaw is in Cincinnati. Mr. Martin has received one of his trunks which he thought lost.

Dear Father, will you advise me what I must do with regard to some debts I owe for mending shoes twice, for a few quires of paper to translate the conduit, and for medicine.

Dear Father, pray for your affectionate son in Christ.

Brother Mary Joseph

48. Brother Anselm (17) to Father Sorin

Madison, Indiana April 16, 1845

Reverend Father,

I have not yet received the trunk you sent me, and indeed I don't know whether it is only astray or lost. At all events you would do well to go or to send some competent persons to the stage office of South Bend, and ask the stage-master whether he has sent that trunk or not. Also to require him to write all along the line and inquire from all the stage-masters or stage-drivers what they have done with such a trunk addressed to such a one in such a place and tell him to tell them to send it on in haste for indeed I am in the greatest need of it.

My Levite is all torn, and by cutting the lower part which was all raggy and full of holes, I have made it look very much like an old Redingote, insomuch that I am indeed ashamed to go to town with it.

Reverend Mr. Delaune advised me to tell you to make the inquiries hereabove mentioned, telling me that it was the only way to find out whether the said trunk was lost or not. Then be pleased to make them as soon as you receive this letter, and you will oblige me very much.

Last Friday at 2 o'clock in the afternoon a remnant of the fever I had last year seized me and continues sticking to me very closely. It's more than 6 days I have it now and notwithstanding all the medicine I take daily, I don't feel any change in the intensity of the fever.

Last Wednesday week I received a letter from Brother Mary Joseph through the politeness of Reverend Mr. Shawe who was going up to Cincinnati to get the holy oils. He stated in his letter that he had been very sick, but did not tell me which kind of sickness. Mr. Shawe told me that he had a bad cold when he left Vincennes. He told me also that he did not get a cent from the farmer of St. Peter's.

Mr. Delaune requests me to offer you his respects.

Give my love to all the priests and to all the Brothers of Notre Dame du Lac particularly to Brother Vincent.

Do not forget neither the good, humane and charitable Sisters of Bertrand, as well as that of Notre Dame du Lac to whom I am very much indebted for their services.

Tell Sister Mary of the Sacred Heart (or Marie du Coeur de Jésus) that I have found out how to make du papier à calquer [tracing paper] and that I will bring her some and give her the receipt when I will go up. Tell them also that in the sickly state I am in, I would be excessively glad to be with them, but as I cannot go, tell them to be so kind as to pray for me.

In your answer, pray tell me what is the stage fare from Detroit to South Bend. I would like to know it for I have a mind to go to South Bend by water, that is from here to Cincinnati, from Cincinnati to Portsmouth, and from Portsmouth to Cleveland, from Cleveland to Detroit and thence to South Bend. This route is undoubtedly a great [MS torn] longer, but then it is as cheap, and [MS torn].

I am, Reverend Father, with much respect your humble and obedient servant,

Brother Anselm

I recommend myself to your prayer[s] and to those of the whole Community. Goodby. The fever is coming back with a vengeance. Answer me.

49. Brother Anselm (18) to Father Sorin

Madison, Indiana June 15, 1845

Reverend Father,

At last I have received that so-much-desired and so-long-delayed bundle, and also your letter of the 30th of last month for which I return you my humble thanks. Three days before the reception of that bundle, despairing of ever receiving it, I went with Mr. Delaune to town and bought myself a summer habit, which when done came to 6 dollars. In the bargain I had my old Levite mended.

I do not know whether you will be pleased at my having bought that summer habit or not, but as necessity compelled me on one side, and as I had waited long enough for that so-long-sent and so-long-delayed bundle, on the other, I therefore do not feel much afraid of your displeasure knowing well that you will not be displeased.

I am very glad to learn from your last letter, as well as from Brother Vincent's, that the establishment of Notre Dame du Lac increases, and above all, that all its members are in good health.

Since about 3 weeks I feel very unwell. Last Monday week immediately after Mass, Mr. Fever (*my old tyrant*) came to pay me a visit and obliged me to dismiss the boys and go to bed. Towards the evening, the fever having left me, I took a good dose of medicine and the next morning, though very weak and sick, I resolved to teach school. I have taken medicine every day since that new relapse, and now I begin to feel a little better.

I do not know how I will go up to the retreat. I think that if I could get a good horse to borrow or to hire cheap, it would be the cheapest way, but I am very near sure that I will not find any horse to borrow here in town for less than 9 or 10 dollars or even more.

If I do not find any horse, I will be obliged to go stage, or to go on a steamboat as far as Cincinnati and there take the Miami Canal (if it is finished). If it is not, I will be obliged to go to Portsmouth and thence to Cleveland, and after that to South Bend. The passage by water from here to Cleveland is, I believe, 5 or 6 dollars.

I spoke to Mr. Delaune about your museum, and he told me that he could not give you anything for the simple reason that he had nothing. I could probably, if I took the trouble, procure you several kinds of petrifications which are found on the hills around this city, namely petrified shells, wood, insects, and even reptiles.

Reverend Father, I wish you would answer this letter soon, and tell me which way I must follow in going up to the retreat.

I am respectfully your humble and obedient servant,

Brother Anselm

PS Pray have the goodness to remit to Brother Vincent the following short letter.

P [PS] The *friend of Religion* comes always through here, on account that those who sent it to you do not know how to direct it to you. Instead of South-Bend, they write South-end, etc. As I am in need of a pair of pantaloons, I will probably buy one before I go up if you do not forbid me.

50. Brother Anselm (19) to Brother Vincent
[Translated from French]

Madison, Indiana June 15, 1845

My dear Brother,

Finally I've received the package you sent me last March 15. The long awaited package doesn't contain all the things you promised to send me. On its reception I found only my levite, my accordion, a pair of shoes, and one pants, but no collar, although you had told me before I left that you would send me one. You also told me that you had a box of paints for me in addition to the beautiful chromium yellow that you sent me, but this box was not in the package, at least not when it got to me.

Have the kindness to please tell me what you did with these paints because I'd feel very bad if they were lost.

I am, dear Brother, your very devoted and affectionate friend,

Brother Anselm

PS Remember me, if you please, to all the members of the Community and tell them to pray for me. Also my greetings to whomever they are due.

51. Brother Anselm (20) to Father Sorin

Madison, Indiana July 10, 1945.

Reverend Father,

I thank you for your readiness to answer my last letter, and I heartily wish that you would be as quick to answer this one as you were to answer that and much more so as the time for the retreat is nearer now than it was then.

According to your request, I have asked Mr. Delaune whether it wouldn't be in his power to buy me a young horse worth from 25 to 30 dollars in payment of the $50 due. He told me that he couldn't possibly do it before I'd go, that his means were very short at this time of the year, but that nevertheless he would do his best in order to have the money ready when I would go up, but that he could not have it ready soon enough to buy me a horse.

Now that Mr. Delaune cannot buy me a horse, what shall I do? Shall I go in the stage, or shall I hire a horse? Shall I go through Indianapolis, or through Cincinnati, Portsmouth, Cleveland, Detroit, or from Cincinnati to Paulding on the Miami Canal, and from there to Fort Wayne, thence to South Bend? This would certainly be the cheapest way, but I do not know if the Miami Canal is finished. The route from here to Cincinnati, Portsmouth, Cleveland, would certainly be long, but very agreeable in this time of the year and every way as cheap, if no cheaper than that I took last year to come here. I can go from here to Cleveland *in the cabin* for 6 dollars. The passage from Cleveland to Detroit cannot exceed $2 and that from Detroit to South Bend 4, making $12 dollars in all, whilst if I go through Indianapolis it will cost me 12 dollars for the stage and at least 4 for meals and beds making in all $16.

Mr. Delaune would be glad that I would come back for the 1st of September or at the latest for the 15th.

Mr. Baquelin was here yesterday. He told me that you would come to Indianapolis (if he could find a house for you) in September next.

I had a great dinner here on the 4th. More than 100 children were admitted to it and behaved very well. The most respectable ladies of Madison helped me to serve at table, and before the dinner sent me pies, cakes, and crackers of every kind. They appeared to take a great interest in it. I dare say, Dear Father, that you had not such a dinner at the Lake.

After the dinner we marched 2 by 2 through different streets of the city. Three girls of about 16 or 17 years of age carried the banner which I had made the night before, and which though made in hurry, was, I have been told by several, finer than any of those the other schools had.

If you think that it would cost to[o] much to go to the retreat, pray allow me to go some place where Mr. Delaune would send me. I would like to go up very well, but when I reflect that my going and coming back will take more than one half of what I earn for the Community, it makes me sick, and I would deprive myself of the natural pleasure which I would have in seeing you as well as my dear Brothers and above all of making my retreat in order to save a few dollars for the Community.

Pray answer me and tell me what to do.

I am respectfully your most humble and obedient servant,

Brother Anselm

I long to see you and my Brothers. Pray for me.

Excuse my bad writing. I am in [a] hurry. Anyway this letter will cost you but 5 cents.

Mr. Delaune sends you his love and respect.

52. Brother Augustine (4) to Father Sorin

Notre Dame de Ste. Croix August 4, 1845

My dear Father Superior,

After what the Reverend Father Rector told me three weeks ago, I expected I should be on sea at this time, but some cause unknown to me has determined him to defer our departure until he receives a letter from you, which, if you have not written in the last month, will delay us here this winter. I spoke to the Sister Superior this morning. She requests me to say that after her two months voyage in this country, she collected but very little. She told me also, judging from Reverend Father Rector's sentiments, that she did not believe we would leave here this winter. According to her recent evidences, this delay will injure materially the collection which you intended I should make in the several cities of the United States, for if I should arrive in New York in September, I would have time to make the necessary delay in each city and then I could arrive at New Orleans at the season when the sickness disappears, but as this is prevented by the legitimate voice of obedience, it consequently will result to the greater glory of God at the end. Reverend Father Rector commenced his retreat last evening and is entirely invisible to every business. The retreat of the priests commences on the 7th and will terminate at the Assumption. Since my arrival here there has been an increase of a priest and two seminarists and also a decrease of as many. The priest who is arrived is come expressly, he tells me, to make his novitiate and then to go to Notre Dame du Lac. His name is Mr. Baroux. He is well acquainted with Father Granger and Mr. Guesse. Probably you are already aware that I have the permission to study the Latin. During the last four months I attended with the boarders the fifth class and made considerable progress although being nearly constantly employed with the boarders. I told Father Rector some time ago that I was disposed to make a vow of perpetual obedience which would remove all danger of instability for I do assure you, my dear Father Superior, I have no other idea than to consecrate my life in the mission of Notre Dame du Lac. The arrival of the Sisters without a single line from anyone from America to me made me feel very lonesome. Nevertheless I supported it in the opinion that it was caused by the hurry of affairs for their departure. I see occasionally in the Catholic Herald mention of the college and of your conversions. I feel anxious to be once more enjoy[n]ed with those dear orphans and boarders of our young college. I offer my most respectful sentiments of affection to the priests, Brothers and boarders of the Lake and to yourself, my dear Father Superior. I offer myself to be your most devoted son in the hearts of Jesus, Mary and Joseph until death.

Brother Augustine

53. Brother Charles (1) to Father Sorin

Brooklyn September 6, 1845

My dear Father,

The first person on my arrival here that I had the pleasure to see, whom I knew, was the Reverend N. O'Donnell, who received me very ungraciously on account of a letter he had just previously received from Brother Mary Joseph, addressed to Mrs. Parmentier, in which he is pleased to say:

1. That I have been seen drunk several times.
2. That wine had been missed from the chapel for a long time past; that a bottle put there in the evening would be gone in the morning.
3. The Reverend W. Clarke of Peru told him that I was intemperate.
4. That he and others had heard me use the filthiest language, and that Mrs. Parmentier ought to be put upon her guard against me to prevent trouble.

In addition to this, dear Father, what are my feelings on this occasion? Judge how the zeal with which I left and the good intentions I entertained on leaving are thus cruelly and unjustly blighted, and my own reputation, in the only neighborhood where I am known, not the less blasted.

You well knew the only motive that I had in leaving for a short time. You knew my intention of going to England before I took the habit. You knew of the renewal of that intention in November last, and you knew the time that was deemed fit for my departure, for it was in a great measure if not entirely acquiesced in by yourself.

I leave you to judge then what my case is and how injured I am by the officiousness of a calumniating Brother, making his charge behind my back and, unmistrusted, without permission thus so grossly to libel me.

Thus repulsed, as I naturally should be, by Mrs. Parmentier, and Father Nicholas neither having the convenience, and what to my mind, is still more bitter, considerable less inclination to entertain me, I am here pennyless, dispirited and unhappy.

I therefore wait with impatience your answer, and remain desiring your prayers, your faithful friend and humble servant,

Brother Charles

Please to direct to the care of the Reverend N. O'Donnell, Brooklyn.

54. Brother Charles (2) to Father Sorin

Niles October 3, 1845

Reverend Sir,

Not wishing to do anything rashly or with precipitation and really desirous to avoid any ulterior action, which would lead to great public exposure, through the courts of the country, I have visited this place and have placed myself under the advice of Mr. Adderly, a gentleman who has proved himself to possess a lively and disinterested zeal for the welfare of your institute.

By his advice, I again renew, for the *last* time, the proposition I made you in my letter of the 1st instant, namely, for you to furnish me with the means to proceed on my contemplated journey to England, and he further suggests that the party originating and the parties sanctioning the malignant and outrageous libel made upon my character should be reproved and a public apology be made to me, exonerating me of the damning charges so unjustly and so basely preferred against me.

This done, I shall be satisfied, and should I be spared to return, all shall be forgiven, and you will find in me till death the zealous brother you confess I have hitherto been.

Anxiously waiting your answer, which I hope will be without delay,

I am, Reverend Sir, yours very respectfully,

Charles W. Riley

55. Brother Aloysius (1) to Father Sorin

Vincennes November 3, 1845

Reverend and dear Father,

We opened school on the 29th of September with 28 scholars. At present we have 50 names on the book. On an average we have about 30 attending, some sick, and some working. There are a few of the boys learning spelling, reading, writing, and ciphering. This school is badly provided for. We applied to the bishop for the necessary things. He said he would settle it with Mr. Martin, but we got nothing yet, nor can we get the boys to provide wood for the fire. We suffer great inconvenience for want of a watch. I often regretted for not applying for my watch before we left, but I thought the clock would suffice, and that is almost useless. Dear Father, we are both unwell most of the time since we came here. We attribute it to the da[m]pness of the school. I know my constitution, and you know it is different from that of Brother Francis. I fear every day is too long for me to remain here, so in the name of God I wish to be called home. At least if I do not feel better in two or three weeks, I wish to have the means at hand to return to the Lake.

I have said nothing to Brother Francis of what I mention to you lest it might discourage him. He left here on Friday morning last on a visit to his parents. I expect him back on tomorrow evening. He expects to recruit [recoup?] himself by his visit.

I hope you will write to me as soon as possible. I am, Reverend and dear Father, your obedient and humble child,

Brother Aloysius

56. Brother Francis (1) to Father Sorin

Vincennes November 18, 1845

Dear Father,

We have received your letter on the 17 of this month, out of which we were requested to state som of our school, etc. We will therefore give you an account of the principle of them and commence with our journy though briefly. The first day of our traveling was good enough, but Brother Mary Joseph was too full of gab with the driver. This it is that caused some dissadisfaction for when we came on the other side of Lafayette, we came to be going in the night, not knowing w[h]ere to stop when Brother Aloysious spoke to driver to drive faster, but in place of doing it did much harm. The driver spoke harshly to Brother Aloysious and said to him none of your lip, etc. Brother Mary Joseph spoke then very roughly, etc. I was scilend. Brother Mary Joseph scolded me for not speaking, etc. The driver acted very badly in all cases.

As for our school, we have not much to say, only that the school-room is not in a healthy place, that the boys are very bad, very ma[n]y not knowing their prayers, and that those who know them say them very badly, etc. Their parents are very careless about them. Some of the scholars are sick, and others are at work, and others run off from their parents, and what is still more is that we have very poor books. We have an old dictionary 50 years. I spoke to the bishop. He said to gave the note to Mr. Martian. Did so, but we have none yet. As for our health, it is not very good though meny in town are sick. We have great difficulty in getting wood, and also in not knowing the time. The clock is not good. As for my happiness, I am happy onought. I have a great desire of studies. We have meny things that come in our way but for the glory of God we must suffer meny things.

I spoke to the bishop about the share which is in the bank. He said "that he could not do anything to it and that you must be there." The case which Mr. Thomas had with Mr. Robinson is not in a very good case, for Mr. Robinson is gon to New York. Mr. Thomas wrote to the sheriff before Mr. Robinson had left, but not long ago Mr. Thomas was at Washington and got a degree aginst Robinson, and Robinson has left the old deeds with Mr. Camper who is in Washington and them degrees sayag [saying] that if you will pay Mr. Robinson for his improvements, he give the land up to you. Mr. Thomas will write to you and inform you better than we may. I spoke to Mr. Marsille about Mr. La Pios and Potter. He said to me "that he has paid the first" and about the second he said, that Father Cointe gave him a note or some money wich was not good. The value of $13. He found out that it was not good, and so he brought it Father Cointe from whom he got it. Brother Lawrence was in his room and some others. And that he gave Mr. Marsille a note of $13 for him to give to Mr. Bierly. And that he thinks that Father Cointe made an error whēn making the account with Mr. Bierly.

Mr. Marsille will write to you and state the facts to you. I would have much more to say about our school, scholars, etc., but as you have so much to do and I not having time to write more, on account of not being able to speak to Mr. Marsille, but in the next letter I hope to give you more information about the school, etc. I or rather we hope that you will pray for us.

Your humble and affectionate son in Christ Jesus,

Brother Francis

57. Brother Francis (2) to Father Sorin

Vincennes November 24, 1845

Dear Father,

On the 22 of this month I was going to speak to the bishop about wood for we had not so much as to make a fire, and the time was very cold, but the bishop was not at home and will only be on the 29 of this month. So I spoke to Mr. Martian. He said, "I have nothing to do with school, that the school allways found its own wood and he said as much as that the bishop would not furnish any." We have spoken frequently to the scholars about their fuel, but three brought it and that which they brought was very little. As for the school furnishing its own wood, since the Brothers firs[t] kept school, we have been informed that Brother Anselm got his wood from the bishop, but we cannot vindicate this fact, and as for Brother Mary Joseph wc were informed that he wend in the river frequently when the whater was high to get wood, but we have no means to do so. Firs[t] we have no boat to go in the river. Second the watter is too low and no wood [MS torn] and moreover we did not like to do such a thi[n]g withou[t] your permission. On the 23 of this month when I was going in the chapel, Mr. Martian called me in the vestery and said that we could have some wood of the bishop's, but we were obliged to chopp it, but as soone as the bishop will be at home, we must ask him. We do not know what the consequence will be. We have two bedrooms but there is no way of making a fire in them, and the schoolroom is about 6 feet in the ground, and when it rains much we have the floor covered with wather, and to have the place so wet it is not healthy. We therefore ask you with the simplicity of a child to know what to do. I for my part am happy for the greater the sufferings are, the more I should be happy. We are well enough, but we hope that this letter will find you in better. Brother Aloysious is expecting an answer to the letter which he wrote to you. You know how much we are attached to the good community. We would therefore be glad to know how they are. Pray for us, dear Father.

Your most affectionate and obedient son in Jesus Christ,

Brother Francis

58. Brother Francis (3) to Father Sorin

Vincennes December 25, 1845

Dear Father,

I desired to write to you on the 20 of december but sickness prevented me of doing it. In your last letter you requested me to give you a conscientious account of the state of affairs. I will do so but not without faults and errors. After having spoken to the bishop, he replyed: "You may have wood, but I am not obliged to furnish the school with books." The books for which we asked you are not for the schollars but for us to learn them their lessions. "You may go and buy books of Mr. Hayes, and I will mark it against Father Superior." If we had done so, we would have acted against the rules. Nevertheless we have bought an arithmetic and key to it, but not from Mr. Hayes, and it is payed. The number of the things we asked are, 2 spelling books, 2 readers, a dictionary, arithmetic and key, pen-knife, and a pencil. The cause for which we bought a key is for to facilitate our study in the arithmetic and not to loose so much time which we would have to do if we had no key. The bishop gave some books to be sold. They are the first and second reader, universal reader, and some little prayer book. We are not so badly off now for books as we have been. I have been speaking to the bishop about good notes [?]. He gave me thins [?] enough of things to redeem the good notes [?]. As for the time we are poorly off about it, but as soon as the weather will be fine we will be better off. As for the usual difficulties which we may expect, I thing that they are of very usual, and if there would be any of some usual consideration, I that they shoud be taken by us in a very easy way for the bishop is better disposed than he had been. The books which are of pious reading and which we have are the lives of the saints, Chablener's meditations, the New Testament, the following of Christ, and some others. The school books which belong to the school are a dictionary, a geography, ancient history, arithmetic, grammar, bookkeeping, and slates with some paper. But I think the paper was bought by the brothers that were before us.

We have received some new schollars, who never have been to school but our number is not yet very grate nor will it be so till the weather will be fine and some of the parents sented their children to some other schools because they did not learn fast. Others kept them at home because they had no shoes, and some others make their children work. There are some very hard boys in this school, but we have hopes of their becoming better. We take as much care as we can to instruct them. Most of them seem to do pretty well since we commenced. My health is geting better, and when I was sick, they took grate care of me. I had a grate swelling in my throat with a hard fever. Brother Aloysious is well and seems to be happy. I am happy enough to what regards the place. Butt [for] the best part, I am yet very weak, but with the blessings of God [and] that of the Blessed Virgin and your good prayers, I hope to overcome all the obstacles with which I may meet with in this world. Two priest have been ordained this last week. The weather is very cold and has been so for some dayes, and on one of these cold dayes Mr. Moor's house bourned up. That is the frame house. I was very glad to hear that all were well and that you have 50 borders. Pray for me, dear Father. Excuse me for the poor and bad writing. I must also informe you that our school room is good enough now because we have a grate fire in it, and when we will not have no fire in it, we will be obliged to go to some other place after school is out, and so I hope that our health will be kept good.

Your most obedient and affectionate child in Christ,

Brother Francis

Chapter Five

1846

59. Brother Aloysius (2) to Father Sorin

Vincennes January 14, 1846

Reverend and dear Father,

I have received your kind favor of the 5th January just as I was thinking to write to you to inform you that I had made up my mind to return to New York as soon as the weather will permit which I suppose [will] not be before the month of March. I want to get there as early as I can in the spring. I hope you will not censure me for this change but pray for me and by your generosity afford me some assistance to defray the expence of my journey which you know is a long and expensive one. I assure you, Reverend Father, that it is a great disappointment to me and a severe trial, but yet trusting in God. I am discouraged if you could [not] with safety and with expence to send my trunk and things to me here. It would be much easier for me to go by St. Louis than to return to South Bend. I have lately learned the probability of my watch being lost. If so I am very [sorry] for it was a very useful watch and worth 18 dollars to me. The key attatched to it I could not set a value on. It was the memorial of a dear friend which if lost I shall [have] great reason to regret.

[MS torn] my things some of which I have here the [MS torn] are one overcoat, a frock, and d[r]ess coat [MS torn] cravat, and satin stock, one pair [MS torn] there are one or two for [MS torn] My watch was not included in the bill.

Except a trunk is sent direct by stage to here it [is] in danger of being lost. The bishop told Brother Francis today about the contents of your letter. He told me in the morning that he sent the order. I intend to let him know that I am not prepared until I hear from you again. If you leave this school trusting to Brother Francis, it must go down. We have 71 scholars now and no doubt but there will be 100 when the weather gets fine. If my opinion is of any use, you should send a Brother to fill my place for indeed Brother Francis is not competent to take charge of any kind of a school alone. There is no one here aware of resolution. My dear Father, I cannot [ ] your solicitude for my health which is well now, thank God, as is also that of Brother Francis. Be pleased to write to me immediately that I may know what to depend on and how or which way to travel, and of course to countermand your good and worthy orders.

I am, Reverend and dear Father, with esteem and veneration your humble and obedient servant and child in Christ,

Brother Aloysius

60. Brother Mary Joseph (8) to Father Sorin

Madison February 9, 1846

My Reverend Father,

I hope yourself and all the Brothers are well. I cannot tell why I receive no letter. I have been expecting one these four months. It is true. I received one November 7th, a small note which said nothing about my school, etc. I am astonished. When I ask advice, I receive no letters. In Vincennes I received one in eight months. People were asking about the Brothers and were asking me if I did not receive letters. I said no. I am asked by Reverend Mr. Delaune if I have had a letter, by the Sisters, by Mother Theodore. I say no. They are astonished. Sisters tell me they receive each one every two and three weeks. Reverend Mr. Delaune told me to write to you on this subject, or I should not have done.

I am tired of the mission. I should like to [be] at the Lake, but God's will be done.

Yours truly in Jesus Christ,

Brother Mary Joseph

N.B. Whilst in Madison the first year, I received five or six in the same time when the postage was 18 cents on each. Now it is 5 cents. I have about 50 scholars at present.

61. Brother Gatian (1) to Father Moreau
[Translated from French]

Notre Dame February 18, 1846

My reverend Father,

I'm happily taking advantage of the occasion that Father Superior's departure for France offers me to give you witness of my acknowledging the counsel you gave me in your last letter, to tell you something about our establishment, and to acquit myself of the obligation for guidance as the Constitutions prescribe.

Father Superior's trip doesn't make me uneasy although there's no one here who can replace him and human prudence expects only disorder and ill fortune, because since only I myself of the entire council voted negative, one can piously believe it's the will of God. Father Superior, better than anybody, will be able to make you understand the urgent needs of the house, to come to an understanding with you on the interpretation of certain passages in the Constitutions and on the founding of establishments, and to explain the confusion which the contract with Monsignor de la Hailandière often puts us in.

I'm going to tell you something which perhaps will not please you, but, hating disorder, I'm never afraid of using all imaginable methods to correct it. Many members of the Council, almost all the seminarians and the Brothers, think as I do and often made remarks to me. Fearing that no one is saying a word to you about it, I've resolved to make you aware of it.

Father Superior's great kindness (or his timidity or lack of vigilance) lets him be easily fooled in his moves and in his dealings with hypocrites and flatterers who get from him everything they want. For example, there's been little concern for three postulants or Brothers, never giving them the least public reproach, although their scandalous conduct merited expulsion, but instead of believing them guilty, he preferred to imagine that those who complained were mistaken. They're no longer in the house. One was since married without a priest at the door of the university. Another revealed Council matters from when he had been secretary. Thus jealousies and complaints are created. I have to add, however, that Father Superior is more on his guard this year.

We have no more Brothers this year than last year, but our jobs always increase. So Brother Vincent, for example, is novice master, fruiterer, cellarist, infirmarian, gardener, assistant [superior], prefect, kitchen helper; Brother Gatian is director of studies, prefect of discipline, head of the accounting office, secretary of four weekly councils, and in the boarding-school, professor of the upper division course in which the students know as much as the teacher, supervisor of all recreations and of a dormitory, and professor of French to boot. You can guess how the jobs are done.

Send us reinforcements: a robust cook, a good blacksmith, ten or twelve postulants, priests, or Brothers fifteen years old who can learn English to perfection and be other Anselms; and send also some young priests not only pious but wise, who have good heads and are capable of filling the head places. For those spots it's necessary to have more industrious men here than in France.

I'm feeling pretty good although my classes and the supervision, joined to my somber and irritable temperament, exhaust me a lot, and by the distaste they cause in me, they sometimes make me want to play the fool (which I'm not doing) so that I could be relieved of some of my duties.

I still have my same taste for studying languages, mathematics, etc., but I don't have a minute to study them. I'll be twenty years old in a month. Consequently, it's a good time to push myself if I'm going to develop, because, ruined by teaching, I'll become good for nothing.

I really believe I'm out of place and called to the ecclesiastical state as I've always believed, but that's not so much my affair as it's yours since prudence and the vow of obedience likewise oblige me to follow your orders.

As far as my spiritual exercises, etc., in re-reading my last letter, you can see where I am.

Your Reverence's respectful and obedient servant,

Brother Gatian

I hope that our communities at Ste. Croix won't forget to pray for Notre Dame du Lac. I haven't forgotten the old coadjutor Brothers of Ste. Croix, nor Brothers Hilarion, Hilaire, Chrysostom, Francis Xavier, etc.

Brother Gatian

You ask me if I'd not go eagerly to teach English in France. I answer that it doesn't matter much, but if I had to choose, I'd prefer to stay where I am. Anyway, you don't need me right now since Mr. Steber is going to stay at your place.

Have you received my decennial pledge that I sent with Mother Superior?

62. Brother Joseph (1) to Father Sorin

Indianapolis March 26, 1846

Dear and Reverend Father,

In my last letter, I forgot to tell you a word about the present subject. Besides I was not much inclined to writing and discussing matters.

In your last letter, you tell me that you will send me Brother Francis for the day school and for the French. Brother Francis, of couse, is good for the French, but for the English I am certain he will spoil the broth. He speeks worse than I do. He knows no grammar, no arithatic, no geography. We must keep pace with the other schools. There are already some Protestants who think my school superior to their own. Now instead of increasing the good opinon, we will lessen it.

If you can send Brother Bernard, it will be much better. Then the day school will be secured. As for the French and German, I believe I can do, if Brother Francis speeks the French better. I know for certain that I understand grammar fully as well.

I have no objection to your sending Brother Francis for the French, but the above named Brother for the English. If I will show you that we will have the best school in town. However you will do well to come and see before you do anything, so that no blame may fall upon me.

Tomorrow I shall begin to give lessons to the governer (in German). He seems to be very favorable to our establishment in this city.

Receive, dear Father, my love and respect with which I am your most obedient but unworthy son.

Brother Joseph

Please tell Brother Vincent to send me a scolding in a letter, that I may have at least a letter from him.

It seems that the Methodists beginn to put themselves under the patronage of the Blessed Virgin Mary. I am glad to see it. Very likely though I think that they have denied her long enough. There is in this town a little Methodist house of education called St. Mary's Seminary. I never knew it till I saw it in The School Friend, a paper which I receive every month gratis from Cincinati.

The fever has once more seized upon me. I was well for about four weeks, but I took a relapse on Easter and was very sick on Easter Monday.

63. Brother Joseph (2) to Father Sorin

[Indianapolis] [July] 22, 1846

Dear and reverend Father,

Your letter of the 20th has been received but no money. I see indeed there is indeed no reason for not sending at least that which you have. I call these things windings round, zig zag, amusing the people and making fools of them. I wish you will excuse me if I speak this way because it makes me mad indeed; for there is every week something else. In fact there is no end. You want Mr. Phipps to make such an enormous deduction, and you will not give him the chance to pay a single cent of his debts so that he has to pay interest all the time. Permit me to say that this is no fair dealing.

I have put your box on the stage this evening. I have paid $1.70 charges from Louisville to Indiana. You seem to take no notice of what I reported in different letters that I am altogether distressed for want of a cook. Trouble and hard labor have caused me a great deal of sickness since you have seen me. I have to give lessons, I have to be cook, gardener, to get in the wheat and hay. In a word I have to do everything or better I have to be the fac totem. If you bear me any interest at all, at least send me an old woman if you have nobody else. Indeed, I pity the man that is in any way dependent on Notre Dame du Lac.

Little Henry has left me yesterday. In the morning I sent him to market, and instead of keeping his stand, he run about with a bad fellow after girls. When he came home, I sent him to work in the meadow to shake out hay. There he got at the whisky jug of the man who mowed my grass. At dinner he came home so drunk that he could not stand on his legs. Then he spent the whole afternoon in the meadow doing nothing. Towards evening he came to tell me that he would not work for me [for] under $4.00 per month and boarding. I told him I would not give him 50 cents, and if he was not pleased, he might go. So he did, but I kept his clothes back. Never a human being abused me and gave me such bad language as this little rascal did. But today he was sorry for it. He waited for me at noon when

I came from town. He wanted me to take him back again, but I would not. Perhaps I will, if he humbles himself well.

I am, dear Father, your most humble but unworthy son,

Brother Joseph

64. Brother Joseph (3) to Father Sorin
[Translated from French]

[Indianapolis] [1846?]

My very dear Father,

You concede that the step August takes is much for a man like him. Then it isn't necessary to require more of him for the time being. Let us treat him with kindness, charity and a little consideration, and I'm sure that you can do with him all you want to. But don't repress him. He's the most easily discouraged man I've ever seen.

Please tell my cousin he has not replied to the letter you gave him. I wrote it myself—that took a lot of effort. Josephine Lande gave me 361 dollars in silver which carries interest of 6 percent. Moreover, I have 400 dollars in notes which are due at different times.

I want to pay Mr. Phipps today what is indicated here.

Brother Joseph

65. Brother Benedict (1) to Father Sorin

Mt. Pleasant, Indiana September 19, 1846

Reverend Father,

Your letter animated my soul with a new gleam of consolation for reading the contents thereof fully pleased me for I think I see the opperating hand of Providence directing and blessing the institution. I suppose you did not get my letter at the mother house for I got no answer though I expected it. I heard you were sick, but I am happy to know of your safe return.

Reverend Father, my habit is fully as good as the day I took it though I wore [it] all the time except one Sunday at St. Mary's and two at Mt. Pleasant. The days were very warm, and I think it good enough untill I go back again unless you wish to respect the Community, not me, but if you send it I will wear it on Sabbath days. I want a book of med[i]tation. The priest has no English ones, but I take my meditation generally on the life, passion, and crucifixion of Jesus Christ or the Gospel of the day.

As for the school, the number of children I had from 8 to 12, sometimes 15 or 16, latterly from 18 to 22. The whole on the list is about 35, some Protes[t]ants. They are kept at home half the time to work. The children are morally good and virtuous, but the parents in general have no love for the practice of virtue or religion though many go to Communion every second Sunday. They are very ignorant although very good neighbors. The children would be much better if they could come regular. They attended the chapel very well on Sunday, twice a day. There is a fall off now. The priest does his duty well to compel them to come.

I taught the boys to read Latin, and we all read Vespers every Sunday before catechism, which induced boys and girls to come regularly each Sunday. I taught all in common to read Latin for one hour before Vespers. Several big boys and girls would not go to dinner to attend the reading. Old men and women often attended in the afternoon.

Now, Reverend Father, I will tell you how I act. When the priest will go to Mt. Pleasant, I am up at 5 o'clock, in the chapel in 15 minutes. Say some vocal prayers till 5:30, prayer O Infinite. Meditation till 6 or 6:15, continue other prayers till 7. Morning prayer in common in the chapel with the children and people. Catechism till 10:30. Then rosary, the gospel and epistle of day. We unite with the church. Return home, particular meditation till 12. Vespers 2:30, catechism 2:30 till 4:45. Finally rosary for the conversion of bad parents and bad children.

I then recreate myself for half an hour. I then return to finish my obligatory devotion for half an hour. I take in the scholars at 8 AM, continue till 11:30. One o'clock we go daily to the chapel to say the rosary for the conversion of sinners. Reverend Father, it would delight you to see their actual piety. If any shew levity or bad conduct, I punish by not letting him to the chapel that day.

I was often sorry to have so few to attend on at school. I thought if you knew it, you would not leave me here. But, Reverend Father, I am very uneasy because of the debts I owe in Ireland, because of the difficulty of getting and sending the money there. But I wrote lately to the South for the money in such a way that I hope I will not be disappointed to be sent to Reverend William Starrs, he being so convenient to manage the thing. I will write to him as you desire it, acknowledging the receipt of the sum received.

Reverend Father, I often wished that I could live and die at the college or novitiate to avoid the snairs and temtations of a wor[l]dly life in which I am exposed at present, that is, I must mix with men and women at table, even with the priest, but when he is away, his housekeeper and daughter are fond of company. The house is often filled, even when eating, [with] young girls particularly. I told the priest I would [want] never to go in that kitchen. He made no answer.

I often thought to ask you to employ [me] at the college or novitiate to live and die there. Amen.

Reverend Father, I send my cordial love and affection to you and all the reverend clergymen in Jesus Christ and all my Brothers and Sisters also. So pay a visit to Sacred Heart of Jesus and Mary and you may salute me there. Amen.

N.S. Reverend Father, when you did not write to me I thought I would tire you, reading mine as a penance for that fault. I subscribe myself, your prodigal son,

Brother Benedict

Let me know, did John Baptist die? Let me know also, did Brother Aloysius go away?

66. Brother Mary Joseph (9) to Father Sorin

Madison October 26, 1846

Reverend Father,

We arrived in Madison on Saturday evening at 5 o'clock. I was told that Reverend St. Pallais was sick and was boarding at a house in town. Brother Francis's feet were a little sore and he could not walk, so I went alone to Reverend Mr. St. Pallais and left Brother Francis with the family with whom Reverend Mr. Delaune boarded whilst in Madison.

Reverend Mr. St. Pallais was in the sitting room. I presented to him your letter and he asked me who had told Father Sorin he wanted Brothers. I said that I had, that the people were asking me everywhere when I passed through, when they would have two Brothers. I said that if they would write, that they would have either one or two from South Bend, and that the representations I had made to you induced you to send two. When we arrived in Madison, the people were glad to see us all except two persons who wrote against Reverend Mr. Delaune to the bishop and one of them, Mr. W. Griffin, has circulated through the town that Reverend J. Delaune had taken the people's money from Madison to buy the college and farm in Kentucky.

These men boasted on Sunday that we would not be received by Reverend Mr. St. Pallais. I asked Reverend Mr. St. Pallais if he would permit us to teach catechism on Sunday. He said it was not necessary. I said, very well. On Sunday we went to High Mass. Everyone welcomed us to Madison. They asked us when the school would commence as their children were running wild for want of a school. Others told me they were sending their children to Protestants' schools, but would send them to us as soon as we should start the school. There were over 40 children in gallery at Mass and there has been an increase of several families since I left. All told us they would assist us. Some offered us rooms if we would accept of them. I told them I would wait till I would know what the priest would tell us.

Brother Francis and myself went to Mass on Monday morning after we went to see Reverend St. Pallais to ask him if we should start school as the children were at the school door waiting for us. The school and desks were all ready. He talked with us some time, then told us that his house was not ready yet and he wanted to ask you about the terms. I told him the terms were $50 for each Brother for 10 1/2 months schooling. He said he wanted to see the people about it. I told him the people had sent their children to school and that they had paid well last year and said they would do the same this. He then said his house was not yet furnished and he wanted us to live in his house and he would rather we would return to South Bend. He would pay the expenses back and would send for us when he wanted us. He wished us to leave Madison, and I said we could not leave untill we had an answer from the Superior. He said he would take that upon himself and would give us a letter to you which would be satisfactory.

Brother Francis and I thought it would be best for us to write to you and wait untill you should tell us what to do in this matter. The members of the congregation are very much displeased. They say that Mr. Griffin and Mr. Blenkinsop have prevailed with Reverend Mr. St. Pallais to send us back. You will not believe this possible perhaps, but if you knew these men as well as I do and how they have troubled Reverend Mr. Delaune since his first arrival in Madison untill this day and even now are trying to blacken his character by saying that he took the money of the congregation away with him, but no one believes them because they knew Reverend Mr. D. too well.

You perhaps will say what has this to do with the school? Why when Brother Anselm was here, Mr. Griffin went to him and wanted him to make more of his children than the rest. Brother Anselm refused. He sent them to a Protestant school. When I came here a year ago, he did not like to send them, but Reverend Mr. D. said he must. He sent them. They came to school 7 months, behaved bad, would not conform to the rules of the school. Reverend Mr. D. told me to punish them. I did so. He took them from school and sent them to Protestant schools. He refused to pay Reverend Mr. Delaune his school money that was due, but abused when he was asked for it. Mr. Blenkinsop has no children. I could say much more, but I will wait for your answer. I remain, Reverend Father, your respectful and obedient servant,

Brother Mary Joseph

Since writing the letter in which this [is] enclosed, Brother Francis had an attack of the fever and ague. About 4 o'clock we heard that Sr. Liguori was dying, so I went to enquire how she was. Whilst I was there, Reverend Mr. St. Pallais sent for me. I went. He told me he had written a letter to you and that he believed all would be settled. I told him that Brother Francis was sick. He seemed to doubt it, said he would send the doctor to see him, and he would know whether he was able to travel. I said also that I wished to have a letter from you before I left Madison regarding something which I wished to ask you. (This was whether you would allow me to go [to] Kentucky as I had not settled the matters we agreed to.) He said he could not see why I wanted to stay. He said it appeared that we did not want to leave Madison. I deny'd wanting to stay in Madison. I said that I thought it was necessary according to our Constitution to write to you before leaving any place. I told him I had done so regarding Reverend Mr. Delaune. He then said in an angry tone, "I as parish priest of Madison and as Vicar General of this diocese order you both to leave Madison immediately." He said that he "would defray the expenses." I said that perhaps you might have some other destination for us. He said that "he would defray the expenses back." He said these were his last words. He said that "he had nothing against us but that if we were to stay 6 days waiting for your answer, the people would want to detain us to keep school and he would not do it."

As soon as Brother Francis is able to travel, I shall leave here (according to your first intention) for Kentucky. I will stay with Reverend Mr. Delaune as you told me.

I remain, Reverend Father, your respectful and obedient servant,

Brother Mary Joseph

N.B. Please to write to me.

67. Brother Gatian (2) to Father Moreau
[Translated from French]

Notre Dame November 21, 1846

My reverend Father,

I'm writing to you to wish you a happy new year and a happy feast-day, to fulfill my obligation for article 352 [?] of our Constitutions, and above all because as a member of the administrative council, I believe I'm obliged in conscience to do so.

My health is fine, and I'm subject to no spiritual aberration; I'm more serious and at the same time more happy. My jobs keep getting multiplied: I have a regular class, and I'm at the same time professor of French, bookkeeper, secretary of four weekly councils and one monthly council, which take up the whole night, director of students and prefect of discipline for the Brothers, supervisor of all recreation periods and sometimes office head, a job that alone could occupy me continually. With so many jobs, you must understand that it's difficult to attend to my religious exercises. However, I do them better than in the past. Nevertheless, these jobs increase my soul's activity and make me set aside many of my silly ways; regarding the ecclesiastical state, I have the same inclinations as when I wrote you my last letter. I haven't received the decision you'd promised me. He who ought to communicate it to me no doubt has his reasons for not doing so. While waiting, I sleep peacefully, because I'm ready to do whatever you command.

Now I'm going to give you some information on our administrative acts as I understood them, with all the frankness I'm capable of, because your last letter and recent ones led me to believe you'd be happy to know everything of possible consequence to our America.

Father Superior told us on his return that he'd been received coldly at Ste. Croix because it had been insinuated to you that we wanted to separate from the motherhouse. Although nobody spoke in that sense in my presence, I nevertheless have to tell you that in my opinion Father Superior has gone too far in translation of the Constitutions. He believed he had the same powers as you and that Notre Dame du Lac would govern its subjects and establishments [MS illegible] council and in the same way as Ste. Croix [MS illegible].

I nevertheless believe that Father Superior hadn't made these changes and many others except with the conviction that he'd get your approval. I'm cutting my signature off of the account you sent us on Father Superior's return. I'd tried to introduce in the verbal statement some words which note the manner in which the account had been made, but they made me copy it down up to what has disappeared in full. Father Superior decoyed me like the others by the pretended necessity of showing that the accounts he'd given to Ste. Croix were proper. But the account was done from memory by Father Superior and Brother Lawrence, and I assure you if a bad memory exists, it's Father Superior's. Besides, we have no books here except the foul copies of Father Superior, which he didn't even want to use himself although I asked for them with hue and cry. I've since discovered considerable errors of which I'll cite to you some examples, not being able to say anything with precision about others for want of books:

We have at the lumber merchant's instead of 3000 francs as we reckoned, a 4000 franc error for	1000.00
In the account of a Bertrand merchant, an error of	1000.00
The cooper is owed	2500.00
We haven't counted what we have to give a defrocked Brother	3500.00
Total	8000.00

Outside of these errors there are probably others. We're not sure that Mr. Vincent Badin donated lands estimated at 15,000 francs or when he had donated them. They're not worth a cent to us presently because they can't be sold. We'll probably have to buy some land soon for 30,000 francs as I'm going to explain to you later. Finally, Father Superior ordinarily estimates our properties for more than they're worth, and moreover he let himself get trapped with his print shop which is more bothersome to us than useful.

Administration

All those who know our business believe that our house will crumble, and the councilors generally attribute its preservation only to a special protection of Providence. They think with good reason that our misfortunes come from our bad administration, but the councilors throw the blame on Father Superior who, like Father Badin (to the great embarrassment of Father Superior himself he ought to have written to you), *does everything by himself.* I'm very young. It's true. But fearing no one has the courage or imprudence to speak frankly to you about these affairs so as not to wrong our establishment, I'm going to tell you what I, as well as the majority of the Council, think about them. To put order in my ideas, I've divided my subject under three headings, and I've forwarded nothing without citing at least one example.

Father Superior does everything by himself

Father Superior, for the least complaint and the most frivolous reason, caves in to his employees and takes their jobs on himself. They're given to persons of good will, already overburdened. He undertakes important matters without consulting the Council or without its advice. He sometimes misleads his councilors in making them see only the bright side. And finally, he proposes certain money matters to the Minor Chapter alone, from which, seeing the members that constitute it, he can expect no opposition.

I. Father Superior has a very bad memory, and takes charge of every kind of job and mandate. Consequently, he does nothing good and moreover causes everyone to murmur because of his forgetfulness. He mixes up details about subordinate officers, crosses these people for no reason and takes charge of their obediences. One example among others. Father Superior had named Father Gouesse director of infirmaries at a council of professors. A loaf of sugar was secretly taken by a Sister. The infirmarian complained. Father Gouesse, in accordance with his rule that forbids anyone to enter the infirmary and take anything without his permission, not knowing who's guilty, sends the following note to Sister Mary of the Cenacle: "A loaf of sugar was taken from the infirmary; if it has fallen into your hands, please have the courtesy to send it back." Sister of the Cenacle, who had taken it herself, gets angry, and Father Superior, who likes this good Sister so much, crosses Father Gouesse and takes his job away, but is he replacing him?

II. Father Superior holds to his opinion too much on what concerns the administration and acts without consulting when he foresees that the majority will be against him. Thus all his projects for orphans and apprentices, etc., etc., are made to vegetate and put an obstacle in the work of Holy Cross, not to speak of hospitals, asylums for the elderly priests, manufacturing, a boardinghouse run by Sisters who can't speak [English ?], and other enterprises that we've been obliged to abandon or which are a burden to us. Once enterprises are begun, he finds himself perplexed and asks what to do to maintain them. I could include in this category a museum which cost 4 or 5000 francs and which now doesn't pay its rent. There's more. Father Superior sometimes goes directly against the advice of the Council. An old councilor just told me that the museum had been purchased against the unanimous advice of the Council. It produced 150 francs in two years. The two following cases prove that one isn't blessed when one doesn't conform to his Constitutions. The priest in Madison [Indiana] had written to Father Superior to not send Brother Mary Joseph before he had written to him that he was ready to receive them. Father Superior, without paying attention to this letter and without consulting his appropriate Council, sends Brother Mary Joseph and with him a French Brother who barely knew how to read, and this other one against the decision of the Council. The unhappy pastor kept them only a few days and then sent them back, but the Brother, disgusted with the management of our house, instead of coming back here, defrocked.

The second case is not a new one: it seemed inevitable to have at least one fire a year. After having deliberated for a long time, we decided four weeks ago that our stoves were fine and were sufficient to heat the college; so there were no chimneys. But Father Superior who always believes American rogues in preference to his councilors, because like the good Sisters, they know how to flatter him, lets himself be persuaded that a chimney of single bricks works better than a stove, has one made at Father Gouesse's place at the end of the college building, and two days later one in the middle and another at the other end, all on the second floor. The next day about 3 pm, smoke begins to show up in the corridor and some bedrooms but is attributed to the chimneys. At six o'clock the smoke having soon filled all the apartments [ ] the fire on the first floor, on the second, on the third, and on the fourth, and all the fires are put out, except that of Father Gouesse, where there was hardly any smoke, but where's the fire? The alarm is given, and the frightened boarders leave through the smoke and set to work. In an instant all the buckets are filled. But the fire was still hidden. "The fire is in the belfry," cries Brother Vincent. They go up there. Nothing! Meanwhile always a bit skeptical, I walk around slowly outside, examining the roof and the window casements, when suddenly I saw flame leaving Father Gouesse's window which was open. Soon I warned two or three people who took the time to go see for themselves before believing me. I then enter hurriedly into the secretary's office which is under Father Gouesse's bedroom: three square feet of the floor were already on fire. I take my books and papers in haste, and I throw them out the door. I lost nothing. I'd scarcely finished when plaster, bricks, and water started to fill the office. It was then 7 o'clock, and the fire was put out at 8:30. The fire had started under Father Gouesse's hearth by the heat of the bricks and stayed hidden between the ceiling and the floor. The chimney in the middle was since removed, and we found the burned ceiling, but because a fire hadn't been made since the combustion, the fire which was in the floor had been put out. If a fire had been made in Father Gouesse's place before making it in the other chimneys, we probably would have had three fires at the same time, and in the middle of the night to boot. The havoc and losses amount to 2300 francs. Father Superior, in spite of this accident, wants to keep his chimney and will have it repaired by the mason. Wouldn't we do better to throw it out the window?

III. When it sometimes suits Father Superior to consult his Council on important matters, he takes care to let only the bright side be seen. The matter of Mr. Stephen T. Badin is an example. When his gift was proposed to the Council and Brother Lawrence raised the question of some hidden circumstances, Father Superior treated him like a fool, and having thus shut him up, he wheedled the others into believing it was worth at least 60,000 francs and that we had to pay only 2000 francs to Father Badin annually. However, since Father Badin complained so much about us, we began to doubt some conditions and asked for the documents on the return of Father Superior, who first pretended to look for them, then said they were in Louisville and he'd write for them. A month later I asked him in Council if he'd received them, and he replied that the ones in Louisville didn't contain the conditions. Later I asked him for those that contained them, and he set out to find them. "Oh," he said, "Father Badin has everything." I continued to pursue him, and after many ambiguous phrases and useless maneuvers, he was obliged to confess that besides the payment of 500 francs quarterly, Father Badin had the right to 125 francs more if he didn't receive his money on the same day, and that secondly, the contract obliged us to add to our properties three pieces of land estimated at 30,000 francs and that we wouldn't have to [pay] 40,000 francs if we bought them in our own name; meanwhile Father Badin's pieces of land had been sold for only 30,000 francs. This gift, without counting all the trouble it has caused, is really a burden for us, because the pieces of land are not very useful, unable either to be sold or cultivated, and it forces us to add a big debt to those we've already made and can't pay. Some councilors think there are other conditions. But what did Father Superior do? Instead of showing us the documents when Father Badin came to see us, he closed the door to all opposition in discovering the conditions and the difficulties they entailed to the Minor Chapter whose members agree to everything wished, who never agree, and who aren't capable of seeing what is shown them at the end of a finger, as I'm going to prove in the following paragraph.

IV. I know those who compose the Minor Chapter are members of the Administrative Council, because, as you know, they are the same with the exception of Father Gouesse and myself. But Father

Granger and Father Cointet rarely see the mistake of a question and ordinarily change their opinions many times on a single proposition, even as each gives his ideas. Thus they are of Father Superior's opinion until Father Gouesse has spoken and change when this last one gave his opinion. They come back to Father Superior's opinion when Brother Vincent speaks, because this good Brother for some time now seems to line up only with Father Superior. Then they change a third time when I explain my viewpoint. The remarks I just made apply more to Father Granger than to Father Cointet, and I can assure you that I believe they act very conscientiously in their repeated changes.

Brother Marie [Francis Xavier] is almost a zero. Brother Lawrence and Brother Joseph have good ideas, but they express them in an odd and ridiculous way which Father Superior uses adroitly to diminish the influence their observations could have. Good grief! It's to a Council composed of such members that Father Superior proposes the most important money matters which, according to the Constitutions, belong to the Administrative Council which must, if not discuss them, at least know about them. Otherwise, how do you wish us to vote for a purchase of whatever if we know neither the big expenses that have been made nor those about to be made? I could cite, for example, the business with the bishop of Detroit, with the bishop of Vincennes, with Dr. Canalli, and with Mr. Badin.

In finishing I can tell you that all the councilors, with the exception of Brother Vincent, who has never expressed himself clearly, have noticed the same faults. Three weeks ago, Father Superior being absent, I made them consider these irregularities and convinced everyone of the truth of what I observed: Brother Vincent himself didn't dare defend the superior. It was decided unanimously that I put in writing everything I had pointed out so that Father Granger, as Monitor, could admonish Father Superior. You can be assured of their sentiments by sending them the following questions, but since there's been a Minor Chapter in the meantime, I couldn't vouch for their frankness, unless you give them direct orders under pain of disobedience.

1. Does Father Superior take too many jobs on himself and doesn't he busy himself with too many details?

2. Has Father Superior undertaken many things without consulting his Council or even done things without their advice?

3. Does Father Superior always explain as he should the questions he proposes and in such a way to make us see the advantages and disadvantages?

It would perhaps be good to apply these questions to particular cases because things have been better the last fortnight.

Probable reasons for Father Superior's conduct

I. Father Superior is *too* good. He always seems fearful of offending. Punishments and humiliation are almost unknown. He prefers disorder to correction. He lets himself be dragged along by Peter and Paul and is not much on his guard against subtle flattery and the assurances of Americans whom he believes in preference to his Council and with whom he often shares plans before saying a word to those in his house, except sometimes to Brother Vincent. It's so true that in many circumstances we know his administrative acts only by reports that outsiders make to one another.

II. Father Superior has no *confidence* in his councilors. The bad opinion he has of his Council comes 1) from some folk not really understanding temporal affairs 2) from the scorn he has for Brother Lawrence because of his natural blunders 3) from the opposite and different character there is between him and Father Gouesse, our better administrator: Father Superior, good (*too* good), forgetful, neglectful and variable, forgives everything and lets himself be led by those who know how to say kind words to him. Father Gouesse, on the contrary, firm and regular, wants to follow the Constitutions in everything and submit everybody to them, 4) from a certain prejudice he has against Brother Joseph because of his excessive rigor 5) from his humiliation at the liberty and perhaps crudity with which I make my observations to him in Council, because I tell him everything without evasion and without ceremony so he'll have no excuse. The others, who wouldn't often dare to make the same remarks, add to poor Father Superior's mortification by affirming that what I say is true, Brother Vincent, his mediator, saying [only] that I ought to have more deference and respect. I regret having spoken so harshly sometimes, but when one is pushed to shove, one isn't always master of himself.

III. Father Superior's Monitor doesn't have enough influence on him because of the bad opinion Father Superior has of his experiences in temporal affairs. Thus it's very easy for Father Superior to refute the observations he [the Monitor] thinks about making to him [Sorin] for other people, and Father Granger, the only one knowing how to speak up, is obliged to keep quiet.

Remedies

It'd be very desirable if we had responses in writing to the following questions so that all the councilors would know if Father Superior is obliged to conform to the Constitutions or not, and also how we have to interpret the passages that treat of his authority.

I. Doesn't Father Superior have to conform to the majority (Article 50, Constitution 6), and in case he doesn't want to hold to the decision of his Administrative Council, doesn't he have to appeal to the Minor Chapter (Article 67, Constitution 8), or can he act independently of all counsel?

II. Doesn't Father Superior have to propose to the Administrative Council everything which concerns it (Article 43, Constitution 6), and don't all money matters have to pass through this Council before being proposed to the Minor Chapter (Article 43, Constitution 6)?

III. When Father Superior has something which concerns the Administrative Council, doesn't he have to assemble his Council, if possible to do so, and in case the Council can't be assembled, doesn't he have to give an account of what he did at the next Council meeting (Constitution 8, Article 69)?

IV. In case Father Superior doesn't want to present certain purchases and other questions which concern the Administration to the Minor Chapter, which he could very often do in the future, having little opposition to expect from this Council and much from that of the Administration, doesn't he have to make known to administrators the decisions which concern them? (See the reason for it on page 4, paragraph IV).

We should have a priest-administrator as Monitor, a priest whom Father Superior could consider his equal or even more able than he is in the handling of affairs and for whom he had a certain deference because of his seniority in the house: a person of Father Chappé's style. We should also have a councilor in the Minor Chapter capable of countering Father Superior's arguments when necessary.

It seems that you had ruled at Ste. Croix that the Sisters would no longer be seen in the stairways and apartments of the college. Well, you can still meet them every time you turn around, even after nightfall and after supper, sometimes in the stairways where there's hardly any light. Thus a Protestant boarder aged 18, coming back from places at 8 PM, met three of them under the porch. Many are shocked at these comings and goings, but what seems more scandalous is to see the new Sister Superior spend hours with Father Superior, often in his bedroom, although he ordinarily receives nobody except in the office. I'm making you aware of this disorder because I have in mind that you wouldn't tolerate it if you knew about it.

I believe I also have to tell you, because it seems to me you don't know too much about our affairs, that the former Sister Superior was esteemed and admired as well as loved by everybody. As long as she was superior and present, the Sisters were good to the priests and Brothers and almost never appeared at the college. The change has singularly astonished all, and I fear Father Superior regrets having asked for her. Nevertheless, I hope Providence has permitted everything for the best and that Mother Superior will shape up little by little and won't be so unpleasant in the future. I'll have to observe to you in passing that Father Superior is an enthusiast and often considers only the bright side. I wish consequently that you'd see that all the undertakings he speaks to you about are not approved by Council, lest you see there the signature of the councilors.

You'll pardon me if I make another observation to you that all the councilors would gladly repeat. It's that when you have something to rule on for our America, it'd be good if you had the opinion of our Council with all the information possible, because being on location we can see the difficulties better than you can in France.

Different arrangements with the bishop especially bother us, and the arrangements were known by the councilors only when they had been signed. Father Superior himself said he was not consulted regarding the Indianapolis novitiate, but I have trouble believing him. A fortnight ago on Wednesday (November 30) he left for Vincennes in order to reach an agreement with the bishop on this Indianapolis business. I don't know all the difficulties of this thorny affair, not being at the Minor Chapter where it was discussed, but I believe there's an advance of 20,000 francs to make, and we didn't have two cents when Father Superior left for Vincennes.

We'd be very obliged to you if you were able to answer more promptly certain requests that we make to you. Father Superior ought to send you a decision of the Council and a petition by the Council of Professors to have varied what they read in the refectory, etc. It seemed as if you had decided that Father Superior wouldn't have [ ] so many Brothers. I don't blame this decision because it's in accord with [ ] *French*, but I dare propose that Father Superior has as much need [of them] as the Rector and that a single person, like the [ ] everything. The English Brothers know nothing about [ ] Our yearly allowance is a little better than last year [ ] professors and often no books, because Father Superior seems [ ] can grow careless like everything else. He [ ] neglected, our ignorance and our bad government [ ] is more than 100 leagues and even to New [ ] of drunkards and lazy bums who certainly put the [ ] college where one freezes in winter and where one is eaten [ ] in summer. We have 33 paying boarders. Our establishment of Brothers only vegetates, the [ ] number than last year. Our novitiate is [ ] there's no religious spirit among our Brothers; obedience [ ] in its perfection.

Fever has all of us [ ] Father Cointet, the former Mother Superior, many others in danger of dying. Brother [ ] was three months without being able to work. Brother Anthony died four months ago. He died of old age. A postulant [who came] from France with Father Superior died because he drank some [ ] he had fever. Brother John the Baptist died on the feastday of our Father Superior. The [ ] and Brother Marie [Francis Xavier] were very sick. The first looks old, the latter won't live long. Brother Lawrence is [sick]; he worked with fever last summer. The [ ] five or six apprentices and more of the work that he can't [ ] Brother Justin doesn't yet know enough English to make himself understood. Brother Théodule and Brother Placidus [are our] great hopes for work. Brother Benoit has not worked much, having had fever out in the country.

I haven't spoken about Father Superior because I believed that [ ] to be from the house, because I don't want anything of it for him. I believe [he does all] for the best with all good kindness and simplicity, but lets himself be deceived. He seems to know neither his [ ] Don't do anything about what I said to you, but consult [ ] make them tell you everything without reserve. Having [this] information, you can control everything, but I [think] you ought not to make rules for our America [ ] votes of our councilors, because being on location, [ ] they'd be six times less true; they could still judge better.

In case you don't judge it appropriate to answer this letter, I'd prefer that you make me aware (by another letter or otherwise) that you've received it, because I believe Father Superior sometimes intercepts some, although he lately denied it. About two years ago I found an old letter of Brother Joseph's at the bottom of a trunk that Father Superior had ordered me to empty, and I showed it to him saying that he had probably forgotten it and reminded him that you had told us to write when we wanted to. He replied that he hadn't forgotten it, but that Brother Joseph was a buffoon.

I'm so busy that I was obliged to write this letter by stealth, setting myself to it and putting it off more than a fortnight. Please consequently excuse my Englishisms and my other faults, and receive the assurance of the sincerity with which I have the honor of being your Reverence's respectful and obliging servant,

Brother Gatian

If my father or some of my relatives want news of me, tell them what seems good to you, repeating always that I'm happy and completely joyous at having left my country to serve God, and that I love my new homeland as much as and even more than France. I have a younger brother named August in whom I've always believed I'd discover great inclinations for knowledge and piety. Although he's probably too young to be judged and I'm too young to judge,

I'd be very glad nevertheless if my brother [father?] gave him a good education.

I hope you'll make our priests and Brothers as well as our Sisters and Ste. Croix boarders pray for their confreres, their associates and their sincere friends from our dear American colony which has so great a need of heavenly blessing. They shouldn't forget to pray especially for those who formed the first colony of which two are no longer in this world and of which no one has abandoned the work. They should remember especially he who is in age and unfortunately in virtue also the least of these generous pioneers.

Sister Mary of the Heart of Jesus is cut off from the Community of Sisters. Father Superior attributes to her many observations which are made at Ste. Croix about our America. This poor superior could say well founded things, but she shouldn't have been trusted because being superior made her proud: she was hated by everybody and stayed the favorite of Father Superior, from whom she got everything she wanted. Her absence during Father Superior's stay in France scandalized many. She lived in Detroit where she went to the bishop and a benefactress, making them understand (which was true up to a certain point) that the donations destined for the Sisters had been used to buy pretty little birds (the museum) of which one cost more than 200 francs. Please pardon me the freedom of my remarks; I'm always frank with my superiors and councilors, and with all other people I seem to be ignorant of everything and incapable of making an observation.

Observation. Neither account books nor books from the secretary's office are in order for two reasons: the first is that if I'm in charge, I don't have the time to touch them, and the second is that even when I have all the time necessary, I couldn't touch several of these books because Father Superior has all the documents, and this good priest guards them all, although I've asked him more than twenty times for them. I thought in spending some white nights [?] taking on my other jobs and making my child [student helper] write, I could've been able to do at least a part of what there is to do.

N.B. If I've written so lengthily, it was so as to be able to speak with profit about things I had to talk about, their being, in my opinion, very important.

Brother Gatian

Chapter Six

1847

68. Brother Joseph (4) to Father Sorin

Logansport January 11, 1947

Dear and reverend Father,

I am obliged to inform you from Logansport how [the] matter stands with our journey. From South Bend to Logansport we have met with the most horrible roads. They are so rough that I expected to break down the wagon at every step, and, if it was not for the stuberon efforts of my two dear little mules, I should still stick in some mudhole. The fact is that you have no idea of the roads. I was told that for twenty years back no man has seen them so bad.

My poor little Jack has a very sore shoulder, thanks to the kindness of Brother Lawrence who has given me a collar which is a great deal to[o] large for the poor little fellow. It might do on a level ground, but not on such a monstruous road.

I have to stay a few days with good Mr. Autrant in [and] wait for news from the south. The mail from Indianapolis and Lafayette could not come in since ten days, not even on horseback. Nearly all the bridges from Logansport down to the Ohio are s[w]ept away. The railway from Indianapolis to Madison is in many places ruined and broke through. All the mills in Indianapolis are s[w]ept away so that the barrel of flour cost five and six dollars. I do not know what I shall do. I do not like to come back, and still I do not like to expose myself to a danger which no one dared to encounter.

I am, dear Father, your obediant but unworthy son,

Brother Joseph

69. Brother Joseph (5) to Father Sorin

Indianapolis January 11, 1847 [II]

Reverend dear Father,

I have no doubt but that you feel somewhat bad on account [of] our mutual disappointment, but don't be discouraged. The said depot is not more than about 300 yards east of me, and Monday next the Peru depot will be located. The commissioners of the latter can not help themselves to locate theirs west of the farmer, so that whatever may be the consequence, the value of our property is tribled by the very fact. I saw Squire Solivan yesterday. He told me to hold on for a few weeks until the wether gets better. He is certain that I can make from 10,000 to 12,000 dollars of this property.

Let me know what you will do now, or if you let me free to do what I find most advantageous. We have lost nothing by waiting so long.

I did not send you cousin because you did not answer me the question concerning him. I wish he were a member of our Institution, but he does not like to be Brother, particularly since some preists told him that the bishop will take him to Vincennes.

Write me immediately. I remain, dear Father, your most obedient but unworthy son,

Brother Joseph

70. Brother Joseph (6) to Father Sorin

Indianapolis January 19, 1847

Dear Father,

I arrived last Sunday the 17th in Indianapolis after great labor and trouble, through swamps, creeks, holes, broken bridges, cross-ways, difficult by-roads, mud and water; in effect, the roads have never been as bad as they are now. After 3 or 4 hours I had left Logansport, the fever took again possession of me and keeps me since. I suffered indeed a great deal on the road, and to increase my misery, my wagon broke down in going down a broken bridge at 26 miles from Indianapolis. Brother Thomas was of great service to me in this, in many other difficulties where I could do but very little on account of my fever. I hired a man and a team wagon to take wagon and all to Indianapolis, which cost me nearly [ ] dollars, but the poor man almost ruined his horses.

Brother Thomas left for Madison yesterday night in the evening. Little Henry is with a gen[t]leman in town untill I start again, and I stop with Reverend Mr. McDermet. He is an excellent man. He and many others absolutly keep me here right away to teach their children; he would board me for teaching him German and 5 or 6 others would make up $100 for the school. I saw different lots in town and round Mr. Barret. I believe they can be got, what is called at Indianapolis cheap, but the cheapest, the most advantageous and at the same time the most beautiful location is Mr. Merrill's place. It has, in fact, advantages which no other piece of ground in and round the town have. Mr. Merrill will not sell the part on which the house stands, which is a square of eight acres, which eight acres taken from twentie seven leave ninteen. These ninteen he will sell us for $150 per acre. This is a high price, but it is by far the cheapest that can be got. He asked first $3000, but when I pressed him to tell me the lowest price, he said he would take $150 per acre. There is on these 19 acres a little barn; 6 acres (the best part) are planted in locust trees, the balance is in wood. Now if we will make an establishment in Indianapolis, we must avail ourselves of the opportunity, lest we miss it as it has happened to the bishop. He wanted, but when some knew that he was the Catholic bishop, they soon took their measures and the good bishop missed it.

I which [wish] to know what is to be done. It is true you have never told me to make a bargain, but I would like you would purchase these 19 acres whilst you can have them or give up the enterprise all at once. Please to write me immediatly. My fingers are getting stiff and my feet cold. I must go to bed.

I do not believe I shall be able to proceed on my journey; no man can have an exact idea of the roads, if he has not seen them. The flood has completly ruined them, and still I shrink at the thought to return on that monster road to Logansport. However, I am ready to go on. I on[ly] wish to have your opinion. At least I might go by the railroad to Louisville to get the books for the college, or I might bring some apples and peaches. They are cheap here. This is a good fruit country.

Jack is the very worst fellow. He has really a bad spirit in his belly. When he sets in, he has given me a great deal of trouble. He will not stop when the wagon is stopt against something. He will rather upset or break everything. Please present my respects to all the priests and my love to all the Brothers in particular to our old ash-haired Brother Vincent.

I am, dear Father, your unworthy but most obedient son,

Brother Joseph

71. Brother Joseph (7) to Father Sorin

Indianapolis January 25, 1847

Reverend and dear Father!

Since I wrote you from this town,I had the opportunity [ ] lots. Among others I saw the property of a gentleman named Fib's [Phipps]. He has 27 acres, most excellent land, a splendid situation. The line of the corporation passes right through the middle; 15 acres are cleared. There is a good little orchard with all kinds of fruit and a good many grape vines on it (tame grapes). There is a nice well, good sized, new brick house just finished, a good cellar under it, a nice frame house added to it which would serve as parlor, refectory and kitchen, a good porch at the end of which a shed for wood and other things, a wash-house, a new bake-oven, a new barn with an excellent stable, a grainery, cow-houses, sheds for carrages and wagons, and a good cistern, and a good well. In a word, it is the most complete thing that can be desired. I was assured that the gentleman has layd out 3,700 dollars for improvment, and he will give it for $4000.

He will wait for half of the payment 6 or six months and for the other have [half] 6 months longer or a year from now. Or he would make an other bargain, viz., the bishop has a lot in town with an old sloppy frame house on it. This man would take it at $3,000. You can get nothing better and cheaper. I will wait for [an] answer to this letter. Please write me speadily. There is prospect for a good school for different languages. There are many more Catholics in this town than you thought. If I had known your opinion I [would] have written to the bishop, but...

I can get dried apples at 68, peaches at 1.25, as many as I please. I have a notion to trade off gentleman Jack and lady Dulcine. I think I can get a good span of horses for them and something to boot.

Bad health continues to trouble me some. I am, dear Father, your most humble but unworthy servant,

Brother Joseph

72. Brother Thomas (1) to Father Sorin

Madison Jan. 28, 1847

Reverend dear Father,

After a fatiguing journey of two weeks and one day, I arrived safely in Madison on the 22nd, in the absence of the Reverend Mr. St. Palais, who arrived only last evening, having been nearly four weeks absent.

I have nothing particular to say with regard to myself, except that I feel more fervent every day in my exercises of devotion, as I meditate on the necessity of prayer, mortification, and retirement.

The school will commence next Monday. It is uncertain yet how many scholars I will have, but it is said between 70 and 80. I am very well contented so far, and I hope will continue so.

When Brother Joseph and I parted, he gave me four dollars, expecting that I would have enough left to buy a pair of shoes, but being detain[ed] in Oldenburg one day on account of the cars not being ready, I have only 75 cents left and stand in great need of shoes, and have not enough money to buy a pair with.

The reason for which I write, before being fixed, is to inform you that two gentilmen of this congregation wish very ardently to enter the community, and would like to be apprised before starting on what conditions you will receive them.

The youngest is only 19 years and by name is Charles Nodler. His Father Martin Nodler desires very much that his son may become a Brother. The other one who wishes to become a member of the institution is named Godfried Hermann. He is a man of good health and a vigorous constitution and is not in his 44th year and is said to be one of the best shoemakers in Madison. Mr. Hermann has a son that he wishes to bring with him to put him [to] some trade and get schooling. The boy is 12 years old. His mother has been dead 5 years.

In expectation of an answer, I remain your obedient child,

Brother Thomas

Mr. Nodler's father is a grocery keeper and himself a cooper. If you receive him, he wishes to get some schooling.

73. Brother Joseph (8) to Father Sorin

Indianapolis February 2, 1847

Dear and reverend Father,

Perhaps you will scold and be dissatisfied with me in reading the following, but I can not help. I would be afflicted if you were dissatisfied with me, but I could not repent for what I have done. I have concluded the bargain for the property mentioned in my last letter. It is concluded in the manner you have read in the said letter. In order not to break the whole bargain, I had to buy from the same man for $450 lo[o]se property. This consists in: one splendid two horses carrage which has cost, when quite new, $400. There is certainly not a better and nicer one in the county of St. Joseph. One very good wagon of the best make, full of iron, one pair of beautiful black horses, one wind-mill plough, one side plough, one cultivator, one harrow, two hoes, two forks, harness, quieres, etc.

Now Mr. Fib's [Phipps] would actuelly not sell me the property if I would not buy these things because he would not know what to do with them, and to sell them at auction for nothing, he did not like. I did not like to take them, but to break the bargain on this account would have been the hight of foolishness because I could find nothing like it for less than $6000, and you know 2000 dollars gained or lost is not a trifle. But you will ask me why I did not wait till you told me. I will tell you: the Methodists had a revival (retreat) in this town, and they were storming the house of Brother Fibs in order to prevent him from selling his property to Papists. I tried to get ahold of him, and we concluded the bargain because the Brothers and Sisters (Methodists) would not pay his debts. Now it is bought, and you have to keep it. I will soon send you the land-deed of it.

We must take possession of the property the first of May. I am making preparations for housekeeping. The priest is going to board with me. I have an old German lady, about 50 years of age, who gives herself to the Brothers for life. She is an excellent housekeeper, and an postulant about of the same age who will take care of the farm.

I have plenty friends here and even friends of note. I have given to the Catholic ladies in town a sewing party. They make me all my bedding and all I have to do for nothing. You don't need to trouble yourself about me. I will get along till you come yourself and fetch me some help. I will have a good day school for children, and a good evening school for young men who will learn French and German, $2 a quarter per child.

I tried to sell the mules, but I do not think I will get more than 100 or 110 dollars.

In the expectation of seeing you soon, I am, dear Father, your obedient but unworthy son,

Brother Joseph

74. Brother Joseph (9) to Father Sorin

Indianapolis February 8, 1847

Reverend and dear Father!

I have received your letter from the 20th of last month: in it I easily can perceive that you must be sorry for my having concluded the bargain with Mr. Fipps. However I can not be sorry. My only wish at present is to see you, to communicate to you my views and to show you all the advantages we have in our hands. I believe your presence, at any rate, indispensable. If there be any possibility at all, I wish to see you in the course of 10 days.

Let nothing trouble you for you will see that everything is gliding smoothly along. I will have some cash boarders and a good school for French and German. This requires help. If I had Brother Lewis, he would do me great service for the children school. I could easily teach him at home. It would relieve me a great deal and give me leisure to tend the French and German which will put every month 20 or 25 dollars in my hands. Besides I will have enough to do for the concerns of the house, if you leave me here. I have written to Cincinaty for school and other books. I would like to have a new hapit [habit] and my stocks. I want nothing else. I can get it cheaper here. Brother James has my little trunk. There are a good many things in it, of which I want: the French prayer books, my stocks, and the have [half] of every kind of seed that is in it (the half at least). There are different kinds of seeds in my desk in the printing office. I wish to get them. Do not cheat me out of them. Brother Vincent may take charge of all these my wants. If you send Brother Vincent here next spring, besides Brother Lewis now, we will manage tolerably well. [Letter incomplete]

75. Brother Thomas (2) to Father Sorin

Madison February 13, 1845 [1847]

Reverend and Dear Father,

It is not by relying on my own strength that I am justified to say that I will endeavor to meet your expectations to their fullest extent, but on the grace of God and the intercession of the Mother of God. I am weak, but God is strong.

Here is a list of the articles left by the Brothers Mary Joseph and Francis.

Habits	2
Shirts	2
Night-cap	1
Handkerchiefs	3
Drawers	1
Pictures in frames	23
Holy water pots	21
Brass crosses	28
Little framed crosses	15
Medals	48
Statues	3
Plaster pictures	2
Pairs of beads	69
Geography and atlas	1
Grammar	1
Mrs. Herbret's book	4
Gospel books	28
Hales's History	5

These are the things that were left by the two Brothers, and I would be very glad to know if I am allowed to give any of the pictures or medals as rewards to the school children and whether I am allowed to sell the books or not.

Mr. Charles Nodler will start on the 15th for Notre Dame du Lac. He is leaving a plentiful home to follow in the footsteps of him who has promised eternal life to them that forsake all and themselves.

Reverend Father, I have also to inform you that his parents are very uneasy with apprehensions that he might loose his vocation, if he has any.

Mr. Hermann cannot be ready before next Monday. He will start then for sure.

As to the number of the school boys and their proficiency, Mr. N. will faithfully inform you.

N.B. Reverend Father, pray for me that I may daily become more humble and meek of heart.

Reverend Father, one of yours,

Brother Thomas

76. Brother Joseph (10) to Father Sorin

Indianapolis February 24, 1847

Dear and reverend Father!

I did not like to write you since some time because I thought Father Gouesse's writing would justify my conduct with regard to the property I purchased in Indianapolis. As far as [I] can see, I think that some or all were disatisfied with my conduct. They think that nobody knows as much as themselves, but it does not matter much what they think or say because I well know that they do not see farther than their noses can reach. If they are still disatisfied, I wish you would give me liberty to act as I may please in my own name, and I will show you that I can pay for it myself.

If you will allow me to lay out 5 or 6 acres in lots of 1/3 or one-third of an acre, I can sell them right away and bring the acre from 225 to 300 dollars. 5 or 6 lots are assured. If I had $300 cash, I could make a good stroke in purchasing eight acres of land joining ours. A part of these would squerre [?] ours and leave us enough to lay out for $2000 of lots. The man asks 1200 dollars for the eight acres, 300 dollars in hand, and 300 dollars in ninty days. For the other 600, interest could be paid.

I am certain I could sell more than 20 lots to Catholic families round our house. I do not know if you will let me sell and trade off wagon, carrage, or such things as we do not want for our own use.

I keep house for myself. I have a good, smart family. My old Dutch grandmother is an excellent housekeeper. She is clean and extremly economical.

Today is the second of my keeping school. I had 22 scholars, and in as few days, I shall have about 30. I have $12 per scholar per quarter. If I had Brother Bernard here, I could gain a good deal in teaching French and particularly German. There is a great call for German here, and in fact this language is indispensable. I hope you will send me assistance.

It would be worth 500 dollars if I could see you but for 4 hours in Indianapolis.

In this sweet hope, I am, dear Father, with the greatest respect and love, your most obedient but unworthy servant,

Brother Joseph

Please give my respects to the priests and my love to all the Brothers. Please answer me immediatly.

77. Brother Vincent (17) to Father Sorin
[Translated from French]

Notre Dame du Lac December 29, 1847

Very dear Father,

It was necessary indeed to make me speak up through obedience because it is so difficult and even dangerous to examine the actions of a superior who can have special motives which make him act, which can be known only to himself. I'll tell you then very simply things such as I see them for you to meditate on with the good God during your retreat.

1) I find you sometimes too reserved regarding your assistant; for example, to go on retreat without telling him a word of it, neither the place nor time you intended.

2) You don't show enough submission to your nurses when your health requires particular needs.

3) I find that you don't follow through on the plans you form; for example, you had promised to go take your supper every Friday at the novitiate. You had promised the college Brothers as well to give them a spiritual conference at least once a week. I don't doubt that you have motives in not continuing these things, although it always lessens confidence when one doesn't persevere at least for a certain time, and when one arrives only at the end of the time that one had proposed.

4) People complain that you don't observe college rules, that you gave permissions without informing the one who had the right to know; for example, the prefect of discipline. I have to tell you these complaints have happened very little since the beginning of the semester.

5) I believe it would be necessary for you to make yourself accountable more often on the state of the house either in Minor Chapter or to the members you know to be most interested in the development of the work of the trade masters, even if nothing is happening or there's no abuse to correct.

6) It would also perhaps be good if you were to give either on Sundays or at chapter an explication of the vows, particularly obedience and poverty, since our poor Irish Brothers don't have Constitutions to study.

You have to put the above observations into practice after you've conferred with God in your retreat. We didn't forget you yesterday in our chapter; both today and tomorrow we'll continue to pray for you.

You likewise, if you can find a moment, write to me what I have to do for my own good and to sanctify myself as far as God wants it of me.

Your very humble and obedient servant,

Brother Vincent

78. Brother Thomas (3) to Father Sorin

Madison March 6, 1847

Reverend Dear Father,

Your paternal letter tuched my heart more then the reading of any pious book could do, Father, but for bashfulness I could have bursted out into tears before all. Pardon me, Father, my weekness. You wish me to be very meek and humble of heart. Father, I wish it myself from the very bottom of my heart. I beg of you, Reverend Father, therefore, that I may not only consider myself unworthy of what God in his Providence has called me to, but also that I may become pure of heart as Jesus and His Blessed Mother were. So pray for me.

Mr. Nodler's parents were very glad to hear from him, in so much that when I told them of his good dispositions, they burst into tears of joy. Mr. Hermann could not leave Madison before the 7th of March on account of the bad weather. You will please be so kind as to ask Mr. Hermann if he stands in need of snuff because he says that he is perfectly ready to do without any, but that he has been use to snuff all his life.

Father, will you be so kind as to reccommend me to the prayers of good Brother Vincent, Father Granger, Reverend Mr. Shawe and to all those who have any regard for me, for it is likely that God in his infinite goodness will take [me] to himself.

I have not taught school for three weeks, but I will commence tomorrow morning, God willing. Mr. Hermann will tell you the reason why I did not. In your next letter tell me, if you please, the price of the articles which you gave me permission to sell. Excuse me, Father, for writing on this dirty piece of paper, for the Reverend Mr. St. Palais is not at home this evening to give me better.

Reverend dear Father, I remain one of yours in Jesus Christ,

Brother Thomas

79. Brother Joseph (11) to Father Sorin

Indianapolis March 7, 1847

Reverend and dear Father,

Whatever is coming from you is sweet and pleasing to me. Scoldings and praises are equally well-come; therefore, whensoever you think that I deserve a scolding, I wish you would do it without hesitation and fear. I did not know for some time what to think that I received no letter, but I perceive that I have but to be a little cross and I will soon get a sweet littlie scolding by letter, and this is all I want in such circumstances.

I send you Mr. Robert Collet, a boarder from St. Louis. His brother came with him from that city through Indianapolis with the intention to go on with him to South Bend, but as he met me at Indianapolis, he left me [in] charge of his brother and of $60 which he paid me down for him brother. From this 60 dollars, I paid $6.50 for the stage from here to South Bend and $3.50 for a pair of boots for him so that $50 are left for his board and tuition.

The mules are sold. I prefered to sell them cheap than to have them all the time on my expenses. Besides they were a dayly trouble to me, they being always kept in good feed. Jack became so wild that nobody could do anything with him. He run away ever so many times, and Father Gouesse wrote to me that he would not come back through Indianapolis.

I think we can have the deed for the lst of May. At any rate I suppose you will let me take possession of the property on the 1st of May which is the time agreed upon. However, I hope I will see you before that time and then we may talk about it. Do not forget to send me a habit, my French and German prayer books with the seeds mentioned in a previous letter.

If Father Gouesse come by Indianapolis, he may take the 50 dollars of Robert Collet along with him. If he does not come, they will do me some good till you come for them yourself.

What will be the succes of a noviciate in this town I do not know. (However there is more chance than at South Bend.) But a day school now and in very few years a seminary will prove successful.

There is a great deal of good to be done in this town, and I do not know why we should not have in this town if not a noviciate, at least a good establishment. I was the most opposed to an establishment here, but now being on the spot and seeing what can be effected, I am rather inclined to it. However, I was only opposed to the arbitrary measures, procedings, and pretentions of the bishop.

I am, dear Father, with the greatest love and respect, your most obedient but unworthy son,

Brother Joseph

80. Brother Joseph (12) to Father Sorin

Indianapolis March 15, 1847

Dear and reverend Father,

The bearer of this (Robert Collet) ought to have started two weeks ago, but could not on account of bad road. I have stated you the expenses I had to make for him. There is at present something more: 37 1/2 cents I had to pay in a house where he boarded two days, $1.00 in the tavern where he slept, $2.00 are due for boarding with me, $1.00 I have given him for his journey, which he will give you back if he do not use it on the road.

Mr. Hermann, whom Reverend Mr. St. Palais announces in a letter of his, stays with me in Indianapolis. He was afraid to proceed on his journey for the road is almost impassable. He is a shoe-maker, and he suits better for me than for you because he is a German and you have shoe-makers plenty. He has his son with him, 12 years old.

I long for a Brother to keep the day school. I must also state you that I am not such a mean fellow any more as I was at Notre Dame du Lac. I have become on a sudden *Father Joseph.* I have a great name in this city. Therefore I wish you would have a little more consideration for me than you had hitherto. When you write to me, it would do you no harm to write *Reverend Father Joseph.* If you had done so for the past, you would have confirmed me in the public opinion for I must tell you with grief that some persons have already corrected their mistake and they call me now *Brother Joseph.* I wish you would be more caucious for the future.

I laughed many a time on this account, and it is wonderful how people look upon persons from whom they expect money. In fact, I could get in this town anything I wanted.

I am, reverend Father, with the greatest respect, your most obedient son but unworthy son,

Brother Joseph

81. Brother Thomas (4) to Father Sorin

Madison March 18, 1847

Reverend and dear Father,

Be not angery with me for troubling you so often for it is not without necessity, although I love to write frequently, yet I fear I am a burden. It appears almost useless to ask you to pray for me for you have often told us that you never forget anyone that has devoted themselves to God in the institution.

Mr. Hermann's brother wishes to know where he must send his brother's clothes which yet remain in Madison. It is reported that Mr. Hermann when on his way to the lake was stoped by one of our Brothers at Indianapolis and not suffered to go on to the Novitiate of Notre Dame du Lac where his son might be taken care off. Mr. Hermann's brother and friends are not pleased at the Brother who, they suppose, asked so without your concent. Mr. Hermann of Madison wishes to know if you intend to order his brother to Notre Dame du Lac, where according to your letter of February 1st you expect him. With regard to others who are wishing to go to Notre Dame du Lac in August, I believe they are in number 5. I cannot say anything more with regard to them untill your answer arrives. My love and respects to all.

Reverend and dear Father, your affectionate and obedient child,

Brother Thomas

82. Brother Joseph (13) to Father Sorin

Indianapolis March 20, 1847

Dear and reverend Father,

I have received your letter with great satisfaction. It always gives me great pleasure when I hear of sweet home, just as it happens to a little child when he hears the charming voice of his mother.

In answer to your letter, I must tell you that I did not look any longer for Father Gouesse for Henry. I am not much concerned about him because he is just as well here as at the college. I make him work on the farm with my old man. Every day I make him learn a lesson in catechism and give him a lesson in reading. I have a boarder who is learning the German. He pays me 2.00 per week. The shoe-maker (a postulant) is going to work for a storekeeper (Mr. Preston, a real friend of mine who comes to my French class). Mr. Preston furnishes the leather and all and pays him 60 cents for a pair, but I have to take it in store goods, at least the most. This shoemaker postulant (Herman is his name) was a married man. His wife is dead since five years. He has a little son who is employed in helping Grandmother or his father in making shoes when she has nothing to do for him. I teach him morning and evening.

If only I had a brother able to teach the day school. I am insufficient to teach the day school, to keep a French and German class in the evening, and look about for the business of the house is more than I can do. I had a good deal of expenses since I began housekeeping. We are now seven persons and in a few days we shall be eight or nine persons. Then, of course, I had to buy a good many things. I laid out for kooking stove and kitchen utensils and whatever belongs to a kitchen with good house furniture which I nearly all bought at auction extremly cheap. For instance, I bo[ugh]t a bureau at $8 for which Brother Mary would ask 20 dollars. 6 chairs at 50 cents apiece which generaly cost 1 dollar. I have bot a splendid clock for 5.75 which cost even by the dozen $8 apiece as a German watch-maker told me, but if you b[u]y but one you cannot get it under less than twelve or 15 dollars. For the tables to suit me I had to have them made as well [as] bedsteads, because I want them singles. I have bot a good deal of bed clothes, towels, etc. and clothes for me and Henry, for we had nothing.

For the advise you give me with regard to the property of Mr. Phipps, I am very thankful. However, I dare say that I am more cautious than if I was to act for me indivdually. You need in no way to be affreight. I will assure you that you will not hear, in this town, that I have been cheated or overreached. On the contrary, I can say (not to my praise, because I know what I am, my daily weaknesses show me) that I am looked upon as smart and keen and have by my way of procedding t[h]rough the mercy of God secured to the Community a good name and credit and to me respect as, you know, it is needed in such circumstance.

A good and warranted deed for that property will be ready for the 1st of May. My greatest trouble is that I can not converse with you about what we could do and what we s[h]ould do.

I have applications for French, German, and Latin, by Ladies and Gentlemen, but no time. If we had a little seminary here, I know for certain we would do good business, but I hope that time and circumstances will bring all round.

If we had here two priests, a master of novices and one to teach and 2 or 3 teaching Brothers, we could do a great deal more, with less trouble than at Notre Dame du Lac. Notre Dame du Lac, I hope, will always be the center of our institution in the new world, and it is from Notre Dame du Lac that we always shall look for help in all our wants, though not so much from the place or its inmates but from her whose name it bears. My heart is overflowing and my eyes are actually beathed in tears, when I think of *Notre Dame* du Lac. (Super flumina Babilonis illic sedimus et flevimus, dum recordaremur Sion.) But Indianapolis will always be more advantageous.

I have a notion to exchange the carrage for [MS blurred] about the middle of the town, if I can do it with advantage, so we might be enabled to have a seminary more handy and have the advantage over all other schools in this town.

If I come to Notre Dame du Lac, it will be a useless journey; therefore it is requisite that you come here as soon as possible.

In this expectation I am, dear Father, your most humble and most obedient, but unworthy son,

Brother Joseph

83. Brother Joseph (14) to Father Sorin

Indianapolis March 29, 1847

Dear and reverend Father,

I am actually not impatient because I offer all my little crosses and contradictions up to him who died on the cross for me, but I am sorry to see in your last letter that you are not able to come to Indianapolis some weeks yet, and that I am left to shift for myself as well as I can. It is not concerning that property I want to see you, but I want to see you for things of greatest importance. It seems that kind providence, who always watches our interests temporal and eternal, has spread before us a field which by our labor we may improve and reap a plentiful harvest. The chance we have in this town is not little. We must improve it, and if you are not able to come, send either Father Granger or Brother Vincent before you come yourself. You promised me an assistant after the return of Father Gouesse. By this I only want [to] remind you of your promise because I need an assistant for the day school. I am insufficient for all the work.

After my day school, i.e. from four to five o'clock every day, I have French class in which I have (I will have moreso after Easter) persons of all ranks and conditions: merchants, doctors, lawyers, governers, etc (and ladies into the bargain, if you say so). I had applications from the first ladies in town, but I refused with the exception of one, and I suppose you will approve of my conduct in this circumstance. She is the lady of Judge Weak, our present senator in Congress; she is a person of the most refined education, converted to our holy religion by Reverend Mr. Baquelin not long before he died. I suppose she [is] somewhat cooly received by her Protestant relations in town, and this made her cool too in the practice of her religion. At least I saw her but once (on Palm Sunday) in the church. I go to her room every day from 5 to 6 in the evening to give to her and to a boy a lesson in the French language. I will be well paid for my trouble, and at the same time I can tell her now and then a word wich gives her comfort, and she likes it better than the French lesson.

I hope that Robert Collet is at last arrived at Notre Dame du Lac. I believe that young man would spend money enough, if he could get it. He wrote to me from Logansport for money, telling me lies in his letter, which I clearly discover in the letter of Reverend Mr. Autran, and from my inquiry in the stage office.

This letter will reach you before Easter Sunday, and you will [have] the chance to send me Brother Bernard immediatly after Easter.

I remain, dear Father, your obedient but unworthy son in Christ.

Brother Joseph

84. Brother Benedict (2) to Father Sorin

Washington March 29, 1847

Dear Father,

Thinking it my part of duty for your consolation to let you know about myself and the school, I enjoy good health (thank God) at present. I am also well pleased with the people. They are highly thankfull to God's Providence and your good will expressly manifested by allowing female children into my school, so much so that words cannot tell how happy they feel, but, Reverend Father, many are displeased for not allowing all their female children to come together and they even say if all their girls are not allowed, they will keep all at home or send to some other school. Nay, even Mrs. Britt speaks so too.

I have at present about 24 or 25, and they say I will get 50. They expect a great deal of good to be done here. And, Reverend Father, the bigger they are, the more ignorant. Now I reflected on this matter. If you allow all to come till the first of August, the school will be fixed and permanent forever here. If they must divide their children, it will, I fear, uproot our foundation. This I meditated on maturely. I consoled them till Easter till the priest comes home, but what can he do? So I resolved to write again. Reverend Father, permit me to speak once more in their behalf in the charity of God their Redeemer. Remember Abraham and the angels of God. If you do not wish to give a written permission, at least give a tacit one if your conscience can allow it. I speak in the bowels of mercy.

I lodge with Mr. Campbell. I like all things well. Write as soon as possible. Yours truly in Christ Jesus,

Brother Benedict

N.B. Let me know if you received a letter from South Carolina on my account, and as for the thirty dollars Reverend Mr. Starrs handed you, I do not understand about it. I am uneasy about the money I owe in Ireland.

85. Brother Joseph (15) to Father Sorin

Indianapolis March 31, 1847

Dear and reverend Father,

I have received your last letter with a grateful mind, though a thunderbolt could not have had a more terrible and paralising effect upon all my physical and mental powers than this letter. I read it over and over in order to sooth my grief, but in vain. The more I read it, the worse I made the matter. In truth I immediatly lost the appetite of taste of all food, and I was for several hours nearly out of senses, not with anger or rage, but with grief bordering on despair. I looked upon myself as an apostate and a reprobate, and nothing but the thought that my intention and my news in all my doings were innocent upheld my courage and strength and soothed me, late in the night, into a little sleep. For mercy's sake, for God's sake, do not overwhelm me with grief and despair by sending me another such letter. Come yourself, examine the things I have done and judge me, here, accordingly. Whensoever you think me guilty, give me such a pennance as you judge proper and let the guilt lie whatever, without telling me a great deal about it. Command me what I must do and forbid me what I must not do.

Mr. Herman had $11 left after his expenses paid at Indianapolis. They are two, he and his boy. The stage from here to South Bend cost $13 for two persons. Then they must have at least $3 for their other expenses when the roads are so bad it takes the stage 3 or 4 days to go through. He liked better to stay here than to go farther. I have had a great deal of expenses with him, to accommodate him and to set him at work. If you take him, he will have to take whatever I bought on his account so as to pay you.

Concerning the mules, I can say that Henry would not undertake it nor even Father Gouesse, so he told me when he was at Indianapolis. Then what could I do? They are out of my reach now. They have been sold again in Cincinati for less than you would have for them.

Now whatever may be my case, I am resigned to submit whatever you shall dictate to me, and if I have done wrong, I will do all that lies in me to repair the evil. But I am certain that my case is not as bad as it is thought at Notre Dame du Lac. I will give you an account of all my doings when you come.

I am, dear Father, your most obedient but unworthy son,

Brother Joseph

86. Brother Michael (1) to Father Sorin

Vincennes April 1, 1847

My dear reverend Father,

Aware of my obligation of writing to you at least once a month, yesterday on which I intended to write, I forgot it so here it is. That is not wise to deffer any business to the last moment.

It gives me trouble to see the carelessness of the children in attending to school and their other duties. I hope, however, God will not char[g]e it to my account. The number in daily attenda[n]ce this quarter is about 25. I will hold an examination next week. The clergy being so busy this week as that they could not attend to it. I will keep no class these three last days. The service in the church will occupy the most of the time. I will go to the holy communion at the 9 o'clock High Mass with the intention of gaining the indulgence of the jubilee. I fear that I do not advance in perfection. It is well if I stood my ground but now at least I intend to begin. The ague has attacked me. I had it in the fore part of this week, and last week I shook outright. The money you gave me is nearly spent in little thing[s] that I could scarcely avoid. It cost me 50 cents to get my shoes repaired, and at present I need a pair in the worse way.

I hope you will pray for me. I am in a hurry to get home. It would be a comfort to me if you write.

Yours truly,

Brother Micha[e]l

87. Brother Gatian (3) to Father Moreau
[Translated from French]

Notre Dame April 20, 1847

My Reverend Father,

I'm very grateful for your response to my long letter because I was convinced of the truth of what I wrote to you; I didn't know if it would have been more religious to hide from you the affairs of our establishment and our superiors, but your letter dissipates my doubts and makes me resolve to hide nothing from you in the future. If I'm fooling myself, let me know.

I didn't answer you right away because I figured you had written about everything to Father Superior or to Father Granger, and I wanted to see how things would turn out. Father Granger and he have shown themselves very perplexed in regard to this letter, but they have finally resolved to abolish the Administrative Council. Father Superior, having heard the reports that had been made about his vexation, supposed he must say nothing about your letter, even more so because you didn't note the manner in which I had to conduct myself, but I tried to lead them to the reforms which you speak about in your letter to me, Father Superior and Father Granger, and I made Father Granger understand most of the things. The Minor Chapter was set up after about three weeks of deliberation, and I even succeeded in getting Father Gouesse admitted a fortnight later. That done, I took the side of waiting since you had given positive orders to Father Superior or more precisely to Father Granger for my admission. Father Superior seemed to have understood nothing in all these matters. To a Council of Brothers a month ago he made Brother Théodule and Brother Placidus come at my request so they could explain the difference between General Chapter, Major Chapter, and a Minor Chapter. In a word, after all I've seen and heard, Father Superior has to be a consummate liar, or the explanations given to him at Ste. Croix weren't clear.

Another fact inclined me to say nothing about your response, and here it is: I believed I saw a general discontent among the members of our last colony, discontent which comes from irregularities of our government and from the disregard for rules. It also seems that some of them had said to Brother Vincent that they'd write to you on this subject, which soon reached the Superior. He called together all the French Brothers and noted his astonishment about seeing them in such dispositions, saying that he'd hardly understood Father Rector, how he paid attention to similar reports, and that this'd be a very sad way to administrate; that moreover in his own judgement he wouldn't be either exhilarated or depressed by them. He also said to them that with time and patience they'd get accustomed (which is unfortunately very true) to what by necessity and circumstances isn't done as the motherhouse does it (that is to say our irregularities) and that in America it would be necessary to follow the customs of Americans.

Father Superior was in Vincennes last December, found Monsignor in good spirits, and tried to pacify him and make him delay the Indianapolis foundation, since we had neither funds nor personnel. Father Superior succeeded, and Monsignor proposed to make a Brother travel around like a peddlar to sell Catholic books, adding that he'd give two mules for this purpose. Father Superior had a mind to test this new and odd enterprise, laying out all the advantages. Everyone concurred with his opinion (Father Gouesse was absent) except me who, taking everything as a joke, kept silent. Two days later Father Superior had already named Brother Joseph and made him buy a cart, and for the venture to succeed, he proposed it for the first time at the table. I wrote a nasty note immediately to Father Superior, telling him that other councilors, as well as myself, hadn't taken what he'd said as a consultation. He called the Council together immediately and started again to make us see the bright side without talking about the dark side; the councilors who had already moved forward did not pull back. Father Gouesse said nothing for fear that it wouldn't suit his ordination. I raised five arguments that everyone realized were well founded. I said among other things that we were going to advance 7 to 800 francs which would never be reimbursed and that frankly the enterprise wouldn't succeed. But Father Superior said, "You can only do good by risking it." All voted for, except Father Gouesse and me. Father Superior then said (seeing that his vote didn't defeat the enterprise) "I vote against and thus the responsibility rests on those who have voted for." "Ah, Father," one of them said, "If you believed the enterprise is useless, you shouldn't have proposed it, and if you believe it bad, you shouldn't undertake it." "Too bad," replied the Superior, "You've voted; it'll be carried out." It turned out as I predicted it would. The Brother could go no further than Indianapolis where he found himself with a broken cart, a rather serious illness, and without money. There this poor Brother found a piece of land which, to his liking, was suitable for our foundation, and without paying attention to our debts, without waiting for any directive, he bought it for 22,500 francs, adding to our debts, which are growing to about 30,000 francs, or 14,500 francs, since the bishop promised to pay 8,000 francs. Brother Joseph stayed at Indianapolis where he runs a school waiting for whoever is going to join him.

Father Superior was in Detroit at the beginning of the year for Mr. V. Badin's gift. Following the advice of Doctor Canalli, clearly a cheat, he chose a good Presbyterian as a lawyer and put matters in fashion to scare the bishop of Detroit; but he wasn't afraid. He declared to his lawyer, Mr. Van Dyke, an honest deist, since elected mayor of Detroit, that he'd give up nothing except at sword point. A few days after Father Superior's return, Doctor Canalli, who alone can serve as witness, having done Mr. V. Badin's accounts and business affairs, got all worked up and threatened us with a lawsuit. It became necessary to pacify him; Father Gouesse was given the job, since the doctor liked him, and he succeeded. It was only a question of ceding him a certain sum that he exacted for his services, because Father Superior had tricked him with fancy words which he hadn't stuck to. Father Gouesse believed his demand just, but you have to imagine that the Superior thought otherwise. Father Gouesse explained to Father Superior who settled the affair with the Minor Chapter, which Father Gouesse didn't attend, although he was the only one who could speak impartially, because he wasn't a member. The doctor's request was refused, but I don't know the result of the refusal since I no longer help at any Administrative Council.

The discipline at the boarding school is in the worst state ever. The insubordination of the students is insufferable. They came to blows once with the Prefect of Studies. They abandoned the chaperone many times while out walking and left sixteen at a time for town, etc., etc., and all these faults were not punished in a way to make an impression. This insubordination, in my opinion, has for its immediate cause the little unanimity and uniformity which exist among the teachers, but for the first and principal cause, the lack of tact by the Superior, his overly great complaisance for the teachers as much as for the students and a lack of firmness which makes him put aside a rule a few days after publishing it and which makes him give permissions and privileges wrongly and contrarily without reaching an understanding with the Prefect of Discipline. The Prefect of Discipline, who alone is loved, respected and obeyed, seeing that the superior undid what he did and that the Director of Studies is more busy with missions than his boarding school, has lost courage and often leaves everything go helter-skelter. We don't have enough good professors: we have too many who are weak and without zeal.

The Brothers' novitiate instead of growing is shrinking. Since the retreat of August, 1846, Brother Mary Joseph and Brother Francis as well as Brother Peter and Brother Charles Borromeo have defrocked. Brother John Baptist and Brother Anthony are dead. Since that time we have had only two postulants of which one, who had been [ ] took the habit at St. Joseph with the name Brother Charles Borromeo. Brother Basil has also defrocked for the second time with five year vows, but he returned and Father Superior made him make his profession with Brother Bernard about three weeks after his return. My job as Director of Studies doesn't give me much trouble because there're only three Brothers, one postulant, and still I can hardly find a professor. Two of the Brothers are German and could never teach English; the other is Canadian and is little disposed to study. The postulant is also German but speaks English rather well. Our little world has to be augmented since the fevers, which had stopped at the beginning of winter, have again struck Brother Marie [Francis Xavier], Brother Stephen, Brother Louis, Brother Dominic, etc., and although they don't avoid doses of quinine, they can escape from it for only a week or two at a time.

The imaginary sickness of Brother William, which plagued him last August, still endures.

You can conclude from what I just told you that jobs are fulfilled with much negligence and that we are overburdened. For example, four months ago I asked for inventories of clothes and furniture, the statement of our credits and debits, necessary information for the chronicle, the obituary and the register of benefactors, but it seemed that neither the steward, who is too old, can't speak, or has lost his memory, nor the tailors or seamstresses, nor the superior, have the time to think about it. I'll be told, "Next week, tomorrow, we'll straighten out this matter, these accounts," but "Tomorrow never comes" says the proverb. Moreover, I have too much to do myself to be always ready when they are, because outside of my job as secretary, I'm often employed eight hours a day at the boarding school, but I also remark that for each of the professors, I've also been *kindly* given charge of the bookkeeping, arithmetic, algebra, and geometry courses which, arithmetic excepted, I had never taught nor ever learned perfectly and for which I consequently need lots of preparation: I took geometry and algebra lessons for only six weeks at Notre Dame de Ste. Croix.

My job as Prefect of Discipline is purely honorary because how can I fix any disorder among the Brothers, spending only three quarters of an hour with them a week?

As for our deliberation regarding Louisville, it would be possible that Father Superior hasn't sent it. I asked him many times if he had done so, but I can't get a direct response.

Your nota bene "that we must build nothing, nor buy, nor transfer without your permission" hasn't been observed up to now, and I believe it'll be difficult to make it observed in the future. We must buy, according to the contract made with Father Th. Badin, two pieces of land which border us as soon as they're up for sale, which will add at least 25,000 francs to our debts. They just built a wooden stable, 30 by 15 feet, and a cart-house 86 by 20, which is going to cost, without counting part of the wood we took from our farm and the work of our carpenters who have to finish it, 1750 francs. This building was put to a vote last December: four voted for and four against (Father Gouesse was absent). The double vote of the superior carried it. I believe they're thinking about building a beautiful church which, without counting what we can furnish and make ourselves, is going to cost, according to the estimate of Father Superior who didn't exaggerate in a similar case, 5,000 francs at least. When the question was put to a vote, there were three negative votes and two affirmative, and thus the question depends on the superior who asks for time to reflect.

We'll have to return Brother Peter's dowry to him in May	[in francs]	2,500
We have debts amounting to		30,000
Our Indianapolis purchase		22,500
Two pieces of land (if there aren't three) to buy		35,000
The cart-house		1,750
The church, if it's built		5,000
Yearly allowance for Father Badin		2,000
	Total	88,750
But we'll have almost the means to pay all that if we win the lawsuit that (I think) we're going to make against the bishop of Detroit		60,000
	[Total]	28,750

Since you'd like us, reasonably enough, to give you an account of our business affairs as well as the changes that we can make in the rules, and as you seem not to have known several important items, you'll have to require someone in the Minor Chapter to keep you up to date and that man will have to have the freedom to write you at all times.

I saw Father Superior refuse a letter which came from France, but I don't know to whom it was addressed: that explains perhaps how it comes about that several men have never received an answer to letters they wrote to you.

Although you assert you only imitated the superior in the agreement with Monsignor, he always denied it and moreover it seems we'll have to do the translation at our expense. But how can we make a similar foundation without personnel?

The Sisters continue to appear very often at the college. Moreover three are continually in the building: the one who cleans the dormitories, the two infirmarians, and sometimes the cook. The infirmary is in the body of the college, on the second floor, facing Father Gouesse's bedroom, although six months ago we decided to put it in the apartments attached to the print-shop, but those bedrooms aren't ready yet.

The print-shop, which especially bothers us and which since vacation has done nothing, was sold with a loss of two or three thousand francs. Nevertheless we've been praised for having been able to strike a good deal for it.

I'm in the same disposition regarding my vocation. I have the same attraction for studying languages and mathematics, but I don't have time to apply myself to it. It's true these abstract studies and my jobs wither my heart, and I'm consequently lukewarm in my religious exercises, which I do more by obedience than by taste.

I'm happy my parents were made aware that I'm doing well and that I continue to be happy. I don't like to write to them because I've lost the habit, not having written for two years, and because I've received no news from them since I've been in America.

I don't forget former benefactors, Mr. Marchand, pastor at Chéméré-le-Roi, and Brother Vital.

I believe I must tell you that Brother Théodule was elected a member of the Minor Chapter to fill in for the absense of Brother Joseph.

Our armies continue to be victorious in Mexico. It's odd that although only the ninth part of our population is Catholic, the army chaplains are Catholic priests.

Since I still have some paper, I'll tell you the winter hasn't been rough this year, snow having been on the ground only five months.

My reverend Father, please recommend our entire establishment to the Association's prayers and our boarding school to the prayers of the one at Ste. Croix, so God deigns to heal our sicknesses, both spiritual and temporal.

I'm writing in a style only slightly coherent, but that comes from my having to steal time. Excuse the freedom I took in sending you letters so long and so poorly executed.

I am your Reverence's respectful and obedient servant,

Brother Gatian

88. Brother Benedict (3) to Father Sorin

Washington April 22, 1847

Dear Father,

With pleasure I received your letter bearing [the] date March 30th which reanimated my spiritual and natural faculties. I wrote a letter to you three weeks before Easter. I expected an answer. I got none. I asked permission to allow other girls older than twelve, but the parents, I think, wrote to the bishop. He granted a tacit permission to teach them. You asked how many children I had. I have got 44 on the list. Five classes: 22 writing and cyphering, 7 at English grammar and geography, 4 others prepared to begin. The people all seem happy to have me here.

I am well pleased with both priest and people. The country people are sending in their children to me and some boarders. Nay, even Protestants. I pay a visit betimes to some of the principle persons in the town. I like Mr. Campbell's family well, but we have more or less strangers. Every day they introduce me. They talk to me almost at every meal. I do not like it—all are full of worldly conversation. I am as frail as any other person. Now if I do not talk, they seem displeased and I am becoming forgetful of my rules.

The children obey me to the letter. That is, they attend every Sunday at 9 o'clock AM and 2 PM or afternoon. They are doing well. They seem happy, and many others come to be instructed on Sunday from town and country. I told the priest to tell the people so he done so too. They hope to have a large school here in winter. If you will send me any other place, let me know before I go to the retreat that I may take my trunk with me. I am now and shall be your spiritual son in Christ Jesus,

Brother Benedict

N.B. Mr. Campbell was gone to New Orleans two weeks before your letter came here. The priest says he will build a house for himself and me in summer next. He seems to like me. I paid Mr. Gueguen when he came to town two weeks before your letter came to my hand.

89. Brother Michael (2) to Father Sorin

Vincennes April 24, 1847

My reverend Father,

Since my last, nothing remarkable has happened to me. I expected that you would write to me which would surely give me great consolation. Thirty children attended my school the last quarter, that is daily. Since Easter only about twenty-five. The bishop and all his house continue their kindness to me. The more I know him, the better I like him. I serve his Mass every morning a little before half past five. You will see by this that although I have a great many faults to accuse myself of, lying in bed too long will not be on the list.

Mr. Coryoult has given me the notes for the twenty dollars that was due to you. I received the money this day, not, however, without demanding it repeatedly. Mr. Thomas, the lawyer, had the kindness to go with me. I did not wish, without letting you first know about it, to send it in a letter lest it might be mislead.

My Father, I have a great desire to [see] all of you once more and of going to the noviciate which is the lovliest spot that can be selected this side of the grave. In fine, I beg your prayers and of the community that I may gain the grace of perseverence and true devotion.

Yours truly,

Brother Michael

90. Brother Joseph (16) to Father Sorin

Indianapolis May 23, 1847

Reverend and dear Father,

I still continue to entertain that feeling that Providence does not wish us to lose the property in this town. The more I look into it, the more I see that it will turn at last to his greater glory, and to our welfare, and I nearly consider it as something providential. Whatever may be the case, I give thanks to his infinite goodness for having given me more cheering hopes since two days and for having heard, as I believe, the sighs of my oppressed heart.

I have found the means to relieve you and me from a heavy burden: I have spoken yesterday to Mr. Bades, the richest man in this town. He will buy the notes from Mr. Phipps or lent us the money, but the deduction Mr. Phipps will make will be for himself, not for us, but we will have no interest to pay but from the time we will get the money and will have it for one year (or 12 months) or he will take the deed from Mr. Phipps for himself and give us a bond as Mr. Phipps has given me one so that if we can pay in one year from the first of June next, he will make us a deed, and if not, he will keep the property. He says that he wants us to have the property, but he wants to be secure.

Please write me without one day's delay what I shall do. You may be perfectly sure that what I will do in this matter will be well done. There will not be the least danger. I will employ neither Chapman nor Dr. Neckly. If you should want me to have anything to with them, I wish rather you would come yourself. Judge Weak is a better friend to me than all these fellows.

I had the satisfaction to see Father Gouesse. He will come back this way. I will make him say Mass in honor of St. Joseph in our house. I do not know what to do concerning the carriage. I have no money.

I am, dear Father, your most obedient but unworthy son,

Brother Joseph

91. Brother Joseph (17) to Father Sorin

Indianapolis May 23, 1847 [II]

Dear and reverend Father,

I hope you will excuse me for writting two letters in the same day. The first was already gone when I received the news that I would lose old Grandmother. Her daughter is so dangerously sick that the old lady has to take care of her. Now I do not know what to do. Do you advise me to look for another or will you send me a Brother? I think Brother Dominick would do very well as he would not half as much to do as at Notre Dame du Lac. Send the Brothers as soon as possible.

I forgot to tell you in my letter of this morning that it is decided that the railroad will take place from Cinciniti to St. Louis. There was a great convention on Wednesday after you left for this purpose in the state house. The governers of three States with deputies were present. If the [State] of Illinois will not grant it, at least it will go to Terre Haute, but there is no doubt but that Illinois will grant it.

Your most humble but unworthy son,

Brother Joseph

92. Brother Joseph (18) to Father Sorin

Indianapolis June 8, 1847

Dear and reverend Father,

I suppose Father Gouesse has given you an account of the state of things at Indianapolis. However, I have to write to you on different little subjects. First, that I [have] given up the day school, and I have some trouble to get the few dollars which [I] get from this quarter. I have no mind to take up another quarter unless $50 are assured to me for each quarter or $200 per annum.

Second, that I had to borrow money to pay for the mending of the carriage which I will have to give back in a few days, and where to take it. If I had about 50 dollars to defray the expenses of the [ ] have to pay these 13 dollars and to buy some other necessary things as fork, shovel, sythe, etc. which I am obliged to have. I will have to borrow it if you cannot let me have it. I began today to send some garden produce to market, but this is just to keep us from starving, and the few dollars which I will be able to make will be for other purposes. I have the firm confidence in God's goodness that we will get along, but not without care and a little trouble. I have lately paid about 50 dollars of my debts in different ways.

Third, I received yesterday a letter from Robert Collet for his trunk which is gone one month ago or more. I went to the stage office inquiring about [it], and from the information I got of it, it seems to lay in Logansport. They will send it. Robert will have to look for it at South Bend.

The governer has written to the Queen of France on Friday last. I have translated it into French. It is an excellent letter.

I am to[o] busy to write you about trifles.

If Brother Vincent had had the charity to send me the seeds I asked [for] particularly some of the large peas. Even the common green peas sell from 1.50 to 2.00 a bushel, but I had to buy for [myself] about four dollars of seeds when I had hardly one cent to spare.

I am, dear Father, your most humble but unworthy son,

Brother Joseph

93. Brother Joseph (19) to Father Sorin

Indianapolis June 21, 1847

Dear and reverend Father,

It is truly unfortunate that there must be misunderstandings and disappointments. When Father Gouesse was here, I told him that the affair with Mr. Bader wou[l]d, from all I could foresee, turn out ill, and so it did. He put his money to some other use, and he tells me now that he could not do it now without exposing himself.

Now what to do? God knows, I do not. Had I received a letter a week ago, I might have done something. Judge Weak proposed me another way of arranging the matter. The judge is gone and will be absent for some time. Now shall we give up the property when in less than one year we shall be able to sell the half of it for the same price we pay for the whole? It is propable that the railroad will pass through our wood pasture about 600 feet from the house, but may this be or not, let us pay the first payment, and we will find the means to meet the second at the 1st of January. I know I will make it out, if you will let me act. I promise this and you may be certain.

I am about to sell the carriage for $230 cash or for 250, and then I will take two good cows, some hogs of a good breed, and a good horse.

I was well pleased to become acquainted with Father Lanier. He is a very fine man, but the news he brought me, when there is no more time to act, were a thunder bolt to me. You wrote more than a week ago to Dr. Neely that you would write to me in two or three days, but these two days swelled to eight, but now the consequences. Judge Weak counsels to make the first payment.

I will now cut my letter short, for I am overgrieved and unable to say any more.

Receive, dear Father, most profound respect with which I am, your most humble but unworthy son,

Brother Joseph

P.S. I have written in several letters and have given a note to Father Gouesse for my habit and other things I stand in need of, but I received nothing yet, though there were different opportunities to send these things to me quite conveniently. Now I beg your pardon if I say that it is heedlessness or willful neglect. Truly I will no more. They may keep it. Please write me without delay. There is no time to lose.

94. Brother Joseph (20) to Father Sorin

Indianapolis June 27, 1847

Dear and reverend Father,

I was truly astonished yesterday evening to find my box in the postoffice empty whilst I was the whole week most anxiously waiting for a letter. I believe I should have received a letter in the circumstances I am; if you had nothing to tell me, at least you should tell me that you had nothing to tell me.

In order not to be long, I will simply ask, do you decline or do you accept? I must know this for next Saturday, if I have no answer, I shall be obliged to act as I deem it most advisable without asking any further advice.

I am, dear Father, notwithstanding, your most humble and obedient son,

Brother Joseph

If you have the first payment, send it and I engage to make out the second. Moreover I pledge my word to pay the whole in the course of a few years if God give me health and life and if you leave me at Indianapolis.

95. Brother Michael (3) to Father Sorin

Vincennes June 28, 1847

My dear reverend Father,

I feel pleasure in thinking that the time is not far distant when I shall be at home once again. The boys are preparing for their first communion. Their retreat will commence next Wednesday. It will, of course, occupy our attention this week. I don't know when it is the will of the bishop for me to go. I am aware that in forming the minds and hearts of the children to piety, I have not succeeded as well as might be expected, in the first place for want of experience, or, which would be far worse, not having the true spirit myself. I trust, however, it is not for the want of a good will.

Though I do not anticipate how I will go home, I wish to walk at least part of the way if I be able. It would save a little expense and [be] good for penance. The bishop was sick last week. He had not said Mass, but he does this week which plainly shows that [he] is getting better.

Yours truly,

Brother Michael

96. Brother Joseph (21) to Father Sorin

Indianapolis July 8, 1847

Dear and reverend Father,

Since I received your last letter, I did all I could to obtain the loan of the money, but I have failed in where I had the most reason to expect it because there is no capital in this town. All the money is invested in something or other. There is a Catholic gentleman in this town who has 14,000 dollars in notes and mostly due, but he cannot controll it. Had I received your last letter before I had spoken to Phipps, I would have dropped by degrees the property, and I had already made a conditional bargain with General Drake for something else on my own responsibility so as not to leave Indianapolis because to leave it now after all the talk that has been made all over town, it would be a deadly stroke to the Catholic cause.

I will suggest you another way, if it be of any service to you. I will take the property in my own name, but you must procure me the money for the present and you will take a mortgage on the property. I will pay the interest and manage the whole. I know for certain that I will succeed.

What they say at Ste. Croix I do not mind. Father Rector is the first cause of it. At any rate, I will stand up to my task, and I know, if God gives me health of life, I will get along smoothly. I have been in greater difficulties in my life, and I have extricated myself honorably. No difficulty shall make me shrink, if only I do right in the sight of God.

If you have any confidence in me, I beleive it will be the best to accept my proposal. If you do not wish to do so, it will be to me the same thing. I will always do what I can. The only thing is that you will have no trouble, and I know I will succeed.

I am, dear Father, with the greatest respect, your humble but unworthy son,

Brother Joseph

97. Brother Joseph (22) to Father Sorin

[Indianapolis] July 8, 1847

Dear and reverend Father,

It is with the greatest satisfaction I mention to you that the Brothers Benedict and Michael are with me. They want to know what you would like the best they should do: to stay with me or to come to Notre Dame du Lac. They would like to stay, but are ready to come at the least intimation of yours. I have likewise a word to say on this subject. If you preferr the two Brothers should stay here, I wish you would tell us what should be my conduct towards them and theirs towards me so that there never the least difficulty may arise between us. I know there will be none with Brother Michael. He is simplicity and obedience itself, but you know that Brother Benedict is very singular or what is called in French "un original." However, I will get along with him. It only depends on you. If you do not design to come here shortly, Brother Benedict will come home. He wants to settle something with you.

I have a man engaged who is splitting me posts (7 or 800) for the vineyard I intend to plant. Last Friday I sold the carriage for $200 cash which I have in hand, if you come in time with the price of the land. If you don't, I will make use of them as justice requires it. I have received $15.25 from Brother Benedict. The little vineyard I have planted this year gives me the greatest satisfaction. It grows most luxuriously. It has already put forth grapes a week ago, but it is to[o] late for them. They will not come to perfection.

I am, dear Father, with sincere love and respect, your most humble but unworthy son,

Brother Joseph

The Brothers send you their humble respects. Is Brother Vincent dead? I have not heard him breathe since 7 months. My love to all.

98. Brother Joseph (23) to Father Sorin

Indianapolis July 13, 1847

Dear and reverend Father,

I am truly sorry that I give you so much trouble, but I thought I had sufficiently expressed myself or I did not understand you. Reading your letter, I understand that you will immediatly send $229 to [ ] a draught on Phil. of that sum and in the course of six weeks 3260 dollars, making together with the premium 1.50 percent (63 dollars) $4252, but I did not understand what you meant by these words "ce que vous pouvez avancer vous-même." I thought it meant that [I] could tell him this for certain. Now if I understood right, then I must tell you that he agreed to the propositions, else I should not have send you a deed.

The carriage is not yet sold. Concerning my projects, I intended to wright to you, though you should not have required it. They are the cultivation of the grape vine. You will very likely laugh at my simplicity, but let me tell you that I made all possible inquiries relating there-unto, and I am assured that there is nothing more profitable and lucrative.

Cincinati is but 125 miles south of Indianapolis, and there is a gentleman there whom Judge Weak knows personally who has made in one year $3000 clear profit. Besides, I will be encouraged by the agricultural society of the State of Indiana. Now to prove [to] you that there is the greatest hope of succes, I will make you everything clear and evident. The grapevine grows most luxuriously in this country. This is proved by the fact itself. My travels in different wine countries of Europe enable me to see which is the best way of cul[t]ivating it so as to adapt it to the soil and climate. One acre of ground can easily receive 2500 stocks, each stock bearing at the lowest calculation 50 cents per annum, if they are well taken care of. We will in this manner render service to the country, and it is in this manner we must work ourselves into favor and gain the hearts of those who differ from us in beleive. It is by an unblemished life and habits of industry the Jesuits have in many places done more good than by teaching and preaching.

I have one hundred stocks growing beautifully, and I have engaged 600 to seven hundred for next fall. In the course of a few weeks, I will have for a few dollars grapes to sell.

I do not know what to do with my kitchen. If only you could send me somebody. If only I had an old Sister but s[t]ill s[t]out enough and intelligent.

I am, dear Father, with all respect and love, your most obedient but unworthy son,

Brother Joseph

99. Brother Thomas (5) to Father Sorin

Madison July 18, 1847

Reverend and dear Father,

Your wish for the attendance of the Very Reverend Mr. de St. Palais at the exibition of the 3rd, will not reach his ears till it will be out of his power to attend. He feels always pleased whenever he hears of your kind considerations. According to appointment he was to have been here last evening, but probable he is detained at Vincennes, and if so he will not be home before Saturday next. As soon as an oppertunity will offer, I will inform Reverend Mr. Molony on what conditions you receive boys as apprentices. According to what he said, the father of the boy is willing [to] give more than is required, but it is not the case with a couple of poor orphans. Their friends are not able to give more money than will pay their way and clothing for one year. Will you have any objection to receive them? They are most excellent little boys, obedient, tractable. Their guardians are willing to bind them for the specified time. I cannot leave here till your answer arrives.

There will not be more than one or two postulants, if any. Those who a few months ago wished to come to the Community have put the idea out of their head. The prospectuses which you sent did not yet arrive. So if they do not come, it will [be] out of my power to give a definite answer to anyone who wishes to send their sons and boarders.

Dear Father, your kind letter, *as I read,* gives me permission to come and kneel in that chapel of devotion, and for past favors, give thanks to our common Mother, at the foot of her statue. "You *might* stop a few weeks with Brother Jo." It is the word might in which I presume permission to continue my course to Notre Dame du Lac. Be so kind to let me know your will positively. I reccommend myself to prayers of all and yours especially.

With sincere respect and love, I remain your son in Jesus, Mary, and Joseph,

Brother Thomas

Mr. Nodler asked me every day or two why his son does not sometime or other write to him. I can never answer for I know not the reason myself. Will you please to ask Mr. Charles Nodler to write to his anxious parents.

Before closing this letter, a letter arrived from the Very Reverend Mr. de St. Palais, stating that he has been detained at Washington, Davisse Country, by sickness, that he will be at home next Wednesday.

100. Brother Joseph (24) to Father Sorin

Indianapolis August 3, 1847

Dear and reverend Father,

I am sorry to send the present by Brother Thomas. I would rather have sent it by the mail and kept him here, but he woud not or rather could not.

I paid 26 cents charges on Father Lanier's big box. I cannot forbear to pass a remark [on] this matter, that, having a member of the institution, you prefer to send to strangers, as if you had no one here, or as if I were not worthy of the least confidence. If such a thing happens an other time, I will not pay attention to the things, should they be lost. I am just as well known as anybody. Send what you have to send subject to my order and it will reach me. But for greater security, send things to Willis Wright or to Smith and Hana or to Drake's Hotel or to any other hotel.

I see that my shoemake shop is not in a fit place because everyone that has to do with the shoemaker goes right in without any consideration, and of course this would be very unpleasant to the noviciate. We need a porterhouse which will be at the same time the shoemaker shop. Besides, the little room which he occupies is not large enough to contain a stove in winter. I need no money to do this if you allow me to sell a lot or two. I had several offers of the kind.

I took Henry back. I could not see him in his filth and dirt. Though he does certainly not deserve it, I will send the little vilain back to you with the first opportunity or when my means will allow it.

I am sorry not to be at the retreat, so much the more so as I have not been at confession for ten weeks, Mr. McDermott being never at home and I have no confidence in the other.

I write this with a very strong fever, else I would say something on another subject.

I am, dear Father, with love and respect, your most humble but unworthy son,

Brother Joseph

101. Brother Joseph (25) to Father Sorin

Indianapolis August 24, 1847

Dear and reverend Father,

I am always waiting for Reverend Father Granger, but I believe it is useless. I received a letter from the bishop stating [to] me that he sends $3000 to be paid to Mr. Phipps under the condition that the titles be examined by Lawyer Smith and that a deed in fee simple be made to C.R.S. Guynamer de la Hailandière, his heirs, and assigns [ ] and that if the titles should not be good, the money should remain in Mr. McDermott's hands. Now it is a whole week since I received this letter, and I see no money. Everything is ready and waiting. To whom has the bishop sent the money? to you or to Mr. McDermott? Mr. McDermott is absent since four weeks and will not be heir for six weeks longer. He is in Cincinati. His horse run away with him and mangled him in a dreadful manner. I received a letter from him today concerning this affair, but he does not tell me that he has the money.

I am in great straits. I do not know what to do. If I had nothing to rely upon but myself or on other men, I would indeed despair. However "omnia ad majorem Dei gloriam," but a man must have courage in such trying circumstances.

Please send me by the next opportunity all the German books I brought to the Community, not that I pretend to have any claim to them, but I merely think that they are more useful to us here than to you. However, I do not want the history of the Church in 32 volumes. We need some English books of piety. The $3000 of the bishop are not sufficient. I wish somebody would come.

I see that it is healthier here than at Notre Dame du Lac.

I am, dear Father, with respect and love, your most humble but unworthy son,

Brother Joseph

102. Brother Joseph (26) to Father Sorin

Indianapolis September 5, 1847

Dear and reverend Father,

I must inform you that I received from the bishop a draft of $3000. He sent it directly to me upon my writing to him concerning Mr. McDermott's absence. I will close the deed tomorrow and leave it in Lawyer Smith's hands till you send the balance. Please to send it immediately.

I am, dear Father, your most humble but unworthy son,

Brother Joseph

103. Brother Gatian (4) to Father Moreau
[Translated from French]

[Notre Dame] September 14, 1847

To Reverend Father Rector and the Major Chapter of Notre Dame de Ste. Croix,

On September 15, the year of our Lord one thousand eight hundred and forty-seven, the members of the Minor Chapter of Notre Dame du Lac, being assembled under the presidency of Father Sorin, local superior, and in the presence of Father Saulnier, submit the following requests to Father Rector and the Major Chapter:

1) Given the distance between places which necessarily causes delays in American affairs, losing good and causing perplexity, because before a response from Ste. Croix gets to Notre Dame du Lac, circumstances can change, thus individuals destined for certain jobs are no longer suitable or are needed elsewhere, the season perhaps too far along to raise buildings which had been requested etc.; given the necessity of a strong union among the American houses and especially among those in the United States, so they can, for example, make subjects go from one house to another according to circumstances, and to help each other in their money difficulties; given that this union is impossible if each of them, instead of depending on one principal house in America, correspond directly with Ste. Croix, moaning for itself with a spirit of egoism, quite natural but also very apt to create jealousies here and suspicions in France; given the example of Jesuits, of Sisters of the Sacred Heart, etc. who take care of American affairs in America; given the unfortunate experience of Notre Dame du Lac; given finally that to judge rationally, it's necessary to be on the spot and that decisions made at Ste. Croix for governing American establishments have for foundation only the reports and decisions of Notre Dame du Lac which can never be expressed clearly enough in writing and which are often poorly understood, the Minor Chapter of Notre Dame du Lac requests, with respect and submission, not to separate itself, but only that Father Rector and the Major Chapter name a superior who, with a chapter formed by the gathering of Minor Chapters from each house or their deputies, can

decree as a last resort on all American affairs, except those the reverend Father Rector and Major Chapter believe absolutely necessary to reserve to themselves, and that the said superior so named by Notre Dame de Ste. Croix and its council, alone has the right to treat with the motherhouse for both temporal and spiritual affairs.

The sooner you give us latitude, the sooner we'll do good things: that's a universal sentiment. I can assure you that none of the councilors is trying to break away from you! We'll live more amicably if you give us the requested power. I don't know the mind of Father Superior, who always more or less dissimulates, and poor Brother Vincent always does and says like him. He's too holy: his obedience is blind even in Council, "Don't be afraid to agree: at the least sign of danger, I'll sound the alarm." Brother Théodule will do the same, if you command him to.

In the discussion, there was a kind of jealousy between the R. P. [Reverend President] and Father Saulnier [Saunier] which I can no longer recall: each seemed to want to pull the provincial to his place. To my way of thinking, the provincial house ought to be one of the most considerable and most central houses. It seems to me that Canada ought to be a separate province because what suits our republican government hardly suits the monarchy of Canada.

In the document I had prepared, I had been ordered not to put in the word "provincial," but when they want the thing, I don't know why they wouldn't want the name. The word "provincial," they told me, would scare you. I have a better opinion of you, reverend Father, and I hope that before rejecting the request enclosed here, which will be made to you sooner or later, you'd do well to come spend six months with us.

Father Superior suggested at the end of the Council meeting that someone should make the proposition to you as if coming from himself. Thus, if you approve the document, you'd be able to take measures to organize the requested Council a first time and choose a provincial. He should be a thinking man who loves discipline, rather young so he can learn the language to perfection, a very good administrator and very wise. Our republicans are all mischievous and make the best bargains in the world. It isn't necessary that these matters be acted on immediately: take your time and let's understand one another well.

You'll have to reserve to yourself the naming of the provincial, his assistant, and his secretary, also all the improvements to do to the Constitutions, the foundation of new novitiates and new colleges, as well as the right of appealing, when it would be done by a Minor Chapter, but I believe for your own good you shouldn't reserve to yourself many other things. You could also reserve to yourself the right of deducting certain sums in case we become opulent, which won't happen very soon. You'd do well not to name our superior as provincial nor Father Saulnier: the first doesn't keep to the rules enough, and the second doesn't understand business affairs well enough.

Please say nothing about my letter to our Father Superior if you disapprove of the plan.

Father Superior from time to time still lacks frankness. Thus he kept your letter of appointments for Louisville until today without saying a word about it, and he wanted to leave for Canada without saying anything, if I hadn't stopped him with a note.

Father Cointet really doesn't do his duty as assistant superior: when he has missions on his mind, nothing stops him. Recently he left for a two week mission when Father Superior was in danger of dying and when Father Granger left for Indianapolis.

Please pardon my reflections: I'm speaking in total simplicity, and I am your Reverence's respectful and obedient servant,

Brother Gatian

September 15, 1847

I'm not writing you a formal letter today; pardon me, but I really am so overburdened with work and feeling so bad, and the mail leaving this evening (they always take care to warn us too late so that undoubtedly few letters reach you), I wouldn't know how to do otherwise.

I'm happy today and very pleased with Father Superior: what he had kept hidden in the beginning, what I had believed to perceive in the translation of the former Constitutions, as I made you aware of in my first diplomatic letter, all that became rather clear yesterday. Father Superior appeared frank for once in his life, and I'm in accord with him. All the councilors hit the snare (if you want to call it that) except for Brother Théodule, except for me, although we both held to the smallest rules. All agreed to send you the request enclosed here with the one we have really sent you. As undersecretary (Father Cointet being absent), I prepared the page and I had begun to write the present fair copy up to the blue ink stage and all still approved it. But a devil made us see that the first request could make both refused; it was necessary to keep the principal one for another time and say nothing about it at the present time; all backtracked, except me who am rarely persuaded by the superior and who, strongly opposed to this low-life cheat, said to myself: this will be known because I know Father Rector must be up to date on everything. (If I'm fooling myself, help me out, Father Rector.) Here's the document. You'll find it very peculiar, no doubt. Well, send us the person most opposed to it, and after six months of residence in America, he'll sign it. I was always strongly opposed to this measure, although it seemed to me the only way to assure our success here, because it wasn't constitutional and Father Superior pretended it was. I considered these thoughts temptations, and I didn't stop myself from fighting them. But finally, as soon as I saw Father Saulnier newly arrived speak even more strongly in favor of this measure than Father Superior, I said to the Council: Let's talk. So much the worse if we're turned down: I have to continue being frank. It's possible that if you settle everything in Louisville, you won't be sent the document in question. I believe all the capitulants are very well disposed toward the motherhouse, but fear being turned down or have suspicions of obstacles in telling you the plans they believe (and they are the most capable of judging them) necessary to their existence or the good of religion. But this prudence seems misplaced among the religious and angers me; that's why I'm letting you know everything. Father Saulnier is returning to Louisville where he'll stay alone until he gets new orders.

They just delayed for a fortnight sending the second request which consisted in asking the motherhouse to let the Lake take Louisville into its care and profit, because the high school ranks very low in public opinion by reason of its insalubrious location. We have some reason to hope that the high school will turn itself around and in five or six years the area will be, so they say, less unhealthy, but prudence prevents us from believing such a thing.

I'm going to tell you something which scarcely concerns me but which is in the air a lot. Our Sisters have to change clothing style every year. They took one recently which is very ugly, and it's not the motherhouse style, at least so Brother Théodule assured me. Why can't they conform when they can? I've also been assured that Mother Superior was really hated in her novitiate: the Sisters are going so far as to complain to outsiders.

104. Brother Francis de Sales (1) to Father Sorin
[Translated from French]

Vincennes September 26, 1847

My very dear Father,

Mr. Chassé, who just arrived from France, brought me sad news. My brother, who held my little piece of land, just died, leaving six poor orphans. His brother-in-law, the chaplain of St. Nicholas at Fengires, wrote to me and seems to want me. Since it was necessary to get a response to him right away, and as I could not consult you, I went to Monsignor. The response was that my piece would be sold, and that they could pass on to me part of the rent due to me. I intend to fill you in on the entire affair, my very dear Father, and to show you the letter from Abbe Phippiaux, when you come for the consecration of the new bishop. You know that this beautiful ceremony will take place on the 24th of next month. Please, Father, don't forget my levite and my pants which Brother Auguste was to have made for me. Also, I don't have a writing model, and Father Granger, who had some for me, has totally forgotten me. Meanwhile, they told me that if I couldn't give examples myself, I was required to furnish some at my school. Mr. Dussaux made some for me so well in the main part and especially in the middle that they would work nicely.

My school won't begin until the 4th of next month. Monsignor and the president of the Trustees tell me that it was dead and it took some time to try to resuscitate it. I visited all the parents I could find, and they all made promises, but many spoke to me about the cellar where their children fell sick as soon as they appeared there. Indeed, it's an ugly hole by many reports. It seems they aren't happy with the school ever since Brother Mary Joseph. He punished them severely, say the Trustees, but that's necessary in many circumstances, they assured me, in spite of your wish, Father Superior, which I shared with them.

I really want to hear news of Brother Gatian and the other sick Brothers. I suffered a lot during the entire trip, but the fever is gone, thank God. I arrived at Vincennes literally without a penny. That's very unpleasant. I've already had to bother Monsignor many times. Please pay the postage for my letters, and so you won't make a mistake about it, I'll abbreviate my name at the top of the address like so: B.F.de S.

School began again at the Vincennes high school. It's not flourishing. Mr. Bellier just left Vincennes forever. A priest, seventeen years in the priesthood and who has already spent many years in the American islands, is to help Mr. Chassé. His name is Mr. Bertin.

Respects and good wishes to all acquainted with me. I am, my very dear Father, your very humble servant,

Brother Francis de Sales

105. Brother Bernard (1) to Father Sorin

Madison October 9, 1847

Reverend Father Superior,

I feel happy in being able to inform you that I have enjoyed excellent health since I came to this city. I opened school on 20th of September and had 40 pupils on this same day, but in winter, I am told, the number will be double that. The people evince very great dissatisfaction at the manner in which the school has been kept, namely, their boys being left nearly one half of the time without school, first, upon the death of Brother Anselm, secondly, by the long absence of Brother Mary Joseph, who, they say, frequently absented himself without their knowledge, and thirdly, by Brother Thomas's frequent sickness. They, with the priest, also say that two months vacation is too long to have their boys idle, running on the streets, contracting bad habits. This idea is confirmed by the fact that the Sisters give but one month. I feel very well pleased with my employment, but the thought of having to go from house to house to collect my fees discourages me very much. The priest and I board with an Irish couple who have no family, within a few rods of the church.

I have had no trouble of mind nor have I had any violent temptations. My predominant passion has not troubled me much, but I feel a great difficulty in keeping a sufficient restraint on my tongue and eyes. I received a letter yesterday from Father Granger. He has had good health since coming to Indiana with the exception of 6 or 8 days. His cars [?] are also well.

If you have received a letter from my sister or Father M. Lessuolt since I left, I hope you will send it to me.

I remain your very obedient servant,

Brother Bernard

Direct to me in care of the Reverend Mr. St. Pallis.

106. Brother Benedict (4) to Father Sorin

Vincennes October 23, 1847

Reverend Father,

I am happy to think that you and all your children are in good health of soul and body. Well, about the pecuniary matter you mentioned in your last letter to me. I did not tell Brother Michael to speak of it to you. I mean the thirty dollars that you received from

Reverend Mr. Starrs, New York, on my account. I know not who has it at present, but you told me that Mr. Bierly, your neighbor, deposited it in New York with whom I know not, but I think you ought to get the bill from Mr. Bierly and write for the money or secure it as you think fit. I wish you to get it as soon as possible. Time is uncertain.

I wrote to the south for to know the particulars before I would send the notes to the bishop of Charleston for collection. I hope to get an answer soon, and when the money shall be handed to the bishop, he can send the seventy dollars to Ireland according to my directions and the balance to you. So, I say, get the thirty dollars as soon as possible.

The school in Washington is doing pretty well, the number about 40 at present. I expect to have at least 50 for the winter and more in summer if I live (please God). They were all half wild when I returned. I had to act roughly with some of them.

I lodged with Mr. Campbell till the priest shall have finished his house next week. I enjoy good health (Deo Gratias). I hoped to meet you here. I am and ever shall be yours in Jesus Christ. Amen.

Brother Benedict

107. Brother Benedict (5) to Father Sorin

Washington December 8, 1847 J.M.J.

I delayed to write, waiting for an answer to my last, but in vain did I await it. In answer to yours, I say, the priest and people settled for the time in paying me twenty dollars and paid or settled with Mr. Campbell for the board two dollars per week. So that all is settled. My fare home cost about six dollars. The rest I gave to Brother Joseph. Mr. Campbell told me the sum he paid for tax was about seven dollars, but the man who cultivates the land will pay in value the said sum. He also told me of [a] neighbor who is willing to buy the land for 400 or 500 dollars and will pay about 200 in hand for the same by getting time for the balance.

Mr. Dupontafice left here two weeks ago. We expect Mr. McDermot every day. Mr. Dupontafice received me very cooly as if I came against his will, continued to shew his angry feelings against me. I bore it patiently and still [am] happy and welcomed by old and young. Nay, even the Protestants respect me. I have twelve of their children. He told me he did not like to have a school here about him or the church, and being angry he told me he wished both me and my school was in Halifax. I did not answer him a word. He kept me in the little chapel till I had to dismiss the school by reason of cold there before he would let me into his room which is now the school place. I'm happy and happily fixed here. I board now with the priest or at his house.

Now if you be displeased for admitting girls over twelve, say so. I will soon dismiss Catholic and Protestant. If you do not quickly, I will discharge every soul of them after Christmas. If I did say so, do not keep [me] in suspense for I shall not do evil that good may come from it.

Brother Benedict

Still am and will be—Spero in Deo.

108. Brother Francis de Sales (2) to Father Sorin

[Translated from French]

Vincennes December 19, 1847 [?]

Father Superior,

As the first of the year approaches, with all my heart, good Father, I wish you a very happy new year, as well as all our priests, Brothers and Sisters. Won't you come soon yourself to wish a happy new year to our new bishop? I believe you would do well to do so. One is at ease with him, I tell you. *He's a second Monsignor Bruté*. Since he's been at Vincennes, I don't know a single time that I've been able to greet him first.

I put a letter in the mail for Brother Vincent the 5th of this month. I'd like to know if he's received it. I told him in this letter that Monsignor fears that you have a bit of Mr. Belier's mannerism, that is you hug too much. He talked to me about the Kentucky establishment; he doesn't approve of it. Mr. de St. Palais also spoke to me about our Sisters passing through Madison. He said that with their disguise, they seem like anything you'd want. The man who took them from the railroad to Mr. de St. Palais's house regretted being burdened with the job because they made him ashamed, he said, seeing them trotting along the streets, taking care to stay close to the sidewalks, fearful, no doubt, of getting a fine.

Mr. de St. Palais looked fine for the first time in a cape for the ordination of two deacons from the seminary. He is vicar general, as you undoubtedly know. He brought some pants for me from Madison, but no habit. I still need one. It seems to me that Mr. de St. Palais told me that the Sisters, while passing through Madison, left a habit. I suppose that it's mine because Brother Vincent promised me that I'd receive the whole outfit. Please be kind enough to talk to him about it.

Let Brother Bernard watch out—I wouldn't be surprised about this—Mr. de St. Palais asked me many times while smiling if he had made final vows and in particular the stability vow. After what I noticed, I believe he's "shaking his sleeve." The same priest also talked to me about the Great-Brothers at Baltimore and asked where Brother Mary Joseph is. I wouldn't be surprised if I learned that he returned with him. I know that he was happy to leave the University of Notre Dame du Lac while he murmured a lot about seeing himself sent to run a school without having been prepared. That's what will happen to all the Brothers, if there are not good leaders, especially a good master of novices. It's annoying that Brother Vincent can't speak good English; it's annoying that he stayed in France all his teaching years! Of all the Community, he alone could make a good formation director. Here's my belief: the most spiritual man, the man most stripped of his self-will and all material things, would never make a good formation director if he hasn't experienced for himself, if he hasn't gone through all the grades, in a word, if he hasn't himself run schools similar to those for which he's preparing the Brothers. Finally, in the matter of spirituality, I have complete confidence in Father Granger, for example, but in the matter of school principals, I have no confidence in him. Why? Because he has no experience, because he hasn't himself run schools.

Father Superior, I have at least 40 students, but when I have 30 of them at a time in class, I consider myself fortunate. Here parents keep their children at home for nothing. A little colic, a little headache, a little pain in the finger, is enough: "It's not necessary to go to school, my little boy; you'd make yourself sicker." That's the usual language of parents of the majority of my students. And the mean tasks that my poor children are required to do rather than go to school!! These are errands that the parents would better do themselves if they had the education of their children more at heart, if they weren't so lazy. It's to run after a cow in order to bring it back around the house. Another time it's after the pigs. They have to go to the mill, to saw wood, to rock the baby, whatever. I couldn't finish the list.

Father Superior, Mr. Andran, who threatened me several times to write you because I don't want to teach catechism in French in my school (having good reasons for that besides being so authorized by Monsignor Bazin), if he isn't there doing it himself all in English and in church! Undoubtedly they made him understand once and for all that was a whim of the parents which he should scorn. This priest has made several rules for the school that I can't make myself observe. For example, to speak only of the first: "No child will be admitted to school without being first presented to the pastor." More than three-fourths of my children came by themselves to school without being accompanied by their parents, and surely not one of them tried to present himself to the pastor. They know very well that my school is a *free school.* Also Monsignor calls many of Mr. Andran's rules: *fashionable rules in Brittany.*

I am, Father Superior, with the greatest respect, your very humble servant,

Brother Francis de Sales

Speak to Brother Vincent about my habit, please.

109. Brother Joseph (27) to Father Sorin
[Translated from French]

[Indianapolis] December 29, 1947

My reverend and very dear Father,

Brother Vincent has undoubtedly made you aware of my proceeding at the chamber of representatives. To obtain anything, I'll have to publish a treatise on vineyard cultivation either in a periodical or in a small brochure. I believe I'm capable of doing justice to this condition. I prefer to do it in a brochure because I could have subscriptions and register it as Community property. The subscription would pay for the expenses, and I could make 400 or 500 dollars selling the others left over.

Permit me to do what I'll find most advantageous. Be assured that I'd do nothing which could in the least compromise me and put me in debt.

They've assured me that I begin to age and I'm not yet better. I fear my hair begins to turn grey before my conscience and my soul begin to whiten.

I wish you'd write immediately what I have to do with my project. While waiting, please accept, my dear Father, the sentiments of affection and respect with which I am your very obedient but unworthy son in Jesus Christ,

Brother Joseph

Chapter Seven

1848

110. Brother Joseph (28) to Father Sorin

Indianapolis January 16, 1848

Dear and reverend Father,

I do not suppose that you have forgotten that we are now eleven persons to eat and that in proportion the other necessaries increase also. We need meat and bread, i.e. we have not been wanting till now and we shall not want yet for a few days. But we ought to make provisions for summer. I bought 260 pounds [of] sausage-meat for 1 1/2 cents the pound, excellent meat without bones and fresh from the slaughter house. I could have bought a great deal more had it not been for want of money, and I do not like to run always through the streets to borrow a few dollars here and a few there. It is not very pleasant. We will be obliged to pay very high in summer. All the eatabiles are very dear here, except meat. The potatoes are 50 cents a bushel, and all other things in proportion. Happily we are well supplied with such things.

I have made great preparations in my garden for marketing, but I have not all I want. I want a little hand cultivator which will cost $2.50 and a little handcart to go to market. If God spare me, I hope I will have plenty of early vegetables for market. Try to draw us out of the mire for l8 months more. I hope we shall not trouble you much then, if all goes well.

Mr. Cullan can make me a little handcart and many other things, if you send his tools. It will be worth a while to send them. Brother

Mary has the key of the box. He should put all the tools in before sending them, if he has made use of them.

Tomorrow I will hear what will be the result of my petition to the legislature.

May I buy 400 chestnut trees for $20 if I can pay for them at lessure with the produce of my garden? I can pay them in two years.

Give my sincere respect to all the priests and my love to the Brothers. I am, dear Father, with respect and love your most humble but unworthy son,

Brother Joseph

111. Brother Francis de Sales (3) to Father Sorin
[Translated from French]

Vincennes February 13, 1848

Father Superior,

Do you know that your "Live your Constitutions" made me grumble plenty? One can only live what one has. I have no Constitutions. You know there were only enough of them for three or four Brothers, and the elders were first in line. Thus I live as I think fit.

I remember that you told me some days before I left that if I had more than fifty students, you'd send me help. I don't have fifty, but the forty I do have give me as much trouble as seventy or eighty (if I had the place to put them). However, it's not the number which troubles me as it's the many sections. I have four for reading, as many for writing and ciphering. I have to divide my time, and I'm annoyed I can't give them more attention. They'd need it to make progress. Three students would like lessons in grammar and in the Rules of Three, but I'm not trained well enough in those things; besides, I don't have the time. Eight, ten or twelve students can't be neglected for two or three children who've been in school only a few weeks. At my arrival, I told Monsignor what I could teach, and he seemed satisfied. Meanwhile Mr. Moore, the head of the trustees, although he agrees that I don't have to neglect my sections for the three newcomers, says nevertheless that since my school is a district school, the teacher has to teach more.

It's unpleasant. I don't know whom I have to obey. Mr. Andran wants my school to be the parish school, and as pastor, he'd like to give orders. Mr. Moore says my school is a district school, and all the students in the limits of the said district have the right to come to my school. And you, Father Superior, you said my school is a school of the Brothers of St. Joseph.

Very dear Father, I really want you to come to Vincennes to settle all this, and for other reasons. Monsignor, who recently wrote to you, undoubtedly told you that I no longer hold my school in the cellar. I believe that I owe this happy change to the general infirmity I caught on Christmas Eve. For two days I needed all the attention of a two month old child. The doctor says that it was the dampness of the cellar and my room which led to that. Thanks to the attention of Monsignor, his priests, and some good seminarians (who were required to brush me to the point of blood), I was infirm only two days. We are as good as one could wish. We all are near the church, have an enclosed court yard and latrines, and enough room to have a good class, taking down a partition wall. Moreover, two small bedrooms and a wood house. But we really need tables. Those we had have gone to pieces, and few can scarcely stand on their feet. Besides, they were never suitable for school. I believe Monsignor must have made five lies per month about our house. He must have been satisfied to have paid for it, and he left the rest for the good of my poor school.

You undoubtedly know, Father Superior, that the College of St. Gabriel now belongs to the bishop. All the seminarians are now there so that I'm forced to eat in the bishop's kitchen. It hurts me a bit to eat thus, because I know it's not my place, but I can't really go to the college to take my board—it's too far, and I'd lose too much time, because my bed is in the schoolhouse. Meanwhile Monsignor and Mr. de St. Palais want me to trot up there every day. Probably Brother Charles, who, as you know, thinks only about Vincennes, is going to come back to the bishop. One of Monsignor's girls left, and the verger's preparing to return to France. If he wanted to carry the models that Mr. Dussault is to have made for me, he'd do me a favor. And meanwhile that sad habit doesn't show up. I'm lucky to have with me this old redingote that you condemned to retirement when I was Prefect of Studies at Notre Dame du Lac.

Respects and good wishes to all who ask about me and to those in charge.

I am, Father Superior, with the greatest respect, your very humble servant,

Brother Francis de Sales

112. Brother Théodule (1) to Father Sorin
[Translated from French]

St. Mary's, Kentucky February 18, 1848

My very worthy Father,

Finally today I have the strength to write to you. I'm up from a great sickness, a heavy fever which wouldn't have taken long to get me to a cemetery. Since my arrival here, finally I'm pulling through a bit, I think. I don't know how and where to begin to tell you about St. Mary's because things are so mixed up by Father Saunier. I have to tell you all the Sisters are very distressed, and they receive no consolation either from their Father or from their Mother at the Lake. Things are not easily put in order. At present moreover Father Saunier imagines he will become president. I believe thc contrary. Besides there'll be scarcely anything to do this year. Mr. Delaune has everything in hand up to the end of the year.

There are 15,000 francs to pay all the professors, the domestics; no other resource but the college. The farm doesn't prosper. It yields only corn. The wheat isn't doing well. Then it's not half as big as the one at the Lake. There are four or five men hired by the year for the farm.

There are 45 or 50 boarders now. Father Saunier will have a Brothers' and priests' novitiate, he says. I don't believe everything's going well as regards religious vocations. There's not a big catch out there. The Jesuit priests took nothing. I found one of their pamphlets. They were down to almost nothing at the novitiate. It's a beautiful house. Saunier always spoke of disbanding Indianapolis [the novitiate] and putting it here. In the letter you send me from Reverend Father [Rector], he says that since Indianapolis has been founded, we have to sustain it. I said as much to Father Saunier on the subject of the novitiate. He no longer talks of disbanding it.

Although far from the Lake and university, I still like it as much as St. Mary's. I don't doubt that if Mr. Delaune stays president, the college will grow because people have confidence in his name so that when they have said, Mr. Dalaune, they have said everything. And at Louisville Monsignor told me that if the parents of children who are at the college knew that Mr. Delaune was no longer involved in anything, they'd withdraw their children. Saunier and Mr. Delaune can agree on nothing. One day Mr. Delaune said to Father Saunier, "I wish they'd send me a man with whom I can agree so we could move on." Father Saunier replied to him that he was the most capable. Mr. Delaune replied to him on this occasion, "There's nobody in your Community capable of running a college." Mr. Delaune needed three or four years with us to help us to put everything on a good footing, and he even wrote to Ste. Croix. He's received no response. All this trouble makes him resolve to set up a college. There are three associates together from St. Mary's, two very rich professors. Father Saunier has no sense of this. Also this professor leaves tomorrow to go have their college built. He's not happy with us, and I tell you Mr. Delaune loves St. Mary's very much and surely he does the best he can in the midst of all for the good of the house. They say because he's opposed on every side, he's very feisty. Once a thing is said, it's over. He no longer thinks about it. Father Saunier has eight postulants one of which heads the farm. He's a man with the worst insolence for Mr. Delaune. I also found him so when I arrived here. He hardly works and doesn't push those whom he was told to make work on the farm. Mr. Delaune wished that they'd leave. Father Saunier didn't want it. Then Mr. Delaune gave charge of everything regarding the people in the house to me. But since I fell sick, he has everything under his control again.

If you knew, my very dear Father, the trouble I have at St. Mary's (I haven't given the sense of it). If the Lake wasn't far away, and with money in my pocket, I'd no longer be here. This trouble was caused by Father Saunier. I'll only say they asked for Father Gouesse. He'd do good here, but never will a person be free under the pre-eminence of Father Saunier. I wish he'd change. I beg you, Father, to do all possible to help us because we need a priest from Notre Dame du Lac. I don't know how that'll go over with the bishop as Mr. Delaune says he won't take any responsibility with Saunier at the head of the college and congregations. You see that all this is important. Father Saunier says it's not necessary to speak English well to be president. We have a new bishop named. He [Saunier] says, "Since he's bishop, he began to defend me. He will continue to do so." This Mr. Spalding is of the opposite feeling. It's possible [MS covered by seal] who'll do it. The other day, a month ago, he came to St. Mary's. He told Mr. Delaune to remain president. Saunier was at his side. Mr. Spalding says to Father Saunier, "What will you do seeing that Mr. Delaune doesn't want to stay?" "What will I do? I'll be president, and a new priest will be president of studies, and things will move along."

Father Saunier isn't prudent. After my trip to Louisville, they told the bishop a French priest said to me, "Tell Father Saunier that he names himself pastor, but he'll only be so until Monsignor has a priest capable of doing it."

These, my Father, are the principal things that I tell you so as to enlighten you about this establishment. I don't write with discontent. A month ago I sent my [MS torn].

In leaving, I forgot my statuette of St. Joseph in the small dining room. Please have mine sent to me, if they find it, or another one at the next opportunity.

My very sincere respects to Fathers Cointet, Gouesse, to Brother [MS torn] Lawrence and to everyone in general. I am with a very profound respect, my Father, your very humble, obedient son in Jesus Christ,

Brother Théodule

113. Brother Bernard (2) to Father Sorin

Madison February 21, 1848

Very Reverend Father Superior,

The father of the boy named Judge, who is at Notre Dame du Lac, was killed a few weeks ago by the railroad cars running over him. As he made no will, his children were in danger of being cheated out of his property by speculating lawyers, had it not been that a respectable, charitable, and good hearted Irish Catholic man administered for the property and took the children under his protection. The aforesaid Thomas Cavanagh (administrator or guardian) begs of me to write to you, stating that there will be 250 dollars left after liquidating all his debts, and desires to know if you will take the three boys, viz. the boy you had before, another of 10 years old, and the one you have already, he giving satisfactory security to you for the reception of the above sum at the expiration of one year (the property cannot be settled in lifetime). As the deceased was a dissipated and drunken character and consequently raised his boys badly, I will not say one word for or against the proposal.

Your obedient servant,

Brother Bernard

Mrs. Hines wishes to know how her son P. is getting on. If he needs any clothes, etc., she is ready to supply him.

114. Brother Joseph (29) to Father Sorin

Indianapolis February 27, 1848

Dear and reverend Father,

As the time when, I hope, we shall see you is fast approaching, I wish you would be so kind as to remember the following articles:

the life of the saints in German and the life of Ann Catharine Emmerich and a German prayerbook with a red cover.

Before I left Notre Dame du Lac, I laid up a great quantity of a[ll] kinds of flower seeds in the desk of the printing office. I wish I could get them. I planted likewise a great number of tulipe and hyacinthe onions. They would be very useful to me. Now more than ever I am convinced that if we had a large garden of all kinds of vegetables and flowers, we could largely supporte ourselves in this town for there is not a single gardner here and great demand for all such things.

Please give charge of these things to somebody that it might not be forgoten.

I am, dear Father, with the greatest respect and love, your most obedient but unworthy son,

Brother Joseph

115. Brother Théodule (2) to Father Sorin
[Translated from French]

St. Mary's [Kentucky] March 1, 1848

My very dear Father,

Following advice from Mr. Delaune, I believe I must tell you right away what's happening at St. Mary's so you can be on your guard. Reverend Father Rector wrote a letter to Mr. Delaune. He received it eight days ago. In it he says that he never sent Father Saunier to St. Mary's to take possession of it, that consequently he abolishes all acts or other arrangements that he has arranged. He says, "I'm not spreading calumny" (this is Reverend Father [Rector] speaking), "I advise you," he says to Mr. Delaune, "and I beg you to continue your superiorship next year." There's big trouble. Mr. Delaune took commitments for next year. Who will then replace him? Mr. Delaune tells me he's sure that Monsignor will not give the college to Father Saunier. Mr. Spalding told him positively that he wanted a man capable of giving assignments. Father Saunier has no doubt that Monsignor will give him everything he wants. I wanted to defend myself on what they said about me to the bishop regarding the capable priest. Father Saunier wants to understand or hear nothing. Father Saunier said to the contrary, "I am sole master of the college: everything is mine."

Reverend Father [Rector] says in Mr. Delaune's letter that he's going to write to Father Saunier in the same sense as his, but this letter is not here yet. You see then that Reverend Father [Rector] gives appointments on this matter because in a letter come to Father Saunier in January, he said, in responding to his letter about the trouble he had had with Mr. Delaune: "You've put me in terrible distress on the departure of Mr. Delaune. I truly don't know whom to send you for a superior. I'm preparing a colony for you of four Brothers and as many Sisters." Meanwhile he says to Mr. Delaune that he's sending nobody. Father Saunier says that he can make that all happen all alone. You see Reverend Father's disposition: it's not to take over St. Mary's all by ourselves. Mr. Delaune says that for himself, he doesn't want it, and that he's convinced that they'll offer it back to him, if there's only Father Saunier to take it. I don't know how everything will end. God knows. Mr. Delaune says that since he received the letter, Father Rector is appointing Father Saunier. He had to leave for France. It would be the best way to end the affair with Reverend Father [Rector]. Father Saunier doesn't want to hear any talk of it. He'll walk alone. All this is going to overpower Father Saunier. He said, "I'm the great president of St. Mary's." I'm happy that Reverend [Father Rector] wrote to Mr. Delaune, so that this may not be thus in regard to Father Saunier. As Mr. Delaune says, "Father Rector is a man who has good sense and a man I respect. I don't understand how he could make Father Saunier the superior. Right now I see that he never had."

I end this because I can no longer deal with it. I still have a very weak head, and all the rest of my body isn't worth anything. Also, like Brother Gatian, I'll soon die. I don't know if you can understand the entire sense of my letter. I don't have the head to arrange my paragraphs. Mr. Delaune asked me to offer you his very affectionate respect. I am, with profound respect, Father, your very humble, obedient son in Jesus Christ,

Brother Théodule

Keep secret the things I communicate to you, please, so that Father Saunier doesn't learn them. I believe I'm obliged as a member of your house to keep you informed about everything. It's by no means to hurt Father Saunier that I write, but so you know how to act in order not to go against the orders of Reverend Father [Rector]. We didn't receive the New Year's circular letter.

116. Brother Benedict (6) to Father Sorin

Washington March 7, 1848

Reverend Father,

I am sorry to impart bad tidings to you. Reverend Mr. McDermot is gone away to Vincennes to the college by order of the bishop. I grieve to tell you we got Mr. Doyle, a yong man lately ordained, to supply the necessity. I am sorry.

Reverend Mr. Doyle being here only one week, he offended me several times. I fear he is proud and wants to domineer over me.

Behold this day, Shrove Tuesday, he came with insulting countenance and bid me go sweep the church. I was highly offen[d]ed and said I never done it and never would and told him if I was wanting only for sweeping now, I was brought very low.

I then told him my children swept it when I told them and helped them myself. But being ordered, I would not do it. But if I must do so, let me know quickly. The first cause was I bought coal for the school. He burned it since he came here. I told him this morning the people were displeased to do so. I suffered before I got it.

I told Mr. Campbell. He told me to stop with him, but I will not until I get your letter. The people like me better than himself, so I will stop here.

When he came here, he had no mony nor value, so I got an order for seven dollars to buy food for the house and poor living here. I cannot collect the school money tho I have a good one, but they will pay money or value.

N.B. He passed his boy and came to me to order to go sweep the church. His boy was idle on the spot. Young and old loved Mr. McDermot. I think I will not stay here with him. I am tempted to quit the State altogather. But still I hope to live and die with you.

Brother Benedict

117. Brother Bernard (3) to Father Sorin

Madison March 11, 1848

Very reverend Superior,

My school progresses very well, so far as numbers are concerned, but the changing of Brothers so often has injured my collection very materially. The matter stands thus: there are a faithful few who are ever ready to pay their school bills, and another class, by far the greater, who are under the impression that they will have a new Brother every year and that by defering their payments to me till August, they may begin a new account with the next teacher. Judging by the promptness with which these few honest men paid me, I indulged the flattering hope of being able ere now to send Father Granger at least $30, but I have not been able yet to collect more than my support.

In case I should return here next year, I am inclined to think that I will be able to remit my superior as much, if not more, than any of our Brothers on the missions. Mr. Pontavice and I agree very well indeed. The people declare to him that their children have learned more since I came among them, than they did for two years before, and yet the probability of my changing encourages the roguish and speculating to defer remunerating me.

Though it may be impertinent in me to make known to you the fact (yet as a faithful subject I deem it my duty) that a very great majority of the parish who have visited Mr. Du Pontavice, since Father Shaw's removal to Detroit, blames you unsparingly as being the ultimate cause of his removal to the Diocese of Detroit.

If you have not yet remited my money to Archbishop Mr. Hale, there is an excellent opportunity offered at present. The superior and one of the Brothers of the house to which I am indebted are in New York collecting for the starving children of their large school. Their mission has been announced in all the Catholic papers. They are expected in Louisville, Ky. (where there is a branch of their house) in the course of a few weeks. The Brothers in Louisville upbraided me very severely for neglecting the matter so long and beg of me now at least to take prompt measures to retrieve my wounded character.

Will you therefore send me $40 dollars that I may present it to them when they will call to see me in Madison? I hope none of your Council will say that it is a total loss to the Community. For let them remember that the Community owed me $20 for manual labor when I joined, and that my services since have benefited the house more than the other half.

Please then, my dearly beloved superior, to send me the money in all possible haste, as I know not how soon they may arrive here so that I may be able to free my conscience of that burden which has so long disturbed its tranquillity.

Allow me again to thank you for your kind admonitory letter. It has proved of infinite service to me. I took occasion from themes to tell Mr. Pontavice to watch my every word and action and apprise me of my defects. Whatever it may arise from, I cannot be half so recollected during my daily employments as when at the college. Sometimes a whole day passes on me without recollecting or renewing my morning resolutions. I confess once a week and communicate twice, as usual. I make very few visits, and then only for a short time. God has favored me with a great increase of patience, so much so that my pupils have never seen me angry (or in a passion), yet I maintain the most perfect silence and order in the school.

Your acceptance of Judge's boys came to hand. Please to let me know if you intend to visit Indianapolis very soon. If so, these boys may return in your car.

I hope you will direct me in your next as to the best means of geting free from numerous distractions, etc.

Your obedient and humble servant,

Brother Bernard

118. Brother Théodule (3) to Father Sorin
[Translated from French]

St. Mary's, Kentucky March 22, 1848

My Father,

Undoubtedly you've received my letter which told you about our leaving St. Mary's. This frightening situation has just ended. I'd told you that Mr. Delaune had received a letter from Reverend Father [Rector]. He put it in the hands of the bishop, who did like Reverend Father [Rector]—cancelled Father Saunier's acts, established Mr. Delaune master, complete master of everything. Father Saunier is like a stranger in the house.

The sisters and I, the servants, soon [will] surely not have the college, because if Mr. Delaune wants it, he'll have it. The bishop does all possible so he can. He never felt like giving it to Father Saunier, and he's not happy with the contract made for Mr. Chabrut. But the bishop says to Father Saunier that he'll give him something better in Kentucky, to wait until July and he'll give him a definite contract.

Here we are, left to hang for three months, and at the end of that time, we don't know what we'll have. If Mr. Delaune wants the college, he'll get it. If he doesn't want it, and they find nobody to take it, they'll perhaps give it to Father Saunier, but I believe Mr. Delaune will take it for several years, and we'll no longer have anything to expect. And why don't we have this college? Because there are no capable people. And they don't send any. That's the buzz, as it were, from the country and from the bishop about Mr. Delaune.

To secure our position in all that, can we go to Notre Dame du Lac without money, my dear Father? Can you come to St. Mary's as we're counting on? It's really possible to find oneself in terrible circumstances and not be able to get out of them. Writing to Father Rector takes three months. That's a long time. Now there's no longer time to think about sending people here.

I am with profound respect, Father, your very humble, obedient servant.

Brother Théodule

March 22, 1848

I think, Father, that you can still call me back. I've received nothing from Reverend Father [Rector] who gave me the assignment for St. Mary's, and when I wrote to him at the end of January, I begged him not to leave me here. I can't take it with Father Saunier. Please see what you can do about it. I have no money. Mr. Delaune is of the opinion to exchange Father Saunier with another priest. [This is] the frightening situation which I spoke louder about and even said that one had to appeal to France.

My very deep and affectionate respect to all the members of the Minor Chapter as well as to everyone.

119. Brother Francis de Sales (4) to Father Sorin
[Translated from French]

Vincennes March 28, 1848

My very dear Father,

You know that when I retired from the students at Notre Dame du Lac, I begged you to give me a manual labor assignment, pointing out to you (in putting before you some of my reasons) that I didn't believe myself adequate to being made Prefect of Studies or a school teacher. I'm confirmed more and more in this opinion, and I have the experience of fifteen years. I'll not give you any reason for my ineptitude to run a school; I have plenty of them, and I wouldn't know where to begin. I'll simply tell you that I see clearly to make a school run it's absolutely necessary that a teacher have talent for thousands of things; and I don't have the style. I see very clearly that a teacher, especially at Vincennes, must have all the virtues, and I find myself destitute of them almost entirely, and too old now to acquire them, not only all the virtues, but even only those absolutely necessary for a Vincennes Brother. Besides, I'm very sad to see myself incapable of running a school, because I know that's what you need the most; I'm convinced that a good Brother and a capable Brother can do incalculable good, even at Vincennes, now especially that we have a local [bishop] as good as can be desired; but once more, I well understand that I am not suitable neither here, nor elsewhere, among young people, either as Prefect of Studies or as school teacher. I know, good Father Superior, that before sending me where I am, you had the kindness to ask me if I wanted to go here. I consented, but down deep I had intended only to give it a last try to see if I definitely could do some good among children. Now that I'm convinced that I can't, I hope, good Father Superior, that you'll have me replaced at the next retreat. I don't ask to be replaced before, because I know that you don't have subjects in abundance. Thus, I'm resigned to go on, finding myself hobbling along as best I can until vacation. I sincerely believe that for the health of mind and body, I have to be employed manually in one of the establishments. I know that I can work the ground, but you need people to run errands in your house.

I received Brother Vincent's letter, and I was pained to learn about Mother Superior's sickness, also your bad health, good Father, because of the bad cold which settled in your chest. May you both get back to health perfectly and promptly!! That's what I want with all my heart. I'm surprised Brother Vincent asks me if I've received my levite and my writing models. No! None of that. That's what I always told you, Father Superior, every time I've written. Before Brother Vincent's letter, I expected to see you here, after St. Joseph's feast. Now I no longer have any hope.

Look here, Father Superior, it seems to me that there is no friendship nor cordiality among the Brothers. Undoubtedly, I am not for the Brothers losing time and money writing to each other, but not a word, not even a hello, when the occasion arises—I find this a bit too much. No, that loving cordiality which is still found very often among the people of the world is unknown among the Brothers of St. Joseph. They came here many times from Washington and Madison, and not a single word, even a hello, for the poor Vincennes Brother. I admit it—I felt a kind of shame in asking for news from these Brothers, sensing as well that the coldness, which generally prevails among the Brothers of St. Joseph, could not escape him I addressed to find out how they were.

They say here that lately in France there's great confusion: that more than 500 people have been killed, that Louis Philippe has been forced to escape to England, that the Chambers have temporarily taken over the government, etc., etc. Surely you are more up on all this than I am.

Please, Father Superior, my respects and good wishes to those deserving them. Your very humble and obedient son in Jesus Christ,

Brother Francis de Sales

I posted a letter to Brother Vincent on March 18, 1848.

120. Brother Benedict (7) to Father Sorin

Washington April 2, 1848

Reverend Father,

Having read yours last Thursday, I deem it prudent to write again. As to the school money, Reverend Mr. Dupontavice made agrement to pay quarterly and to take value for my board also from the people. The contract stands in written agrement, so they promise to pay as soon as they can. They all seem happy with our school and declared openly they would rather do without a priest than that I should leave them for any reason. The school is now reduced in number by reason of the Protestant children being taken away—many declared to become Catholics. Some profess it openly, tho not yet baptised. They say that no preacher or teacher dares to oppose me. The priest says he's glad of that agitation among them.

Reverend Mr. Doyle and I are reconciled and happy. I liked him now well. He acted humbly and declared his mistake. I still support the house by my means.

Reverend Mr. Pearce is pastor at St. Peter's. He wants a school at St. Peter's and at St. Patrick's. He asked me out to settle or tell the conditions. St. Patrick's can have 50 [or] 60 children. St. Peter's about 25. Mr. Murphy is gone out to St. Mary's last week. Mr. Guegaen is at Indianapolis now.

Brother Francis de Sales begged for charity's sake to go see him at Easter. He says he is alone and forgotten by all. He says if I will go to see him, he will again be happy. I will do so. He complains of Brother Bernard.

Reverend Father, one thing only troubles me very much, that is the 70 dollars I told you that I owed in Ireland. I wrote to the South. I got no answer to my letter. I am now determined to write to the bishop in Charleston to find out if that man Mr. William E. Davis is dead. For I think religion would not save me if I do not pay my debts.

I do not like to ask you to pay it, but I must pay it somehow. I think of going to the South for my money, about 100$. It would pay for all. But, Reverend Father, I do not like to be compelled to leave religion for worldly motives, but I say justice demands it, God and my neighbor.

My dear reverend Father, believe me with sincere cordiality yours in Jesus, Mary, and Joseph,

Brother Benedict

N.B. Remember me specially at the alter. I daily make memento for you.

121. Brother Francis de Sales (5) to Father Sorin
[Translated from French]

Vincennes May 3, 1848

Good Father Superior,

I received again, and for the third time, with your last letter of May 19, the circular letters of Reverend Father Rector from the 1st and 24th of February, 1848. Do you know I grumbled this third time? Really, are these circulars so important to make them trot around a third time and thus lose time, money, and paper for nothing? Is it so necessary that I know Father Rector intends to have the remains of Brothers Louis and Cyprian returned to the Motherhouse? Is it so necessary that I know I and my school have to stay put and not leave immediately for France to take part against the Republic or for the Republic?? etc., etc.

You see, good Father Superior, that I'm far from being perfect and approving everything my superiors do. But in the end, I'm telling you I'm convinced you're far from knowing my bad will since you undoubtedly have nothing more at heart than to see your Brothers show you themselves just as they are. I think good superiors must love that. This candor can serve them in government.

Good Father Superior, allow me again a small reflection on some words in your last letter: "Crucify your old nature: it's the surest way to do good in this world." I agree with that for everything except eating in the kitchen because to do good, it seems to me that each person must be in his place. I confirm myself in this opinion more and more. I'm convinced that a priest, whoever he is, who finds himself dishonored by admitting a teaching Brother to his table doesn't deserve to have help in the Christian education of children. I sense with all my soul that a true Brother who does his duty and does everything possible to put in practice the twelve virtues of a good teacher is a martyr from morning to night for the good of children, and these ministers of a God born in a stable believe they have to keep a certain distance from a man so useful to religion and to society!! Yes, once again I believe that a priest such as I'm imagining would be unworthy of having a Brother. As for me, I'll continue to eat in the kitchen until I leave for retreat because I haven't been able and I can't make myself to be forever on the high school road for my soup and tea. Free from having at table in front of me young *bitches,* free from eating my bread dry (it's happened often to me), free from being grumbled at, etc., etc.

I still have thirty-two children, but it's rare when I have all of them together, and it's not rare when ten or twelve are absent together, but there's no remedy, so much the more as I've been lame for a month. My foot is better, but I still have to carry a sandal. Mr. Ducoudray has already given part of our house and courtyard to a family. It's the verger he's given us as a neighbor. He's a very gallant man; however, it's annoying that, not having too much lodging, he takes away part of it and disfigures our small courtyard with a shed for the cow, etc. I don't always prophesy falsely: I told Brother Vincent I wouldn't be surprised that he took the rest of our house at vacation.

The poor Frenchmen of the *dead town Vincennes* are going to look for work where they think they'll find some. Mr. Marsille left for St. Louis where he counts on establishing himself—advice for those who build: "They're more and more tired of the basements that Monsignor de la Hailandière ordered dug, and the French doctor has a good part in these removals." I wouldn't even be very surprised to see the little jewel suddenly abandoned, I mean the basement chapel. They've already begun.

Respects and good wishes to those deserving them. Good Father Superior, I am with respect, your very humble servant,

Brother Francis de Sales

122. Brother Joseph (30) to Father Sorin

Indianapolis May 4, 1848

Dear and reverend Father,

I must let you know something more certain about that railroad matter. It is not determined where the depot will be, on our land or on that of one of our neighbors. I spoke to some of the agents. They say that the committee has not decided yet because there are contending parties, each one will have it on his own land. Mr. Buttler, my nearest neighbor, one of the richest men in town, does all he can to get it on his land, but ours is by far the best situated for the purpose. Besides, I offered to the company for nothing land enough to build the depot if they will build the depot in the centre of the land. If they do so, we will sell every acre all round the depot for a thousand dollars, and we will be certain to make 15 or 20 thousand dollars of[f] our land. But whatever may be the case, the depot will not be 200 steps from our land so that the value of our property will be greatly increased. The fact is that I could sell now every acre of it to two and three hundred dollars.

Now it is not needed to sell all in a hurry for we will make 3 or 4 thousand dollars before we will have to pay the bishop. To manage the matter well, it will be necessary that I remain in Indianapolis even for two or three years. If you trust the matter to strangers, we will lose the have [half] of what this property will bring, as you have seen it to be the case with General Drake. But it is for me a matter of the highest importance to know now if in this case you would leave me, for I should take measures which would secure me a substantial livlyhood. More it will be most beneficial to Notre Dame du Lac.

Please answer immediatly to this. I remain, reverend Father, with respect and love, your most obedient but unworthy son,

Brother Joseph

123. Brother Joseph (31) to Father Sorin

Indianapolis May 18, 1848

Dear and reverend Father,

I wish you would send me these hundred and fifty dollars in some other way because it is impossible to get them at the bank. Since the last meeting of the different branches of the State Bank, that of Indianapolis is doing almost nothing. From what I understand, I beleive it is nearly broke up. I saw Judge Sample of South Bend. I asked him if he could let me have the money, but he said he could not. I do not know what to do. Last week I promised to every one that I would pay them this week. I borrowed $25 for Father Granger. I will have to pay interest if it goes long.

Nothing new about the property. I hope by this time the pilgrims are arrived. I wish them good luck and God's blessing they [be] happier than I. I would write a little more, but I am very unwell in soul and body. In fact, I do not know which of the two is worse.

Receive, dear Father, my respect and love, with which I am, your most obedient but unworthy son,

Brother Joseph

124. Brother Joseph (32) to Father Sorin
[Translated from French]

Indianapolis May 23, 1948

My reverend and very dear Father,

Unless the Lord build the house, they labor in vain who build it. For thirty centuries these words haven't stopped coming to our ears, but our pride never lets them penetrate to our hearts. We know them, but we don't understand them. At least these make so little impression on us that we always want to act without God and to make our plans without Him. Meanwhile sometimes God in his mercy warns us of our powerlessness and makes us know by His design the truth of these words of the king-prophet.

Today between 3 and 4 o'clock we had a hailstorm so terrible that it destroyed all our hopes in the space of ten minutes. It fell in stones as big as a good sized French nut, and the smallest had at least a half-inch diameter. My garden is like a desert, and the apples are mostly on the ground. The windows facing west are broken.

I've been sick for a week. I remain, dear Father, your most obedient but unworthy son,

Brother Joseph

125. Brother Joseph (33) to Father Sorin

Indianapolis June 5, 1848

Dear and reverend Father,

I have received your letter with the check enclosed therein. I sold it as you directed me. I paid the same day 159 dollars 51 cents and a few days previous to this I paid 10 dollars which we were owing for bread stuff. If I had 25 dollars more, I would be rid of all my debts. In fact, I do not know when I will be able to pay all because the hail and all the other mishaps which came over my garden destroyed 4/5 of my expe[c]tations.

Prepare a suitable piece of ground on a southeren exposition for next fall. I shall have between four and five hundred grapevines to send you, all of superior quality. My plantation to this effect is coming on beautifuly.

If you read Chapman's paper, you will see how matters stand with that intended railroad. It is certain that it will go on, but [not] where the depot will be. Lawyer Smith tells me he is one of the principal agents, that wheresoever the depot will be located, it will be near enough to double at least the price of our property.

I have a plan drawn up by Squire Solivan, on which he has laid out the 17 acres within the limits of the corporation into 40 lots which will be worth $100 each, some more, some less. Squire Solivan says that he will take a lot as soon as I will be ready to sell.

I will not be able to tell you much about [it] untill July when the matter will be decided. What is much in our favor is that it is the best situation that can be found for the purpose. Mr. Phipps is almost every day at me for buying a few acres nearest town or giving his property in town in exchange. If you think that I should let him have two acres for the 380 dollars we are owing him yet, I will make a bargain with him, but I do not like to do it.

When Father Granger had [been] with the Brothers, I took a family in the house. They should [pay] for the house rent, the use of one cow, firewood, and the vegetables for the house, board me and my old man, but I soon repented. When I made the agreement with the man, I asked him if his wife could cook and how many children he had. He said, "O yes my wife knows how to cook, and I have three children, but I will leave my oldest little girl with my brother-in-law." Well, the bargain was concluded, and the article signed. They arrived the same day, but besides his wife and his three children, he fetched his sister-in-law, a widow, with two other children. They are indeed very good and kind people, but the little fellows make music the whole day round, and the poor woman is so dirty and so ignorant that I could not stand it. She does not know more about cooking than a child of two years. I broke the agreement because the articles were not fulfilled. They will move again tomorrow. My old man and I keep bachelor's hall since one week, and we will continue so. We don't cook anything in hot weather. We have three times a day milk and butter and bread, like the patriarchs of old. The priest says Masse every day he is at home in our house, and we have the Blessed Sacrament here!

If you make any particular prayers for the Holy Father and the Church, I wish you would let me know. It is very necessary to pray for the ship of Peter in these s[t]ormy and turbulent times. It is very much tost to and fro by the winds and the waves. We are happy to be in this country. At least we are safe as long as it shall please God. I beleive we are approching fast the end of times which not we but the third generation will certainly see.

Mrs. Laux told me to remind you of the little boy you promised her.

Receive, dear Father, my love and respect, with which I am your most obedient but unworthy son,

Brother Joseph

126. Brother Joseph (34) to Brother Vincent
[Translated from French]

Indianapolis June 8, 1848

My very dear Brother,

It's not to surprise you nor give you pain if I don't write more often. There's always one thing or another to stop me. It's been more than a fortnight that I've been staying almost always in bed and always in my bedroom. I've a great pain in my left side near my heart. Sometimes it's so bad I have pain breathing. I took fresh water enemas every morning for a fortnight. I bought myself a syringe for this purpose. The headaches have scarcely stopped for three weeks. I lost sweat in my foot, a bad sign.

The 26th or 27th of this month, it'll be decided where the depot will be put. I have rich competitors who want to have it on their land. If we didn't have the most favorable location, I'd abandon hope to have it on our land, but whether we have this depot on our land or not, I wouldn't want to sell it today for less than 10,000 dollars. I'm sure that we'll get that, selling it by lots.

My garden has recovered a bit from the misfortune that the hailstorm caused. If God blesses it, I'll have a bunch of all kinds of things. I'll have about 500 cauliflower, 3000 cabbages. I'm already sending beets to market. I'll have cart loads of them. I have superb white endive, good to eat. I sold lots of peas. I have early potatoes, good to eat. My vineyard is magnificent. Every day I have visitors who come to see it.

In my last letter to Reverend Father Superior, I told him that I'd have 400 or 500 vines to send you, of the best kinds. Don't neglect to have a piece of land with good sunlight to plant them in as soon as they arrive.

Today is the first day I feel a little better. I don't want to tire myself out writing to you.

While waiting, my dear Broither, receive my sincere love, with which I am lovingly yours,

Brother Joseph

My respects to the priests and my love to all the Brothers.

127. Brother Bernard (4) to Father Sorin

Madison June 23, 1848

Very reverend Father Superior,

After a very long and mature deliberation, I am come to the conclusion that 'twill be more conducive to my salvation to be a member of some other order than that of the Brothers of St. Joseph.

My reasons are as follows: first, I am of opinion that our society cannot hold very long together on account of the dissatisfaction that exists among its component parts, though I assure you I have been always ready to overlook the trifles to which others have objected.

Second, we have no model school or even an individual professor to train Brothers for so arduous and important a mission. Hence it is that when we are aware of our inadequacy to conduct a school in a satisfactory manner, we are forced to seek admission in some society that will afford us those privileges.

You can hardly judge of the vexations and difficulties an imperfect scholar has to meet with in conducting a parcel of intelligent boys.

I will omit to add many other reasons which would seem to you of no importance. I have had a personal interview with the Reverend Mr.________ of an already *approved* society, who assures me that it is perfec [MS torn] practicable for me to pass from ours into his society.

If you wish to retain the Madison school, send a Brother as soon as possible to take my place. I collected a good deal of my old debts, by which I am enabled this day to remit to Dr. M. Hale the sum which your kindness authorises me. I will leave with Mr. Dupontavice a list of my school debts for my successor.

Mr. Dupontavice strongly suspects my final resolve, and as strongly disapproves of it, but my spiritual director approves of it. Allow me to tell you, my dear superior, that I am perfectly satisfied with the deportment of each and every individual of our young society, and that the fear of its final dissolution is the chiel [chief] cause of my seceding from it.

Hoping you will recommend my final resolution to the prayers of the assembled Brothers, and awaiting your answer, I remain your humble and obedient son in Christ,

Brother Bernard

128. Brother Joseph (35) to Father Sorin

Indianapolis June 25, 1848

Dear and reverend Father,

I must inform you what is the prospect for that depot. There is great figh[t]ing for the depot. Each part of the town will have it in its own quarter so as to benefit their property. However, the largest majority wants to have it in the northeren part of the town, but not on our property because some of my more influential and wealthy neighbors want it on their own land. Yesterday I conversed long with Mr. Underhill, who is, in conjunction with Lawyer Smith, the subscription gatherer. These two men are the candidates for directors of the railroad. They are both in favor of having it in my vicinity, but they can do nothing of their own accord. The committee will decide the matter, but the majority of subscribers will appoint a committee favorable to their views. Yesterday when I was informed of all these circumstances and I saw that I could not get an answer timly enough to this letter, I subscribed for one share in your name. One share is $25 paiable $5 per annum. I hope you will not blame me for doing so. The books will be shut the 27 of this month, and I thought I should not lose the right of voting for the sake of fife dollars per annum during fife years. Tomorrow I will engage as many as I can to take a share in order to vote for our side. I have already another man who takes one. There is great excitment in town about the matter. I am afraid that this railroad fever will delay the location of the depot until next spring. I heard something of it.

I am tolerably well now. My garden is going well. I have nearly a hundred cabbage already, several califlower fit for market. Such things are worth money. No one has them but myself. I have made fife dollars this week. If the late frosts and the hail had not injured me, I should have made 50 dollars by this time, but I will make something yet with the accidents I had.

I do not beleive the stage will take these large boxes. The clerk told me to see the director himself tomorrow morning.

I am, dear Father, with all respect and love, your most obedient but unworthy son,

Brother Joseph

129. Brother Joseph (36) to Father Sorin

Indianapolis June 27, 1848

Dear and reverend Father,

I hasten to give you further information concerning the railroad business. I entertain still great hopes to have the depot on our land or at least quite close by, because the party I belong to is by far the most numerous, but it is doubtful that it will be located this fall.

Today the stockholders have a meeting, though not at Indianapolis. I have taken another share for my old man payable in labor. Forty miles will be let out immediatly. The town of Indianapolis alone has subscribed $100,000.

The stage will not take the pagage. They say it would break down the stage.

With respect and love, I remain, dear Father, your most obedient but unworthy son,

Brother Joseph

130. Brother Joseph (37) to Father Sorin

Indianapolis July 2, 1848

Reverend and dear Father,

Though I have nothing of importance to tell you, I thought proper to tell you something in order not to let you in an axious expectation of the result of my negotiations with these railroad men and of my doings in general.

Mr. Underhill, to whom the majority has given the vote for director, is not home yet from the elections. The meeting for the election of commissioners was not held at Indianapolis but at 60 miles from hence. The competition is actually very livly, particularly since they know the proposition I made to the company. The mayor of the city, who always was my friend, he shook hand with Father Joseph everywhere he met him. His lady paid me even a visit some time ago, but now he is a[s] mad at me as a dog. However, I hope all their achintions [actions] will be useless. We hold the primacy in position, and my proposition to the company will save them 5000 or 6000 dollars, if they accept. If not, they must be a set [of] madmen. In a few days you will know.

I do not beleive I will be able to stand it long. We have to[o] much to do for two men. Our garden is very large. I have to cook, and everything about the house tended to. I have frequently to go to town to see how things are going on. The old man goes to market four times a week. We have to rise every morning after 2 o'clock in order to face all our labor. The half of the time I eat nothing for weariness. If you could send me with the wagon Mrs. Drimmer, I should feel very happy, or send me a Brother who can not do much at home. He may do a great deal of good to me. Brother Ignatius would do [for] me.

The week past I made $6.48 in market. I bought eight little pigs so as not [to] lose the things I can not sell. I have a large quantity of vegetables. When the wagon comes, I will send you two pea-fowls, a hen and a coq. I bought them for a dollar a piece from a man who was in need of money and they are very cheap.

I remain, dear Father, with respect and love, your most obedient but unworthy son,

Brother Joseph

131. Brother Benedict (8) to Father Sorin

Washington [Indiana] July 7, 1848

Reverend Father,

Hoping that you and all your children are well (as I am at present, Deo gratias), I wish to let you know how we are getting along here. The Protestants made a kind of display of their school and Sunday scholars. They even exclaimed against Catholic children to join them in marching. In fact, they showed they were secterians (I mean on the fourth of July). Several Protestants and all the Catholics were displeased. I resolved to shew them that I was in Washington. Therefore, I appointed Monday next to let them see. I invited all my children to assemble at the church at 9 o'clock with all their parents, and the chief persons of town and country, with several Protestants, all fitted for a journey of 4 miles to a farmer's house to take dinner, each one family being supplied with dinner wagons, light and heavy. They are borrowing horses, carriages, buggys in town and country. Besides we will have 3 or 4 big wagon[s] to carry the children. (Mass at 8 o'clock.)

All are very thankful to me for the invitation.

The very Reverend Mr. St. Palais visited my school, was well pleased, defended me in all matters. I invited him to come on the twentieth of July to the Examination. [He] was delighted with the honor I paid him in doing so—so that he promised to bring Reverend Mr. McDermot, Reverend Mr. Shassy, Reverend Mr. Ducady, and the band of musick with the big drum with him. He sent me word since to be prepared and to write a week beforehand. So that I hope to have 7 priests that day. He, Mr. St. Palais, proposed to have high

Mass. The children will give a dinner or rather a supper when all shall be over.

They are all in great glee at the hope of the pleasure they expect.

I will go home as soon as possible, and believe me to be yours truly in Jesus, Mary, and Joseph,

Brother Benedict

132. Brother Joseph (38) to Father Sorin

Indianapolis July 8, 1848

Dear and reverend Father,

As the rain prevents me to work out the doors, I will in order not to lose my time, inform you, by a somewhat lengthy letter, of all the particulars of the railroad business. So far the things have a good prospect. We have succeded according to wish in the election. Mr. Underhill is director and Lawyer Smith is president. So then, this fact decides that the depot will be in our neighborhood, but on what spot will not be decided untill fall. Now if we will have the depot, I can not say. It depends on circumstances and in a great measure of ourselves. As I have taken all possible information and am well acquented with the whole affair, I will give you my own views. I am certain they are good and will have good consequences, if followed. Several of my competitors have made the same propositions as myself to the company. The company looks to her own interest, of couse, and takes as much as she can. Therefore, he of the competitors who takes the most stock in the railroad will have the depot.

Now, if you appreciate well what I will tell you, you will see that it is our great interest to act upon my plan. The company takes land for stock, and after or in the course [of] four years, if that land is worth more than what it is put in for, the subscriber may redeem it. If he does not redeem it after these four years, the land belongs invariably, inalterably, to the company, but during these four years the subscriber has to pay the interest of the sum he subscribed the land for, but he will have the fruition of the land all this while and he must pay the taxes, because the company has no other benefit from it during these four years.

My plan is to subscribe four or six or eight acres according to need (so as to beat the others) to $300 per acre because, if we get the depot, in four years an acre will be worth 4 or 500 dollars, and if we do not get the depot, it will not be worth more than $100 an acre, not counting the improvments. Then by subscribing we will greatly increase the prise of the land in the corporation, and at the same time the prise of that out of the corporation. So we should neglect nothing to get the depot. If we get it, I pledge my word, I will make 8 or 10,000 dollars of[f] the land in the corporation and in four years from now I will make 8 or 10,000 dollars more of[f] that out of the corporation. Examine the matter well and let me know what you think to be the best.

If we take stock now, we may sell it again after a few years, if we don't like to keep it. I must remark that I do not want to take a single share, if we can get the depot without taking any. This would be only in case of necessity.

I need help very badly. I will be obliged to hire a man even the whole year round. I am now acquented with what is going in market, and I am certain that I can pay a man, and the property will be worth a great deal more if it has a fine appearance. I have a great many visitors from all quarters, and it pleases them excedingly.

I made $7.50 this week, and if I had been provided as I ought to have been, I would make 3 times as much. The little boy is pleased with Mrs. Laux, and she with him. I have such an abundance of vegetables (but not all the right kind for market) that I do not know what to do with them.

I remain, dear Father, your most obedient but unworthy son,

Brother Joseph

I am interrupted by visitors.

133. Brother Théodule (4) to Father Sorin
[Translated from French]

St. Mary's, Kentucky July 9, 1848

My Father,

There are painful days for man in this life. They'll be sad for you and more so for me. Yesterday we received your answers which were much awaited. The response has a hidden pain. Father Saunier left St. Mary's this morning to go to the Jesuits. He's going to Cincinnati and at the same time is leaving the Community. He gave me his rules last night and everything relating to the Lake. He gave us to believe that this trip is like a retreat that he's going to make for thirty days to know what he ought to do. This morning and then all day long Mr. Delaune told everybody the truth. He counsels him to go in this manner. Mr. Delaune wrote for that. He said that Father Saunier wished to be absolved from his vows as Mr. Spalding proposed to him and to stay here. It's better that he's with the Jesuits. You see, very dear father, the troubles with Kentucky are heavy for each of us. If we all wanted to leave, it'd be crazy. The positions are good. They don't lack money here. The Community is scorned and looked at as nothing. They said to me a few days ago, "The Lake is falling apart: they're going to disperse one of these days." But I cry out the contrary with all my strength, and I don't believe I'm fooling myself; they almost seem like the French in these bad times. They profit from criticism. I believe that these are only proofs that God gives us for our good, and for the good of Notre Dame du Lac. The loss of this college is a blessing. If you knew everything as I do and if our Community had never known this college, it would be a blessing.

We can't leave before Monday the 17th because Mr. Delaune isn't ready to give money. He thinks he's a great friend of mine, and I'm on good terms with him. He gives me much. I'm free to do as I wish anytime. He gave me a horse to fetch letters in Lebanon. But he gets that in the morning for fear of having too much [ ] in the middle of the day in front of strangers or savages. And, my dear father, I assure you that as soon as God gives me the blessing to see

Notre Dame du Lac again, my heart will be happy. I'm indifferent to everything they do to me here. I comply while not seeing.

We'll talk about the rest in a few weeks. I don't know how many before we return to you. I recommend myself to a prayer from everybody.

I am, with a profound respect, my Father, your very humble and obedient son in Jesus Christ.

[Brother Théodule]

134. Brother Gatian (5) to Father Sorin
[Translated from French]

[Notre Dame] August 20, 1848

My Interior State

I believe I have to describe succinctly to you the state of my soul, not being able to do it very frankly out loud:

1) Well! I'm convinced, as you are yourself, that I can correct myself as much as I'd like and that I can do much good here, being able to accommodate myself to all jobs.

2) The inertia in my will is the result of my character or natural inclination which hasn't yet been tamed.

3) My character is a mix of melancholy and sanguine—the melancholy dominates.

4) My melancholy makes me find difficulties everywhere. I see only disorders and troubles in life. It goes with me everywhere. My soul is full of grief and fears. I imagine that people are wretched, that they hate me—that I spend my time foolishly, that I'm not in my right vocation and that although I excel, I'll never come to the end of my undertakings, that I'll be [at them] surely for years, etc. Melancholy takes me especially into discouragement when I consider that I'm already twenty-two and I yet know nothing, that there's a multitude of academic disciplines I don't even know the name of and

even in the areas to which I am most attached, like mathematics and languages, there are young people fifteen, sixteen, twenty years old who are already doctors, soldiers or even generals; that if I were out in the world, I would perhaps be better read in business, etc.; that I've lost all pretention to knowledge and honors to lead a life for which I have no particular attraction and where the sole desire to save myself and blind obedience to my directors have made me stay; that this desire to save myself will perhaps never be accomplished since I'm becoming corrupted more and more each day and that I'm evidently damning myself; that, on the other hand, it would be useless to think about changing lifestyles, all my physical and spiritual faculties being exhausted, and it would be equally useless to wish to become a saint, because I'd never persevere a fortnight. These dark ideas and many others hit me with all their consequences (which I understand in their full extent and beyond) more than twenty times a day and make me think sometimes of plunging myself in infamy to ease my pains, as a drunkard drowns his sorrows in wine; sometimes to return to the world to lead a philosophical, political and philanthropic life where, away from religion, it seems possible I could be happy. I'd gladly get away from life, if I could get away from faith. If I knew I had only a few days to live, I'd easily decide to live well, but as I don't know the hour of my death, it so happens that I ordinarily end my dark musings wanting the madness which would take away all my cares and let me sin innocently: that's why I play the fool.

5) I'm also a bit sanguine in character. From that comes this extraordinary thirst for knowledge which with the melancholy turns into despair that I can't acquire it. From that also come these philanthropic ideas because if I become unfaithful, I'd upset the world (if I could), but this would not be in Robespierre's style, but for people's good with all the humanism of Lamartine. From that comes also my extraordinary attachment to certain individuals, invincible attachment, and which presently is the immediate cause (not the unique cause) of my madness; from that also comes my melancholy's changing this propensity into despair of ever being able to teach. In effect, I can't teach without loving my students passionately and without my heart requiring inwardly that they love me as well, which is impossible for them. This passion makes me consider their faults as

ingratitude, and I punish them as such, which alienates them from me. Then follow the perpetual suspicions of a jealous love. I then have to make a distinction between the good and the bad: the first become favorites and the others consider themselves enemies. They hate both the teacher and the favorites. The favorites, seeing themselves so treated, turn then against the teacher, which puts the latter into despair, if like me he has a strong head but is governed by a will dominated by passion.

6) My two inclinations have been rallying for a long time around John Hays. I can never and I'll never be able to stop myself from loving him, nor from wanting to be loved by him. I know by experience that neither separation nor estrangement will be able to cure me. I've loved other children before him (but never as much as him), and although these children had been separated from me, some three years, others four or even ten years, I still think of them often, but without trouble because they loved me. Nothing but the caresses of John Hays can quiet me. With the child not wishing to love me, melancholy turns this passion into despair. For a long time I had asked God and the Blessed Virgin that the child would pardon and love me. Not having obtained it as promptly as I wanted, I wrote a foolish letter to the Virgin, and I played the fool, and then repenting, I begged again and promised to act better, if I got that. I got a part of it because the child doesn't hate me now and acts very nicely to me. Instead of thanking God for this favor, I then began to go no longer to confession and to send everyone to the devil.

7) From my discouragement or despair, a result of my passion which originated in my sanguine and melancholy character, comes this desire that I've often shown to you, to be put into manual labor, although I know this isn't my vocation, because work deadens the spirit and makes my imagination incapable of its customary wanderings.

8) It's not necessary to understand from #6 that I am strongly inclined to impurity. I haven't had temptations against the sixth commandment for at least two years. Nevertheless I'm subject to illusions at night.

9) As for my vocation, my belief is that I became a Brother, not because that was my inclination, but because my inclination was religious and it was impossible to be a priest, considering my pover-

ty, and the Brotherhood seemed to me to come closest to that of priesthood. I've never even dared speak of my inclination for priesthood, primarily because I believed it was useless, and at other times because I took such thoughts to be temptations. These last years I haven't spoken about it 1) because I thought I was dying last year 2) because for some time I thought myself too old—besides, this despair and my other passions had alienated me from all good thoughts 3) the fate of Steber and of O'Leary had almost convinced me that it was impossible to become a priest after having been a priest [Brother]. I have nevertheless always regretted having taken promises so young, although, following my melancholy character, I've communicated my regrets to no one.

Brother Gatian

N.B. I believe people are sometimes fooled in discussing my character. I read that melancholiacs ought to be busy, but not overworked. I've often remarked that a double [personality] had been the immediate cause (not direct) of my extravagances.

135. Brother Joseph (39) to Father Sorin

Indianapolis August 28, 1848

Reverend and dear Father,

I have but two minutes to give you this notice. I just came from the stage office where they told me that if the steamcars bring no passengers from Madison for the north, they will take that box with musical instruments to Logansport today. They have begun today to lay out the railroad. No other news.

I am, dear Father, with respect and love, your unworthy son,

Brother Joseph

136. Brother Joseph (40) to Father Sorin

Indianapolis September 10, 1848

Reverend and dear Father,

I have no news as yet, but something of importance to ask. You tell me that you pray for the success of my affairs. Nothing better indeed, but what I wish in particular is that the 1000 Hail Maries be said this week at the Community. It is this week or next, if I am not mistaken, that the matter will be decided. Though I will have hard run, I have still great hopes. The surveyors and their attendants are camped in my barnyard this evening. The matter will be decided when they go at it without delay. Of course, I will have no time during the race to inform you of my proceedings and to get answers to my letters, but I beleive you may depend upon me, with God's help. I am certain if they came in with my views, they will make 5000 dollars and we will make 12 or 15,000 dollars of[f] our property.

I had to dig a new well outside the house. My old one failed and caved in. The new one cost me $27, but it is nearly paid. Please give my respects to your visitor. Send him by Indianapolis. I could not make out the last line of your letter. It is still a mistery to me. I will give you news as often as it will be needed, and when there is any chance to do it.

I remain, dear Father, your most obedient but unworthy son,

Brother Joseph

137. Brother Joseph (41) to Father Sorin

Indianapolis October 1, 1948

Dear and reverend Father,

I have no news to give you yet. What I can tell you are only rumors in town that the depot will be in my pasture. The letting of the railroad will take place the 25th inst. The directors are very cautious and circumspect. They give no satisfactory answer to anybody. They do their business in secret, and I find they well [do] because they would be overrun and overpowered. They have very likely their point in view, but they will conclude nothing untill they find nothing better. But I have a question of importance to make: have you the deed of the property? If you have, at least it has not been recorded and transferred to you. Then whose agent am I? Am I yours or the bishop's? Can I give a full and warranted deed to the company for the land I give them, and in whose name? I think I must have a written legal authorisation for agency. Please give me an immediate answer to all these questions and procure me the power necessary that I may be ready for the event.

Mr. Rayan is a very singular being. I never saw so awkward a man in my whole life. The other day being in the chapel, I heard a great quarrel in the yard. When I came to see, I found him quite alone. He was quarreling over a half hour with my other old man whilst, indeed, this latter was absent, and this is not the first instant of folly he manifested.

I will send you in a short time 3 or 400 vines. Have a good place ready for them.

Mr. Fisher has made his retreat here for a week.

Since my last sickness, I enjoy better health than I deed for several years before.

You have, indeed, not made a great acquisition with Mr. Rayan. It is an act of charity to keep him, and this is all. Indeed, it takes a good deal of charity to bear with his singularity and his awkwardness. He eats for two, and works for a half, not because he is lazy, but because he is awkward.

I remain, dear Father, with respect and love, your most obedient but unworthy son,

Brother Joseph

138. Brother Joseph (42) to Father Sorin

Indianapolis October 8, 1848

Dear and reverend Father,

I expect you are as tired of reading my letters as I am of writing them, because I can give you no satisfactory news about this depot business. I saw Mr. Smith the other day. He told me that the location of the depot is delayed untill December, that they have to run the whole line of the road before they can do anything else, but that it will be certain in December. Now what shall I say? Shall we lose patience? It is of no use. If it is a little trying in the present circumstances, we will be more joyful in our success and more thankful to God for it. I dare say that I have as much hope if not more than ever that it will be in my pasture, and we will enjoy it better after having obtained success by hard tryal.

I do not expect that I can keep Mr. Rayan here. He has almost no cloths, so I should cloth and feed him, what I am not willing to do, because he does not earn 15 cents per day, to take it all round. Besides, it is very tedious to bear with his awkwardness and singularity. He is as cross and peevish as an old cat. Please tell me in your next letter if he has brought any money to you. If he has, I will send him to you. If he has not, I will send him anyway.

I have a housekeeper now, an Irish widow woman.

Mr. de St. Palais wants to send one of his seminarians here. I should board him for pay, and Mr. Gueguen teach him. I do not like to do it, but however tell me what I shall do. I am willing to do what you tell me. They have shut up the college and seminary at Vincennes.

I remain, dear Father, with respect and love, your obedient but unworthy son,

Brother Joseph

My respect and love to all.

139. Brother Joseph (43) to Father Sorin

Indianapolis October 13, 1848

Dear and reverend Father,

Now has the contest begun. The committee receives proposals at the railroad office for no less than five acres of land for the depot.

After mature consideration and the advise of my friends, the most clearsighted in the matter, I gave in my proposals, which are as follows: I propose to sell to the company the 5 acres required for the consideration of one share of the capital stock of the company, and to the further inducement to the acceptance of my proposals, I subscribe in addition for 60 more shares of the same stock.

This very likely will seem to you to be an exorpitant sum, and you, with the Community, will be inclined to blame me more than ever, but pray do not judge untill you are well informed of the matter, and you will not blame me then. If I succeed, I will make 15,000 dollars, besides keeping 4 acres with the improvments for us. If I do not make this, I will consent to be disgracefully and without one cent in my pocket, chased out of the Community.

The third day of January, 1849, the proposals will be opened, and the lot selected will immediatly have to be conveyed to the company. Let no one's mind be troubled during this time. I will do my best.

I remain, dear Father, your ever obedient but unworthy son,

Brother Joseph

140. Brother Joseph (44) to Father Sorin

Indianapolis October 27, 1848

Reverend and dear Father,

I had the satisfaction to enjoy the presence of Reverend Father Drouelle for nearly two days. He is a very amiable man, and I am sorry that he went so soon away. We have fully discussed and examined everything concerning our temporal and spiritual interests, present and future. He has adopted all my views in their full extent, particularly so if the things succeed as we fondly anticipate. He will write you, not from here but from Louisville.

Now, dear Father, what shall I say? I acknoledge that if my piety and my virtue were proportioned to the graces I have received, I would be sure of success, but alas this is not the case!...Indeed, my sinful life and my unworthiness make me fear and tremble. In truth, I expect more from the prayers of the Community than from my skil and capacity because I am thoroughly penetrated with that of Davit[d]: Nisi Dominus aedificaverit domum, in vanum laboraverant qui aedificant eam. I[n]deed, the more the time draws near, the more I fear, and however I have not more reason to fear than at any other period previous. Therefore let prayers be said. Three weeks will decide the matter for certain.

I remain, dear Father, with respect and love your obedient but unworthy son,

Brother Joseph

141. Brother Benedict (9) to Father Sorin

St. Mary's December 26, 1848

Reverend Sir,

To fulfill your injunction, I wish to let you know that I still exist on the battlefield, not conquering but fighting. I visited Brother Francis, but [got] a very cool reception. He neither asked me to stop nor to come in to the house, late in the afternoon on Saturday. So I returned back to St. Peter's, ful of shame. I told him you willed me to see him, having no other business. As for the school, there is no great encouragement. The number that comes daily is from eight to ten. We expect more shortly, but it is doubtful. I like all things well, but the small number tires me.

I have many large boys, but they do not come regularly. I have one teacher who come[s] to perfect his studies, also a boy that went to three teachers and could do nothing for him. He can spell now with me after three months. He is about ten years old. He could not bless himself at first, but now he can say his prayers. All his faculties are defective, but now he can speak pretty well.

So, wishing the benediction of the Infant Jesus in your soul springing up to eternal life and to all my good Brothers, I remain yours cincerely,

Prodigal Benedict

Chapter Eight

1849

142. Brother Vincent (18) to Father Sorin
[Translated from French]

New Orleans January 1, 1849

Very dear Father,

I begin by wishing a happy new year to you and all those who are in your care. I must tell you then that the bishop and the directors intend to have a school for the children of our neighborhood. They'll ask you soon for Brothers. Note well that so beautiful a future will not have [MS blurred] if you don't take steps to bring it about. Monsignor is [MS blurred] that there's so much harmony between the Brothers and Sisters. The Brothers and Sisters complain that you don't respond to their letters [MS blurred] particularly Brother Théodule, and Sister Mary of Calvary, Sister Mary of [ ] [MS blurred] then to say the three Sisters. Be good enough then to come if you don't send Father Gouesse.

You perhaps think that I'm in a dark mood, but if we lose the establishment, we'll never find a similar one, and besides I'm sure Brother Théodule won't stay if there's no change. He told me that again this morning. Nor Sister Mary of Calvary. Brothers Basil and Théodule don't go to confession regularly, a subject of complaint from His Grace. Consult your council again if you judge it appropriate. In the first analysis, your presence would do good, but I fear the trouble would begin again a week later.

We need a permanent priest here. The reason for that is although we have a good priest to serve the asylum, many things are known around the bishop's palace, and Monsignor understands our trouble. I know I'm telling you to hurry up. I know that one Sister said she wanted to go find His Grace. Understand we need a priest here who alone can hear our confessions and be skilled in administration and order, which I am not. Again, don't sleep any longer on my information. You'll lay an obligation on him who has the greatest desire to save the asylum, the honor of our Society, my reverend Father, your very humble and obedient son in our Lord Jesus Christ,

Brother Vincent

My God, save us or we'll be shipwrecked. If you were coming with the priest, how nice it would be. You've earned this trip. Bring your chest of instruments and your picture.

143. Brother Joseph (45) to Father Sorin

Indianapolis January 9, 1849

Reverend and dear Father,

The depot question is decided in favor of my antagonist: he had $6000 more subscriptions more than I, but this was not all that was against me. The president went to see at the clerc's office, on finding that Monsignor de la Helandière had never transferred it to Monsignor Basin. He is dead and the land is always in the same name, so they thought that I could not give them a good deed.

Now as the things stand so that nobody will buy anything unless I can prove by record that I can make a good deed. I will write next Sunday.

I am with respect and love, your most humble but unworthy son,

Brother Joseph

144. Brother Joseph (46) to Father Sorin

Indianapolis January 15, 1849

Reverend and dear Father,

In my two last letters, I gave you notice of my defeat in the railroad depot business. However, I must tell you that the loss is not so great a one particularly [as] you at a distancne might perhaps believe. But pray be perfectly easy about the matter. I will show you that in the course of next spring I will make something out of this property because there are many judicious men in town who believe that I have lost nothing because of the vicinity of the depot which is not farther from me as the novitiate is from the college. Beside[s], the Peru depot is to be located this week. This latter must of necessity [be] located on my lot or on the lot immediatly west of me. Therefore, I will make no great efforts to get it because I will be between two or three depots in whatever way it may turn out. The Lafayette depot is coming in at the same point.

Immediatly after my defeat, I went to Squire Sollivan to have the 17 acres in the corporation laid out into lots, but he would not do it. He said I should hold on until spring else I would repent. In fact, we could not sell much now nohow, so it is better for us to wait a month or two.

I am only afraid that you are very uneasy about this matter, but rest assured that everything will go well. You may make inquiries about my procee[d]ings. My opinion is to make a public saile next spring. I mean of lots.

Write to me soon. You have not written to me since more than ten weeks.

I remain, dear Father, with respect and love, your most obedient but unworthy son,

Brother Joseph

145. Brother Joseph (47) to Father Sorin

Indianapolis January 21, 1849

Reverend and dear Father,

It is really a greivous affliction to me to see that all my exertions fail, but I would not repine if I was myself alone involved in the matter because I am still certain that all will turn out well, but my affliction chiefly arises from the trouble it gives you and the Community. May God assist me and you.

I know no better expedient now than to divide into lots all that part which lays inside the corporation line. The most judicious men in town think that we do wrong if we sell any particle of it before two or three years, but they do not know our embarrassment. Whatever may be the case, we can do nothing before March.

I have written to the bishop, stating [to] to him the whole matter, but I will write to him again this evening. I think we will sell the lots well, but slower. The value of the property is greatly enhanced by the depot which is not more than 300 yards from me.

I remain, dear Father, with respect and love, your obedient but unworthy son,

Brother Joseph

146. Brother Joseph (48) to Father Sorin

Indianapolis January 23, 1849

Reverend and dear Father,

The bearer of the present is my cousin. I give him over to you. I have done my share for him, so I will let you do the balance. I do not find in him all the qualities I should wish for, but I hope that divine grace will make him what he is not. At least he promised me that he would do his best to please you and all, and to make himself useful.

He has studied the German and French languages, though he is not a perfect scholar: he has forgotten much of what he has learned, but he will soon get it again, besides acquiring a new stock of knowledge. He has a very good intellect, and I have no doubt but that you can make something with him. Like me, he is of German blood and of course a little hauty and stuborn, but good sense will supply what nature has refused to our character. I do not suppose he will ever be [a] Brother. In fact, he does not come with this intention.

I have dismissed my housekeeper because I am not able to pay her. I have borrowed $8.00 to send my cousin. I have no income at present. I am as poor as I can be, or as the Frenchman expresses it, "queue [pauvre] comme un rat." The taxes came to $19.00, as last year.

I wish you would not be uneasy about the Indianapolis question. I am certain to sell the lots well. Several have spoken to me, let the month of March come.

I am, dear Father, with respect and love, your obedient but unworthy son,

Brother Joseph

Let me know if you are satisfied that I should devide the property into lots. I am sure it is the best.

147. Brother Vincent (19) to Father Sorin
[Translated from French]

New Orleans January 28, 1849

My reverend Father,

We can receive our payment only when the legislature comes to the help of our asylum. Mr. Rasch was happy with your letter. He won't delay asking you for two Sisters. But having a priest is close to his heart. We must have a Sister who is skilled in sewing to help

Sister Mary of the Five Wounds, and if Sister Mary of Calvary is called back, we'll have to have a Sister who has some stewardship and is skilled in keeping order in a large house, especially its kitchen. Sister Mary of Calvary would stay, I think, if there were a priest as director. Again, you know what she's written to you.

The hope that you gave Brother Théodule in your last letter that we'd see Father Gouesse sooner than we think probably invigorated all our expectations, but I don't understand why you wrote to me several days later in a different sense. I don't think the Brothers and Sisters had the least idea of such a disappointment. God alone can direct you in an affair as delicate as what I'm going to tell you about. It's indispensable that whoever you send speaks French. It's the first question Monsignor put to me when you first promised Father Gouesse, because he'll be obliged to help Mr. Pacher both at the convent and to hear confession, almost always in French. If you send two Sisters without a priest, it'd perhaps be good that in fact the Mother Superior bring them; but I doubt they could follow with a council since we are subject to authorities who have the right to give us orders. I'd prefer to wait for some time longer and that a priest bring the Sisters, because I don't doubt that when Brother Théodule and Brother Basil see the Sisters arrive without a priest, they will want to leave. You know Brother Théodule, a good Brother. But you must not push him as to what he says to you. He likewise wrote to Father Rector that without a priest he wouldn't stay in New Orleans. Don't believe, dear and very kind Father, that I want to have Father Gouesse and you against [ ]. No, to please God I have to make you a party to what I know; we must have a priest here who has good judgement and method, without which the troubles will continue.

Don't let Father Barraux come back from France without [settling] the Mr. Mignard business. Moreover, if he could bring back Brother Leonard, that's the man suitable for New Orleans. He unfortunately debased himself in quarreling at the last retreat, which makes me think that Father Rector would let him go. [MS torn] didn't respect Sister Mary of the Five Wounds too much. I often had [MS torn] later than she, since she put the infirmary in order [MS torn] is fine. She keeps the linen-closet in perfect order. [MS torn] to God. May the Lord direct you.

Brother Vincent

148. Brother Basil (1) to Father Sorin

Brooklyn January 30, 1849

Reverend Father,

I am sorry that I have to write again so soon, but the predicament in which we are placed compels me to do it.

I received a letter from Father Granger, in which he has given me no satisfaction in anything I required of him, but he is surprised at my long silences. In the name of God, what is the use of writing and representing our situation and difficulties when there is nothing done to alleviate them? We are ordered to be strict in the observance of our rules, but where are the rules? And if we had them, we could not practice them.

I am aware that the spare time, which the multiplicity of business which you have to do leaves you, is but very little. Still, I hope you will find time enough to examine and consider upon what I shall represent to you.

Since the time Brother Vincent left here, Father Bacon has neither said nor done anything for the encouragement or progress of the schools. As I stated in my letter to Father Granger, he has furnished for us a clock and a crucifix. I asked him yesterday evening if he had received any account lately from you. He said he had not, and that he had not answered your letters yet because he was waiting to see how the schools would succeed. I was not surprised at his reply, because if something be not in contemplation, he would show some little interest for them. If the Reverend Mr. Lafont, pastor of the Church of St. Vincent of Paul in New York, had said such to the Christian Brothers, what encouragement it would [be] for them. Please to examine the Freeman's Journal of the 20th of January, and you will see what [he] is doing for them, etc.

You may judge from the following how we are paid by the schools. Our boarding is 7 dollars per week. It is three weeks this night since we settled up for our boarding, which leaves us 21 dollars for three weeks. We paid 9 towards that which leaves us in debt 11 dollars. Such is the income from 87 boys.

Three months are past, and not a word about hearing the confessions of the boys. Also, it is now the fifth week since I have been to confession and communion. We have lost all heart and courage to do anything, but there is one thing certain, and that is the people who are boarding us are making well by us. Be not deceived: we are sure that it is Father Bacon's intention that the schools shall pay our expenses. The predicament in which we are placed, by sending us here, you could not treat us worse if we were really slaves, and you may be sure that we shall never forget this. What I mean by saying that Father Bacon's intention is that the schools shall pay our expenses is if the parents do not pay for their children, whatever we fall short of paying for our expenses, you will have to pay it. It is unnecessary for me to state any more. You judge from this much how things stand.

Now, Reverend Father, I beseech you to relieve us from our present place. For myself, either send me the means of leaving here or dispense with my vows. I prefer the former, but if not granted, I must resort to the latter. I am sorry to be compelled to say so, but either one or the other must be done. Let me know as soon as you receive this what I am to depend upon as I shall be waiting with anxiety.

What I say here are also the sentiments of my fellow Brothers. If you want the school [to] continue here, you will have to send those who are more competent than we are. Do not direct your answer to this for me to Father Bacon. I shall call at the office for it.

I remain with respect, etc., yours truly,

Brother Basil

149. Brother Joseph (49) to Father Sorin

Indianapolis February 8, 1849

Reverend and dear Father,

I must inform you that I have done nothing yet. The ground is not surveight, owing to the extreme frost and afterwards to the softness of the ground. And now I expect I will have to wait one week longer on account of these different depot locations. My richest neighbors, and those who could do the most for me at first but have abandoned me now, are now obliged to come to me if they will succeed in their operations. They want to have the three depots as close together as possible, but they cannot do it without me. I refused constantly since some time to have anything to do with them, but yesterday I gave them some hope that I would do something, if I would find it advantageous.

They want to have the Lafayette depot on our ground and the Peru depot on that between me and the Bellefontaine depot. Let me immediatly know if I shall make them any proposals, if I find advantageous to do so.

The bearer of this does not seem to be very smart.

I have already lettuce to eat. I expect I will have plenty things before you will have the spade in the ground.

I remain, dear Father, with respect and love, your most obedient but unworthy son,

Brother Joseph

150. Brother Basil (2) to Father Sorin

Brooklyn February 10, 1849

Reverend Father,

I received your tellegraphic despatch on the 9th inst. at half past 7 P.M. You want to know if I require Brother Gatian here. I say *yes.* Thank God that thick, black and heavy cloud which has been hovering over us and preventing the sun of shining upon us since we came here has almost disappeared. I am glad that I have somewhat more encouraging news to communicate to you than heretofore.

I had not said any to Father Bacon about Brother Aloysius not being able to teach his school until this morning. I then told him that I had written to you to send some person that would be able to do justice to the school, and that you had answered me that you would send Brother Gatien. He said that he intended to write in the spring for another Brother and that he must have three if he had to give up his own house for a schoolroom. He says that the people are now well pleased with the schools and that there is no danger but we will succeed here. For some time, says he, the prospect was very gloomy, but now it is not so. He said the Reverend Mr. Sneller from St. Paul's had been to see him twice and that his intention is to have the Brothers next fall, if you send them. He also said the orphan assylum would be commenced in May and that where they intended to build it there are almost Catholics enough to support a priest and that the Brothers should have charge of the assylum. But where are the Brothers to take charge of it, if you do not open a novitiate here, which if possible ought to be done.

We have now about 100 boys in the two schools and for want of room and convenience we can receve only a few more. There are several boys going to the Jesuits' school in New York, who, when Brother Gatian commences will come.

Brother Gatian must be here the last of March so as not to disappoint Father Bacon. Now Reverend Father Mr. Sneller will want at least three Brothers, and whom have you to take charge of the advanced school? I do not know any unless Brother Aloysius can learn enough from Brother Gatian until that time. Brother Gatian is better [to] bring with him what books and cloths he can conveniently, for here we cannot get anything without the money, and we have not sufficient of that to clear our expenses. I am well aware that it will be a great loss to the institution for Brother Gatian to leave, but if you want to do anything here, you will have to make a greater sacrifice than that.

We have not been in good health for two months. The winter here so far has been pretty severe. At present there is beautiful sleighing through the streets of Brooklyn. The house in which we stop is on the Brooklyn Heights and commands a beautiful view of New York City, the North River, Jersey City and Grant Island. There would be two more in it, but the great majority of them are too poor, on which account they are not able to build them.

The new epidemic, called the Callifornia Gold Fever, which is raging in the eastern cities with unabating success, has been very fatal in New York, for it has swept off to that region a great many vessels which were loaded with merchandize, provisions, and gold adventurers.

With respect to our religious exercises, you may judge how we perform them from the situation in which we are placed. (Father Bacon told me in confession that I was taking too much authority upon myself, but did not say in what. I did not ask him, nor do I know myself in what. Therefore, you will not forget, when Brother Gatian comes, to appoint whomsoever you please. I do not want to be accused with the like when I am trying to do my duty.)

Write to us one week before Brother Gatien starts and direct your letter to Father Bacon. Let us know how the Brothers at Fort Wayne are doing. Father Bacon has expressed his surprise why you have not written to him lately, and by request, I present to you his very best respect. Give our love and best respects to all the priests and Brothers, reccommending ourselves to your prayers and to those of the Community at large.

I remain, Reverend Father, with respect and submission, your obedient servant,

Brother Basil

N.B. We are in hopes that something will be done before long that will oblige you to send Father Granger here, which would be the greatest consolation for us, etc.

151. Brother Joseph (50) to Father Sorin

Indianapolis February 21, 1849

Reverend and dear Father,

I have received your letter with that of my sister. I thought well before I opened any of them that yours would give me a scolding. Therefore I opened yours first, thinking that I would get the scolding first and to sweeten it a little by that of my sister.

I will not excuse myself because it is useless, but in answer to your injunctions, I must tell you that next week the 17 acres in the corporation will be layed out in lots. I had two maps drawn of the lots: one for the record office, and the other for me, to sell the lots by. There will be about 55 or 60 lots which should bring at least $100 on an average. This would make $6000, but we must give good terms: either 18 months, as you say, or two years. There are four rows of lots. The first row of front lots will be $150, the second row $125, the third 100, and the fourth $75, and what we cannot sell in the course of 6 months hence must be raised in their price, but I do not think there will be much left. I have not published them as yet, except in the Catholic Pittsburgh. A friend of mine living in Pittsburgh, who has engaged a front lot, has put it in that paper.

Several lots are engaged. I have received $36 on one, but I will give no word untill he has paid me $50. There is a great movement among the Catholics for lots from me because they think they will be near a religious house and that they will have a school. I have no doubt but that Indianapolis will be in the course of a very few years our finest establishment, if we keep hold of the ten acres out of the corporation. If you were witness of the movement in this town as I am, you would be astonished.

With regard to a fixed day for the sale of lots, I can tell you nothing now, but I will let you know in my next what will be the best plan to be adopted.

Mr. Laux and Mrs. Laux send you their best respects. They wish you would sell their lot for $200, if you can get that much. They will pay all the expenses which will be occasioned by it.

I see that the letter from my sister was opened. I wish you had it translated. You would have seen that God has not yet abandoned France. He has never ceased to raise Saints in the most turbulent times to console his church and to strenghen the faithful. There is at present in Alsace a holy virgin like those in Tyrol. Our blessed Savior appears often to her. Her visions are authenticated and recognized by the bishop of Strasbourg and all the clerge of the diocese.

With respect and love, yours,

Brother Joseph

The little cross my good sister sends me has been blessed by our Savior himself. The holy virgin presented it to him for this.

152. Brother Gatian (6) to Father Sorin

Brooklyn February 22, 1849

To Notre Dame du Lac University

Dear Members of the Association of the Holy Cross and my dearly beloved apprentices and boarders,

So great is my affection for you, my beloved friends of the Lake, that I can no longer resist the temptation of opening my heart to you and to give you an account of my adventures since I left my happy abode. I have seen the great city at last, and I have pitched my tent on the seashore in the heights of Columbia Street No. 94 at the Baths of Brooklyn. So you see, being in the Bathhouse, I shall keep myself clean, and one of my consolations is that if I ever be tempted to drown myself, I will have plenty of water on hand, which I can reach before anyone can catch me. But never fear, my good friends, I am not downhearted, and my yearnings after you are great and sufficient to prevent attempts of suicide.

I have been trotting up and down the streets of New York and Brooklyn ever since last Tuesday, 8 o'clock P.M. I am as well accustomed to the turmoil of the city and the fire bells of the nights as if I had lived here ten years. I examine the buildings, streets, etc., as carelessly and independently as the first loafer of the city. In fact, I do not find as many marvellous things as I expected. There are many houses, but what of that? I assisted at the distribution of ashes on last Wednesday: the church was crowded to suffocation, but I am told it is twice as bad on Sundays. It was then I had for the first time a sight of our Brothers' young New Yorkers, hard cases indeed, and I already anticipate hard times: they chatted aloud almost during the whole time of Mass. Still I do not despair: I will drill them. Perhaps they will not be as dangerous to me, as you would have been, my good friends, because they will not take possession of my heart as so many of you have done. Ah, my friends, why are we so far asunder and yet so close together? This is indeed an incomprehensible mystery of love. I think of you more than twenty-four times a day. Think also of me and pray for me that I may not break my neck in the streets of New York, for the urchins that encumber them have been sliding on the sidewalk so that it is very difficult to stand. Some larger rogues have torn off the labels of the streets so that if I go to the city or even in Brooklyn itself four times a day, I will get astray five times. One of these days I expect some knave will direct me to the five points, but what do I care? Now, a word about the circumambulation of the globe.

I left Notre Dame du Lac with all my sweet friends in the afternoon of Wednesday (February 14th) in a sleigh with Father Superior to Bertrand where I lay in a cold bed and slept but little. I suffered that evening, during the night and the next morning in going to Niles. I got at Niles just in time to take the cars from Detroit. I arrived only about half a minute before the cars left. In the cars I was very cold and sleepy, for it grieved my heart so much to leave so many good friends that I did not sleep for eight days previous to my departure, and I did not go to bed after I had slept in Bertrand until Monday evening at Albany.

We had great fun in the cars, but not always agreeable, for we travelled one mile ahead and then two miles backward. It was 7 o'clock when we left Kalamazoo, and we reached Detroit on Friday morning at 8 o'clock. I took my breakfast in a hurry, bought a ticket of $14 to travel thro' Canada, crossed the river, and I stood for the first time on Canadian soil. Here the snow did not put an obstacle to our journey as on the Michigan railroad, but helped us powerfully along. We travelled part of the way in sleigh and part in coaches. At first we had open sleighs, and I tell you I suffered from Canadian goose picking. But we had a young lawyer of Chicago who bribed the driver, and we travelled at certain times 7, 8, 9, 10, and even 11 miles an hour over hills and dales, and across part of Lake Erie. Sometimes the horses had to jump over cracks two feet wide not frozen in the lake.

Thus we travelled across Lake Erie, then down the Thames to London, to Chatham, Hamilton, St. Catherine's, as far as the Niagara

Falls, and then by the cars to Buffalo: 265 miles in 2 1/2 days. I liked our quick travelling, but I was afraid to lose my trunk which they had put on an extra sleigh which did not overtake us until the third day. I was afraid not because I doubted the honesty of the proprietors, who thro' the whole line in Canada were very kind, but because I was afraid it would be forgotten on the way because it is contrary to their rules to forward trunks without passengers, but I recommended mine so well that no accident happened tho' it was half open from Niles to Buffalo, having had no time to get it repaired anywhere until I reached the latter place.

Now four accidents happened on this route, and I was fortunate enough not to fall a victim to any of them. The first was that some of my fellow passengers eat a goose that had not been gutted. The second was that after we had got one mile beyond Hamilton, a short time after my fellows had been expatiating on the disadvantages of an open sleigh and the happiness of having a coach, whilst I was sound asleep with some sweet dream about my friend of the Lake, the driver put us in a ditch. The coach upset, and we all came down on top of each other, but I was on the lower side and my head went thro' the window in the snow, and the first thing I knew was that some were standing on my breast. My feet were entangled in the feet of my companions, and it was some time before we could get out of the coach, and I was the last that came out. Luckily the horses stood still. If the contrary had happened, my head would have been severed from my body, and we would likely have been all killed.

I tell you we quit praising the coach, and we sent our driver after a sleigh whilst we walked ahead in the darkest night until we came to a hotel, when the doctor we had along replaced the ear of one of our men which had been cut off in the upsetting of the coach. It was that night the Extra overtook us for that night we travelled seven miles in eight hours.

The third narrow escape I had was at the Niagara Falls. We crossed the ferry amidst the billows and icicles. We were twenty coming from Detroit, and out of the twenty only five had the courage [to] cross it. I was one of them. The others went down two miles below the falls and crossed on the wire bridge. But I preferred crossing the ferry, because we had been told that if we went by the bridge, we would be too late for the cars, and I would rather have gone to the bottom of the river than to have missed the cars by cowardice.

I indeed was happy to have crossed the ferry, for I took my trunk along and I was ready with my trunk on the other side for the cars, whilst my fellow passengers missed the cars or had to leave their trunks at the ferry, and on that account I was one day before them in New York. Besides, they will perhaps lose their trunks for the man at the ferry is a rogue.

The fourth adventure was that the rogue at the ferry charged 25 cents tho' we had paid in advance at Detroit, and I was cunning enough to trick him out of his wrong tax. On the whole, however, I may say that people in Canada are very kind, and we had fifty miles of very good roads which were m[a]cadamized or planked.

I arrived at Buffalo at 6 o'clock P.M. on Sunday and left it at 8 on the same evening for Albany. By chance I went to a Catholic hotel, took a good supper, got my trunk and my cloak fixed and all that on Sunday (what a scandalous sinner I am sometimes). We had excellent travelling by the cars from Buffalo to Albany, tho' the frequent changes of cars are very troublesome. I slept over half the time, and once I forgot that the conductor had given me a ticket, and I told him I had not seen when he gave the tickets, so I could not return any because he had given me none. He let me be, and since, I have found out that I must have been dreaming at the time for I have the ticket yet, and if I ever become a knave and travel that way again, I will use it.

We arrived at Albany at 6 P.M. on Monday and I slept there. On Tuesday I left Albany by the cars and arrived at New York at 7 o'clock and at 8 o'clock at the city hall. We crossed the state line of New York into the adjacent state and made a circuit of 195 miles in ten hours by the Housatonic Railroad. I remarked that stones were so plenty in that state that people made stone fences. I also wondered that their fences were so low: their cattle must be very tame if they do not jump over them. It must also have taken lots of workmen and time to dig a bed for the railroad, which seems to be dug in the solid rock.

Today was Washington's birthday, and I hope you have had a great deal fun. I wish I had been present to contemplate your happy faces, but I hope to be present for the fourth of July and to participate in your joys. In New York we have had nothing very great, and I think, my good friends, you could have beaten the procession of our soldiers in Brooklyn.

We have plenty of snow and ice here. But the ferryboats continue their work, but at Albany and all other places the Niagara Falls excepted, the water is all frozen, and for my part I had great sleighing down the Thames and crossed the ferry dry foot at Albany.

Some of your folks at home are very kind for themselves and talk without knowing what they are saying, caring but little for poor travellers. Brother Vincent would have persuaded me, for instance, that I did not want a cloak, did not want a comforter. I would like to see him here in his shirt tail. I think he would soon find that we have winter here and not summer. Some of your people seem to be astonished to hear complaints, but I think if they were [here], they [would] complain loudly than our poor Brothers here.

Now, my good friends, I have not much time: it is ten o'clock. The Brothers are making accounts around me. I have had lots of boobies making a fuss in our boarding house. Good bye, my dear friends, good bye my dear bookkeepers, Richard Ferris, John Connolly, etc., my beloved arithmaticians, Francis Wolke, Thomas Richardville, etc., and farewell to you, especially to you, dear apprentices, in whose welfare I take a peculiar delight. May Brother Francis Xavier take good care of you. Amen. I remain most sincerely yours,

Brother Gatian

P.S. I sent the letters to the post office at Detroit and Buffalo, because I had not time to call on the persons. I mean Brother Stephen's, Brother [ ]'s and Mr. Rennoe's.

Reverend Father Superior,

You will please communicate my letter to the Community and recommend our establishment to the prayers of the Association and the apprentices and boarders. I am very busy and tomorrow you will have a business letter. You may tell Brother Stephen that I dropped his bill to C. Merse. I opened his letter and inserted 1/2 doz. Mitchell's Geography and Atlas, tho' I had not asked the Sisters whether they wanted them, but I merely supposed they did. Send me a prospectus of the Sisters or tell me where I can find one. I have forgotten their prospectus at Bertrand.

153. Brother Gatian (7) to Father Sorin

Brooklyn February 23, 1849

Reverend Father Superior,

Let your anxiety cease. Individuals are not so indisposed as you had imagined, but things are, however, in a more precarious state than you seem to have comprehended. No one, however, is as responsible for the ill success of your establishment as Brother Vincent and yourself. Permit me to speak frankly: you generally do things only by halves, and you require real miracles from your subjects and then blame them when these miracles are not really wrought. Brothers Basil and Aloysius were right (humanly speaking) to be dejected; Mr. Bacon was right to keep still and not help the school along; Mr. Twomy was right in being disatisfied, tho' the Brothers did well to leave him. But you were the cause of Brothers Basil's and Aloysius's dejection; you should not have sent them to New York: they were not and they are not able to teach. They have not the least experience in or knowledge of the Plan of Instruction. I don't know more than they in this respect, and if I retrieve your affairs, as I have some hopes of doing, it will be the result of my innate capacity and energy or rather a real miracle. I don't see, Reverend Father Superior, how you manage to be continually getting yourself and others into scrapes, whilst if you would profit by experience and get a man to do business for you with the necessary, business-like nicety, you would avoid these petty difficulties which greatly endanger the reputation of the Institution.

I will at once render an account of the informations and measures which I have already taken and ask you a certain number of questions which you will please answer promptly and exactly that I may not get into scrapes myself. And I am persuaded that if you examine matters closely, you will derive the same conclusions which I and all the individuals I have seen derive from the consideration of the subject, viz., that three persons only are to be blamed: Reverend E. Sorin, Brother Vincent, and Brother Basil.

Reverend E. Sorin is to be blamed for having undertaken foundations which he was not able to sustain; for sending his Brothers before agreements had been concluded and set down in writing; and for putting Brother Vincent at the head of establishments without giving him the necessary instructions. Everyone agrees here that poor Brother Aloysius especially should not have been submitted to so hard a trial.

Brother Vincent's unintelligible method of action has, however, been the direct cause of the difficulties of which you were the indirect cause, and Brother Basil the instrument or the victim.

Brother Vincent's first fault was his attempts at making agreements contrary to the promises or understandings which you had had with the priests. It is thus, for instance, that he explained himself so well to Reverend Joseph McDonough (as I understand from Brother Basil) that he made you pass for a liar, and he did so much with Mr. Bacon that the latter had been in a manner obliged to give up the school and to wait in order to see [how] things would turn out, because he could not make Brother Vincent sensible. This he had confessed to Brother Aloysius and to me. Mr. Bacon had never understood things clearly from you, Brother Vincent or Brother Basil until yesterday morning, when I had a conversation of four hours with him and explained clearly what ailed each of you.

Brother Vincent's second fault was his being in so great a hurry to get a boardinghouse, notwithstanding the advice of Mr. Bacon to the contrary, and his employing Mr. Bayer to urge Mr. Twomy to take a new building. Had he taken these two steps, Brothers Basil and Aloysius might have left Mr. Twomy without hurting the feelings of anyone.

Brother Vincent's third fault was his leaving Brother Basil at the head of the establishment and his coming home without informing you Brother Basil's principal fault, the cause of his dejection, ill success and the disgust which he has excited in the minds of everyone, is his want of candor and his suspicious conduct.

Now to return to the first sentence of my letter. I said that I did not find individuals as indisposed as I had anticipated. It was nearly nine o'clock when I entered Brooklyn and reached Mr. Bacon's house. He received me well, did not blame the school and said there was no occasion of despairing, that he had always told the Brothers, and that he wondered you had sent me so quick, as the Brothers and himself would have been satisfied to wait till the end of March. He did not lay very heavy, specific complaints against the Brothers. He praised Brother Aloysius for his good conduct, but regretted his ignorance of bookkeeping, algebra and geometry and his inexperience. He said Brother Basil seemed to be more experienced in teaching, but that his reserved and suspicious character was very disagreeable and that nobody liked him. He said that he wished merely to have a good understanding with the Institution and that then everything would be right. He regretted very much the faults which I have mentioned on the second page of my letter. When the next day I repeated to him the complaints of the Brothers, he merely answered that he had never been properly informed and that besides he had always been afraid to hurt the feelings of the exceedingly sensible Brother Basil. Mr. Bacon is, I think, generally well disposed, but he seems to be exceedingly quick (he says Mass in 15 and even 14 minutes) and somewhat passionate. In selecting a Brother for director, attention ought to be paid to that: he likes plain dealing.

For a few weeks before I arrived, the Brothers and the priest had been on very good terms. I first saw the Brothers on Wednesday morning: they were in good spirits and only said that they had not asked for me so quick, but that they were glad to have me. They then related their sorrows to me without excessive bitterness, with the exception that Brother Basil said that if he did not get tables for his class, a desk, etc., he would not teach for another quarter. I think he has already changed dispositions since I have planned an agreement, yet I have not had the opportunity of asking him whether he had ever been tempted to leave the Institution. I asked Brother Aloysius, and he said he had never had a serious idea of leaving, but he told me that Brother Basil and himself had been several times on the point of abandoning their school for the want of support from the priest and relief from Notre Dame du Lac. You reproach them without having written to you often enough, but they make you and Father Granger just the same reproach, and they say they wrote twice as many letters as you wrote to them.

I have made several visits in Brooklyn and New York, and everywhere I have heard the same story. Everyone blames Brother Basil and praises Brother Aloysius, yet I do not find Brother Basil guilty of anything substantial or considerable. They say that he is dirty, suspicious, severe, and ill treats Brother Aloysius. I know that the first and last accusations are false. The first originates with Mr. Twomy when Brother Basil was sick. Brother Aloysius tells me that he and Brother Basil have always been on good terms.

The reputation of the school is not excellent because about thirty pupils have been refused, Brother Aloysius being unable [to] teach bookkeeping, algebra and geometry. I have ascertained that the Brothers did not perform their religious exercises very regularly, but I don't wonder at it, considering the state of their minds. On the whole, I say that the Brothers ought not to be blamed; if they have done many things out of the way, they could not well help it. All that you have to do is to blame yourself and then give Brother Vincent a sound scolding. I think, however, that Brother Basil's reputation is lost and that it will never do to leave him as director in any parish of Brooklyn: Mr. Bacon tells me that not a single priest (Mr. Snelles, for instance, who, however, is very desirous to get Brothers) would have him.

You will therefore have to prepare another Brother for next year. That Brother should know the principles of writing, bookkeeping, algebra and geometry perfectly. I will not have time to teach Brother Aloysius algebra and geometry because I will undertake to show the two Brothers how to keep their schools according to the Conduite (tho' I don't know it myself) like two children, and consequently I will have to teach before them, to inspect their children and classify them. They must absolutely adopt this system which is also followed in the other Catholic, etc., schools of Brooklyn, or the establishment will soon be ruined.

I have agreed to take the school on our own account which was, as I understand from Mr. Bacon, your primitive agreement. I enclose the plan which you will please return with the corrections, which you may think absolutely necessary to make, and an authorisation that I may conclude it. For my part, I prefer this plan much to

Brother Vincent's. Mr. Bacon has read the plan, striking out only one line as you may see, and he is very willing to sign the agreement. You will do well, however, when you write to him that you approve the conditions, to appear to attach great importance to having the tables, and desks, privy and place in church regulated promptly in conformity with the Regulations, because the two Brothers are disgusted at his neglect in this respect. There is a condition in it which the Brothers will dislike very much, and that is the care of the Sunday School, composed of over one hundred boys that do not come to school on weekdays, who are exceedingly wicked and who mingle with our own boys in the schoolroom and the church. Mr. Bacon will not give up this point, and I think myself that he is partly right. All that I could obtain from him was that he would give them as soon as possible a separate schoolroom and place in the church, and tho' he would not have the first part inserted in the agreement, because he says he does not think he will ever be able to find a room. You will do well to write to the Brothers that they may submit to this necessity and to the priest that he may make some endeavor to execute his promise promptly. I have not thought proper to oblige the priest to furnish small articles such as a clock, broom, etc. In my opinion these small articles give more trouble than they are worth, both to the priest and Brothers.

Now to show you what the revenue of the establishment of the school will be, I calculate as follows:

Two smart Brothers, one of them knowing bookkeeping, algebra and geometry can teach 150 boys, and they will have this number at Assumption Church. But supposing the average to be 100 pupils, as at present, and taking Mr. Bacon's prices, which, however, we may double, if we have a mind to, as is done in some other schools, we will have about

25 boys at	$1.50	=	37.50
25 "	2.00	=	50.00
25 "	2.25	=	62.50
25 "	4.00	=	100.00

(Mr. Bacon would charge 5 or 6)
But there are 4 quarters in a year $250.00 X 4—1000.00

Two Brothers will cost, taking highest prices for board and fuel during 12 mo. at $7 a week =	364.00	
Clothing each $25	50.00	
Travelling each $60	120.00	
Rewards of boys (mostly covered by sales of books) and other small articles (say)	66.00	600.00
Sure nett gain		400.00

Yet I have taken the lowest retributions and highest expenses and as if we kept house, we could save nearly one third. I say that if things were carried on properly and on a great scale, each Brother could honor a dft of $300 a year.

But to show you that I do not speak at random, I will lay before you the account of the establishment, stating at first that the school has been mismanaged, that many pupils have been refused, that many have been received for nothing, and that our reputation is not good.

The Brothers owe only the board of one week	7.00
They borrowed money from Mr. Bacon	16.38
They received for books sold for Mr. Bacon	17.47
The journeys of the two Brothers to N.Y. cost	40.00
	80.85

I might have calculated 1/2 quarter in advance.

They have cash	16.00
They gave Brother Vincent	16.00
Mr. Bacon collected some of their money, at least	5.00
They have boys owing for past time	60.00
	97.00
Showing nett profit (which would pay for the clothes they have worn out since they came)	$16.15

In my rough estimate, I do not charge the journeys of Father Drouelle, Father Superior, Brothers Vincent, Victer, and Ignatius against the establishment, for they did not do any good to it. A single letter might have done more. If the directing Brother had been smart, he might have come in advance and made the agreement and then the expenses would have stood heretofore as I have marked them. Of course, my own journey has not done any good for the past.

I must also state here that Mr. Bacon will not claim anything of that which he has heretofore advanced, provided we held him acquitted and begin everything anew again. He has very likely advanced different ways above $50 of money and things which he is not obliged to furnish by the agreement.

To terminate what I have at present to say about the school, I will tell you that I do not promise to have your Constitutions before August. Perhaps I will not have time to translate any, having to drill two Brothers and two hundred boys, and also very likely to teach 5 1/2 hours of class besides 2 1/2 hours to Brother Aloysius, to manage all the affairs of the school, which will require frequent journeys to New York of not less than 2 1/2 hours each time, and also spending about 1 1/2 hours each day going to the school room from the boarding house, etc., etc., etc., Besides, Mr. Bayer is absent and I cannot see Dunnigan before he returns.

As to the boarding house of the Brothers, it is pretty comfortable, tho' it is a bathhouse, and we will have to leave it on the first of May. But being so far from the school house, the Brothers cannot take their dinner before five o'clock: they have been unable to find a house nearer. They pay seven dollars, including their washing and fuel. I think their reasons for leaving Mr. Twomy were sufficient, but Brother Basil left him too abruptly. There would not have been any difficulty, if Brother Vincent had not employed Mr. Bayer in the business and if Mr. Twomy had not in a manner been obliged to take the house for the sake of the Brothers. Mr. Twomy has also, I believe, some reasons for being disatisfied. If I believed Mrs. Parmentier, I would have to take the two Brothers for liars. Both of them say they had not enough to eat and that their room was not light. Mrs. Parmentier says the room was comfortable and the food sufficient and that a young man who boarded there was satisfied. Mr. Bacon says he does not know who is right. He does not blame the Brothers, but he thinks Brother Basil left too quick on acount of certain suspicions and without consulting anyone. On the other hand, Brother Vincent himself complained of the food to Mr. Bacon once. I believe, therefore, that the Brothers' motives were good, but the execution badly managed. I think Mr. Twomy was wronged, but having at present a family where the Brothers used to be, I do not think he is entitled to getting much from you. The persons that have most suffered from the transaction have been, if I mistake not, Mr. Bayer and Mrs. Parmentier. If you concluded to pay anything, I think you should do it thro' Mr. Bayer.

I have seen Mr. Erben who is ready to accommodate you with an organ of $2000 as soon as you may have a mind to buy it and to take the other back at a reasonable price. I saw him selling one today like ours for $350, half cash down and the balance in six months. He hopes you will soon be able to remit him the balance due him. As to the remittance of the duty, he asked if you had petitioned or intended to do it, and if Mr. Bayer had not been employed already, he said he would write to you on the subject.

I went to the Truth Teller's office today and got a professor advertised.

As I did not stop for any time in Detroit, of course I did not speak to Mr. Shawe.

I saw Mrs. Parmentier who made a bitter complaint against Brother Basil.

I sent to France the letters which were given to me at the Lake. I returned to Mr. Hugh Kelly his cloth, the receipt of which I enclose as well as the draft which he returned to me. I handed to Mr. McDonough Mr. McCoster's letter.

As I have remarked, you do things only by halves. You sent me to No. 286 in Bridge Street. There is no such number. Mrs. Parmentier stays at No. 280.

I wish you would hand to Brother Stephen and Mr. Shortis the notes which I enclose, and as I think of it, you ought to recommend to Brother Stephen never to write to anyone out of doors without showing you his notes or letters—the one he wrote to Mr. Cherse was full of mistakes. You need not tell him for he would be mad: he thinks he is a great speller.

Once more I will tell you that you give wrong directions over the half of the time. When I asked you [for] $40 for my journey, I was nearer the truth than those who said I would spend but $25. Here is my account:

Feb. 15, 1849		Cars from Niles to Detroit	5.70
"	16	Breakfast 2f, dinner and supper each 3f	1.00
"	16	Fare from Detroit to Buffalo	14.00
"	17	3 meals, each 3f	1.12 1/2

" 18	Breakfast 2f, supper 4f	.75
" 18	Fare from Buffalo to Albany	9.75
" 19	Supper 2f, Bed 2f	.50
	Amt. carried forward	$32.82 1/2
Feb. 20, 1849	Breakfast 2f, Ferry at Albany 2f	.50
" 20	Fare from Albany to New York	4.00
" 20	Carriage from City Hall to Fuller Ferry	.50
" 20	Ferry 5 c, porter 6 c, carriage from ferry to Bacon's church 2f	.36
" 20	Dinner	.38
	Loss in exchange for not having had Canadian money in Canada	.05
		$38.61 1/2
	I received from you	60.00
	Balance in my hands	21.38 1/2

I gave $15 to Brother Aloysius who is our treasurer. Thus the establishment had on hand (February 22nd) $31. I keep the balance to settle your small account viz., $6.38 1/2.

Questions (Send me answers).

Would you not allow the Brothers to have but one class a day, commencing at 9 o'clock and ending at 2 or half past 2 PM, merely giving the boys 20 minutes for their dinner as is done in other schools? Then our Brothers could take a good dinner at half past 2 and they would be sure to have all their boys in the afternoon. Mr. Bacon, the Brothers and myself would prefer this method.

I want you to send me the amount of expenses made for journeys on account of our school and all that the Lake has spent on its account. You will find these accounts in the books in the secretary's office. I want the explanations and exact amounts that I may begin account books and chronicles.

How many copies of the Constitutions must be printed for the postulants? How many for the novices and how many for the professed, and will you have the same number printed for the Sisters as for the Brothers?

I think Mr. Bacon ought also to furnish a stove for each classroom and a clock for each. I forgot to put them in the agreement and to ask them of him, and I do not like to trouble him about that myself, but you may yourself require them of him when you write and then I will insert them in the agreement.

[Final page of 2-23-49 trans. from French]

Can one lend his Constitutions to a priest? I somewhat violated article 194 of the Constitutions in promising to furnish all the small, necessary objects for the classrooms like awards, pictures, brooms, switches, etc., because these conditions could have become a subject of dispute through the agreement. On another matter, we are not obliged to teach class for six hours, but five or five and a half suffice. If I'd forgotten some noteworthy things, you can write to Mr. Bacon and to me. In writing in regard to the stoves and the clock, you could perhaps ask for something for the Sunday School which he absolutely wants to load on us and which the Brothers hate so much, though this would only be to furnish necessary rewards to maintain competition there.

You should write to my two Brothers so they try to conform and apply themselves to the teaching method I'm going to show them. I know they have objections, and I have some fears they'll not submit entirely. We have to choose a Brother director immediately for next year, to make him learn algebra, geometry and bookkeeping or at least one of the three because it's impossible for Brother Louis de Gonzague to learn the three during the summer.

Yours,

Brother Gatian

154. Brother Gatian (8) to Father Sorin

Brooklyn February 26, 1849

Reverend Father Superior,

Yesterday I had a trial of the Sunday School boys of Brooklyn: a more desparate set I never saw. They laughed, talked, fought, bawled out in the schoolroom and mutinied three or four times before High Mass, like so many wild Indians. I have taken charge of them myself, because the other two Brothers do not wish to have anything more to do with them. I do not wonder at their dispositions in this respect, for I almost believe it an impossibility for two Brothers that have 106 boys of their own to take charge of one hundred more on Sundays. However, it is also an impossibility to make an agreement with Mr. Bacon unless we take charge of these boys. He moreover says that it will be so wherever we may go to in Brooklyn and New York, and that if we abandon the establishment, it will be a long time before we again set a foot in the diocese as the bishop and other persons are daily in expectation of a failure or at least are reserved and do not wish to make any advances towards us until they see how things will turn out. These difficulties have induced me to write this morning, that if this letter reaches you before you have answered my letter of the 23rd inst., you may take them in consideration. I may assure you that you will not find one Brother in ten that will be ready to take charge of this Sunday School. If you conclude to take charge of the School of Sundays, which you must do to preserve the establishment, you might perhaps ask for a certain renumeration for this very circumstance may oblige us in many instances to have three Brothers instead of two.

I have also ascertained from Mr. Bacon that Brother Basil must leave, even before the end of the year. Everybody dislikes him, and as long as he has anything to do with the school, people will keep away: his manners, it seems, are exceedingly disagreeable. And for my part, tho' I do not believe Brother Basil very quilty, as I have already stated, yet I think the complaints of ill humour, suspiciousness, and want of courage and good will laid against him are somewhat grounded. He is not obliging. He would have everybody for himself and before nobody, as Mr. Bacon expresses it. And since we must at any rate have another Brother for director next year, would it not be better to make the change as soon as the agreement will have been concluded and to send him on as soon as the navigation opens? If he were here at the end of March, I might show him the manner of teaching, which I am now studying hard every day, and fit him to teach as far as algebra or geometry might be concerned. He should be a good writer, active, open hearted, learned and courageous. I am afraid you have none of the kind to send me, but why did you take the establishment? Brother Thomas, I believe, is less objectionable than any other, but he is a poor writer and too young. I must say that Brother Basil has told me plainly that he would not teach here after another session.

Our board being so high ($10.50 a week), and the boarding house so far as to occasion a considerable loss of time, I have resolved to look for another place, should I find but a hotel or Protestant house. Please object, if you have objections.

The Brothers use the cow hide in their schools, which is against our Rules, but I tolerate this and ask for a dispensation: the boys are too bad. I do not believe that I can wait for an answer, and I think I will have to use it myself before two weeks.

I have consulted Mr. Bayer with respect to the duties paid on the musical instruments, in pursuance to H. Erben's advice, and he tells me that as long as the money was unpaid, there were hopes, but it being paid down, he says the amount would not pay the trouble that would have to be gone through to recover the duty.

About Mr. Twomy's affair, Mr. Bayer does not at all seem excited, and he offers me his services. From him I have partly understood that the Brothers were in a manner requested to look for a boarding house, if they could not be satisfied where they were, but it was Brother Basil that obliged them to come to such extremes by his being so very dirty, unreasonable, sneaky, and rude, Mr. Twomy appears to have been very moderate. He has not complained of the circumstances that have occasioned all your and our difficulties. He has not asked for an indemnity, to which Mr. Bayer says he has a right, but has merely expressed his regret to Mrs. Parmentier once that Brother Basil had so distressed him, upon which Mrs. Parmentier has requested Mr. Bayer to ask you for an indemnity, were it but $20. Mr. Beyer and Mrs. Parmentier have not spoken to Mr. Twomy of this indemnity, but they would be very glad that he should have it, because, as I said in my previous letter, it was in pursuance of your requests and Brother Vincent's, that Mr. Bayer induced Mr. Twomy to move. My opinion then upon the subject, tho 'not absolute, is that $25 should be remitted to Mr. Twomy thro' Mr. Bayer. This would reconcile Mr. Bayer and Mr. Bacon, Mrs. Parmentier, and perhaps some others would feel reconciled. All would be greatly eased by the absence of Brother Basil. Mr. Bayer does not blame any person in particular for our misfortunes in Brooklyn. He attributes the whole to your sending the Brothers before having concluded agreements and without waiting for an answer from him (Mr. Bacon), as you had promised and do with respect to the boarding house.

Times indeed appear daily more gloomy in proportion to my better acquaintance with people and places. I am from time to time inclined to think there is some truth in the suspicions of the Brothers and the rumors of town about Mr. Bacon's indisposition towards us. What I know for certain is that he certainly has the greatest aversion to Brother Basil.

I had an idea of buying at once all the small articles for the schools, such as they are required by the Conduit, but considering the doubtful dispositions of Mr. Bacon and being glad to appear to listen to Brother Basil's advice in order to keep on good terms, until you can effect a change, I have resolved to buy only good points and crosses until the agreement is finally settled.

It is now 10 o'clock P.M. I have been trotting all the afternoon in Brooklyn in the mud and rain, looking for boarding houses. I also went to Mr. Bayer's with whom I have become acquainted for the first time. I expect I shall go [to] New York tomorrow before I finish this letter in order to see E. Dunigan. I have been offered a room furnished, board and light, in a public boarding house near our school for $2.50 ahead per week. If the house is Catholic, I think we shall move, tho' Brother Aloysius objects a great deal to the company which we will have there. But we will save four or five hours time every day and #3.37 1/2 a week: judge the case, if we do not anticipate. We have [a] good many Brethren here anyhow, for we are all Quakers. At least we pass for such, and when we pass thro' the streets, boys and others will say to each other in a low voice: See! see the Quakers. Our dress and that of Quakers are nearly alike.

February 27, 11 o'clock A.M.

I have been in New York this morning trotting in the mud, and I have begun making expenses for our doubtful school, always upon the principle that should it fail next summer, you would still want to keep it until then. I went to Mr. Arnault in Rose Street, No. 10, to get crosses made out of German silver at 15 cents. I bought a tape measure in Liberty St., No. 67, that I may translate the Constitutions and Conduit properly. At Dunigan's I have made a bill of [MS blank] in the name of the school of the Brothers of St. Joseph, for books and paper now necessary to translate the Conduit and Constitutions and also for the use of the Brothers' school. The printing of good points will cost about $5. Mr. Dunigan has received $50 from Mr. Rooney and the dft on the city bank of $8.50. He has given you credit for $4.25 for the things which he had bot of you, but had forgotten it heretofore. The several payments amount to $62.75. His credit is $125.13. Consequently the balance due him is $62.38. I would have enough of money to pay him $12.38, leaving a clear amount of $50 to be paid by Mr. Rooney, but I will not pay until the agreement be concluded with Mr. Bacon.

Tell Mr. Shortis to make the necessary entries in Rooney's and Dunigan's accounts and also in the Acc.of City Bank. I have consulted him about the printing of the Constitutions, and he says that 250 copies of each kind would not cost much more than 100 copies. He cannot say exactly to how much the printing of each will come to, but he calculates that each will cost about $180, making $540 for the Brothers, and those of the Sisters would cost about $100 less for each which would make $240 or for the whole $780.

You must not rely on the above calculation, however, because I forgot to mention that the great part of the printing was the same for the three books. This will make a difference of 3/4 or $585, which would reduce the whole cost of the six books to $195. I shall inquire again in a few days and then write to you.

3 o'clock P.M. I have just been at Mr. Bayer's. He has settled with Mr. C. Meletta: I enclose the receipt. I have paid Mr. Bayer the balance due him so that all the business which I had to do for you in New York is about terminated. The musical books, etc., cannot, of course, be bought before the navigation opens.

I enclose two notes or rather I will write on this page of this sheet for Mr. Shortis and Brother Stephen. I will buy a phonographical reader for Brother Thomas as soon as the navigation opens, if you do not send him to New York. If you sent him on now, it would cost him $4.00 less than it did me because the fare from Detroit to Buffalo was reduced from $14 to $10, three days after I had left Detroit.

In concluding, I will entreat you once more to consider your affair of Brooklyn well which must be carried on a great scale and by smart men in order to succeed. Answer all my letters and questions promptly, for a delay might prove very injurious. I have been here but one week. Many things have been done, but many more, so many more, remain undone. Mr. Bacon will have a great deal to do if he stand to the agreement and gets the necessary tables, seats, etc.

My compliments to all and my love to the apprentices and boarders,

Your obedient son,

Brother Gatian

155. Brother Gatian (9) to Father Sorin
[Translated from French]

Brooklyn March 1, 1849

My Father,

I've finally found a suitable boardinghouse near the church, but not without a lot of trouble. We found ourselves at the point of being put out on the pavement or seeking refuge in some public hotel. When I paid Mr. Mellaugh yesterday, I asked him if he couldn't lower our board, at least during Lent. It seemed that he took offence at that and blamed circumstances which obliged him to tell us last night that they could no longer lodge us after next Tuesday. I, who had already almost made my deal with Miss Murphy in New York, found myself very embarrassed because she couldn't come to Brooklyn for a fortnight. Happily Mr. and Mrs. Malloy, who presently live or will live with Miss Murphy, wanted to offer us shelter while waiting. I haven't bargained with these latter people, leaving everything to their generosity. They're the ones who introduced me to the Murphy family. She is a good Catholic, who lives with her mother, sister, and brother-in-law. Her sister has a little baby. Although this is a private boardinghouse, she's asking from me only three dollars for food, lodging, laundry, and mending, but I had to promise to have at least two Brothers for a year starting in May or to furnish her with two boarders in case we left. This last condition is a little difficult to fill, but as I'd found no other private boardinghouse, I'd have to pay exorbitant prices. It was also impossible for us to wait since we had to leave our boardinghouse and we had nowhere to go. Anyway, I prayed before I took my first steps, and I hope that the Blessed Virgin guided me in the steps I took this morning.

The contract isn't yet written, but I believe there'll be no difficulty. I could have consulted the Lake by telegraph to find out if my letter of February 23 had reached you yesterday, but as I expected that you hadn't received it, I thought I had to finish my deals without consulting you since you wouldn't have known how to respond. We'll gain three hours a day, and we'll save about $1.50 a week, by my calculation. While it's true that we won't have heat in our private room, nor light, the light'll cost scarcely 50 cents a month, and $5 of coal will keep us warm in winter. In summer we won't need heat.

Mr. Bacon continues to be out of sorts; he does nothing for the school. Brother Basil is the cause of it all. Send me $40 so I can send him back to you. The prejudice against him is insurmountable. Send me a capable Brother and above all one who doesn't *piss in bed* because the story is around town that one of the Brothers is very dirty, slovenly, and pisses in bed. Next Saturday we have to go into our temporary boardinghouse. I'd like it to be the last one that notices the bed-wetter. If I were sure of having another Brother in a fortnight, I'd send Brother Basil away immediately. Hurry up because while waiting I haven't yet touched the Constitutions, and I can only get to them when the contract is signed and things are cleaned up. I haven't yet visited the Brothers' classroom, but I'll begin to set that right tomorrow. I don't think I can get that from Mr. Bacon before the contract is signed and Brother Basil has left.

I saw Mr. Dunigan this morning in regard to the Constitutions and he can't give me an exact figure, but the sum won't much exceed $250 (for everything).

I continue to make debts (small ones) for the school, trying to save it, which isn't easy with a priest like Mr. Bacon. I'm not passing judgement totally against Mr. Bacon until Brother Basil leaves. When Brother Basil is gone, we'll see if Mr. Bacon's sentiments are in our favor or not, because up to now, he hasn't complained about me and he praises Brother Louis de Gonzague.

Reply as soon as you've received this letter, by telegram if you wish, because then I'll be ready to tutor a class for a week or two while waiting for the sending of another Brother.

My respects to the priests and Brothers and my best wishes to everybody and especially to the apprentices and boarders.

I have the honor of being, father, your obedient son,

Brother Gatian

Direct your letter to 108 York Street, Brooklyn.

P.S. Should the Brothers be made to recite the various prayers noted in the Conduit? It seems that Father Rector decided that there'd be prayer only at the beginning and at the end. Answer.

156. Brother Gatian (10) [to Father Sorin]
[Fragment of letter]

[Brooklyn] March 1, 1849

To succeed in Brooklyn, we should do things on a great scale and keep a house for ourselves. If we had 3 Brothers at St. James's, 3 at St. Mary's and lay Brothers to cook for them in some room in Jay Street which we could have for $4.50 a month, we would spare a great deal of money and avoid disagreeable changes of boarding-houses.

In each of these establishments, the directing Brother at least should be an uncommonly smart man understanding the plan of teaching perfectly, experienced and learned, and knowing life, especially in the cities of New York and Brooklyn.

Brother Gatian

157. Brother Joseph (51) to Father Sorin

Indianapolis March 1, 1849

Reverend and dear Father,

By the present I inform you of a visit we had from the bishop. He is determined to propose [to] you to change the college into an orphan assylum which, if you consent to, he will assist you with all his might. If, on the contrary, you refuse to do it, he will have part in the profit of the property of Indianapolis. He thinks that this assylum will be more advantageous to the Community and to the diocese. I write to you concerning it that you might be prepared for it.

The pasture is not surveighed yet, but it will be done this week.

I remain, dear Father, with respect and love, your most obedient but unworthy son,

Brother Joseph

158. Brother Gatian (11) to Father Sorin

Brooklyn March 4, 1849

Reverend Father Superior,

Mr. Ryan, lately imprisoned by her Majesty the Queen of Great Britain, has introduced his friend to me, John Ryan, Tenth St. No. 353, N.Y., as a professor of mathematics. He has been a teacher for twenty years either in Europe or in America. He is an Irishman and was professor for three years at St. John's College, Fordham, before the Jesuits took possession of it. He is at present out of employ and wishes to settle in the West. He is married and would take his wife along and his three children, two of whom would become boarders and learn the Latin and Greek. He would take a house in South Bend for his wife and daughter. He wants merely to gain enough to support his two sons at college and his wife and daughter at home. He asks to have his two sons taught Latin and Greek which would be each year

	240.00
He wants moreover in cash	150.00
and for his journey to the Lake	100.00
	$490.00

He would teach six hours a day and would bind himself for any number of years. He is well acquainted with Davies' Course and will give me testimonials to prove the same. I think he is inferior to Jerome Hackett in philosophy and chemistry. He says he knows the theory but cannot experiment. He was going to be a professor at a public academy but was objected to on account of his being a Catholic. If the agreement were made for three years, it would come to about $70 an hour. If you approve the conditions, answer by telegraph that I may conclude the agreement. However, you may answer by letter if you wish, whether you approve or not. But at any rate, answer promptly. You would do well to state in your answer what the professor would have to pay a year in South Bend for his wife and daughter for boarding and lodging.

Yesterday we moved to No. 108 where we will be provisionally taken care of until Miss Murphy, with whom I have not yet finally agreed, shall move to No. 108, for which she has not yet completed arrangements. We are indeed in precarious circumstances. Mr. Bacon does not appear favorable, and our reputation is not good. The Brothers are tired out and homesick. I wish Brother Basil were gone, but I do not like to send him until I have another Brother because Brother Aloysius is frequently sick. He had the fever and ague last Thursday and again yesterday. Today I have again made a fruitless attempt at taming the Sunday School boys. They are cases indeed, and I doubt the success of my persev[er]ance.

Yesterday I examined the class of Brother Aloysius and found the boys generally smart, but the class is a tower of Babel, and next week will determine whether things can be regulated or not. I shall teach myself the class of Brother Aloysius perhaps during the whole week, and I will then take Brother Basil's class and send him to the Lake, if your telegraphic answer to my letter of the first inst. allows me to draw on you for $40 and lets me know that another Brother is coming.

I have not asked Mr. Bacon to hear the boys' confessions once a month because I have understood that he hears them only once a year. And as he is unwilling to do anything for the school at present (and I think he will be in these dispositions until an agreement is made), I do not like to trouble him about anything except that which is indispensably necessary. The Brothers say that Mr. Bacon will let the school run out and appear to speak with good grounds, but my judgment shall remain in suspense until the agreement is made or about to be made. Mr. Bacon says that Brother Basil is the sole cause of the dissatisfaction and distrust.

[Remainder of 3-4-49 translated from French]

This Brother Basil, he says, is fit only to disrupt a community, and if he were alone, I'd gladly have him crucified in the street, and if they hadn't found a house when they left Mr. Twomy's, I'd have taken Brother Aloysius to my house, but I'd have left the other at the door.

Since some paper is left, I'm going to scold you. You told me I'd be told things frankly, and you'd always alleviate difficulties. Thus you had said I'd have no class, and here I have classes ten times as difficult as those at the Lake. All this time, I'm growing old, etc., etc. I've become hard of hearing, and I can hardly see. Teaching is killing me.

Yours,

Brother Gatian

N.B. I have run up a bill of about $15 at Dunigann's for the school, etc.

159. Brother Gatian (12) to Father Sorin
[Translated from French]

Brooklyn, 108 York Street March 12, 1849

My Father,

Eight days ago I wrote you in regard to the professor, and up until now I have no response to any of my letters. I have nothing in particular to write to you about this morning, but I can't stop from opening my heart to you to explain things that you don't seem to act on and you don't seem yet to understand what are, in my judgement, established principles.

I've been unhappy for a week, in the greatest dejection, a prey to the cruellest anguish, but, thanks to God, I haven't yet fallen to the foolish temptation which has frequently attacked me, and I hope nobody's sensed my sadness. The cause of my troubles and of my Brothers' is the insufferable position in which your imprudence has put us, and of your blind haste in the Brooklyn business. It is humanly (enough reasons to omit the word humanly) impossible that Mr. Bacon's establishment will succeed, and it was always impossible that it would succeed, as you would sense yourself if you had wanted to follow the lights of simple good sense and the decisive opinion I gave when you consulted me one evening in the Minor Chapter when it was a question of sending Brothers. It's impossible to succeed here for two reasons: the first is the incompetence of our Brothers and the second Mr. Bacon's presence.

I said our Brothers without exception are incapable of teaching school in the countryside and moreso in a city. I said they're incompetent first, because none (Brother Basil excepted) has method, and second, because they're all ignorant of some branch both essential and absolutely indispensable, or they have flaws which make them incapable of teaching. I could muster all in review for you, and I'd find a flaw which couldn't be satisfied in each Brother. Beginning with me! I don't know penmanship and I'm too deaf for a big class. Brother Victor is absolutely too deaf and too weak in arithmetic and grammar for an upper class. Brother Thomas doesn't know how to write. Brother Anselm is too weak in everything. Brother Ignatius is absolutely too simple. Brother Benoit is too singular. Brother Emmanuel is German.

I have here without question the two most incompetent Brothers, and while they have the best of intentions, they could never succeed. Brother Basil can teach only the low level class, and Brother Louis de Gonzague is absolutely too weak for the highest level class. Isn't it shameful for him and even more for you (my Father) to watch this poor Brother begin to make his students write and then to show them how to write in general terms, then when they finally know how to write, to find writing samples lined with spelling errors? I could have written better, although I myself don't know how to write. Isn't it absurd to watch this same Brother give individual lessons in a class of 58 children who make as much noise as our boarders at the Lake make in one of their ordinary recreation periods? This poor Brother understands his weaknesses, but he doesn't know how to correct them, never having received lessons. I tried to regularize his class (although I was as ignorant of method as he when I left the Lake), and I spent the whole week at it. I arranged them as best I could, but Thursday morning I left his students with him in despair, not being able to succeed in establishing silence there, nor subordination, because, not seeing clearly, or hearing very well, I wasn't able to know where the noise was coming from, and I couldn't understand the lessons they recited to me. He tried Thursday and Friday, with all his heart, to follow the plan I'd laid out, and this morning for the first time in ten days, he taught without me—which proves to me that you were really wrong to endanger the vocation and talents of Brother Louis de Gonzague. In spite of all the disorder and noise in his class, he has influence and is very calm, not abusing anyone with the whip which he uses frequently.

I had merit points printed up and bought some crosses which have been distributed for the first time. If we had two capable Brothers, now classes could turn to instruction. I have great reservations about Brother Louis's class. This week's experiences will make me see if he'll be skilled at it or let it fall into the chaos I've half discovered. I promised a thousand Aves last Thursday if order were reestablished in this class. I wouldn't have the slightest doubt that the Blessed Virgin wished to remove us from shame were it not so much *our* or rather *your* fault. Because it was evidently to tempt God that you made this foundation, and such are the fatal results of this stupid enterprise that you can always say “mea culpa.”

I haven’t examined Brother Basil’s class, and I don’t know if I can do it before knowing if you’re going to call him back. The two Brothers are completely disgusted, and they told me positively they wouldn’t teach any longer at Mr. Bacon’s for the Pope once this year is over. Brother Louis de Gonzague seems even more broken down, and he’s apparently less regular and zealous than Brother Basil: I fear for his vocation. It’s possible however that once Brother Basil left, he’d come into better feelings and he’d consent to stay another year at Brooklyn, provided he not be ill-used nor obliged to teach an advanced class like the one he has at present, above all if I can succeed in showing him the principles of writing or algebra, etc., which I nevertheless believe impossible, as I’ve already told you.

The second reason for the impossibility of success is the presence of Mr. Bacon. Experience proves to me every day the Brothers are very much correct in complaining about him. It’s impossible to get even the basic necessities from him. He’s ill humored, prepossessed, moody and wants everything his way. In the church, for example, 95 children sit where 70 can scarcely fit comfortably, and the Brothers are required to stand during all services. I also find by experience that two Brothers can never take care of their students and the Sunday School children; even now that there are three of us, we can scarcely do it. Yesterday we had about 225 students in our classes which, according to the Constitutions, should have only 123. I now believe it would be imprudent to take assignments with this priest unless he changes his behavior, or you’ll surely lose your Brothers here. I don’t believe you could find Brothers willing to suffer as long as have Brother Basil and Brother Louis de Gonzague. I now share the opinion of these two Brothers: that is, it’s impossible for two Brothers to take care of their own students and those of the congregation [Sunday School]; it’s impossible for children to behave when they have so little space in church, and it’s impossible to continue the school if the classes are not better equipped with tables, desks, and blackboards. That’s why I’m determined to let this establishment sink right now rather than make the Brothers teach Sunday School, before having hope of getting tables, desks, blackboards, and suitable curtains. If you judge it better to expose the Brothers to all these inconveniences which will lose the establishment before the end of the year, tell me by telegraph. If you judge it necessary to lose the establishment rather than the great majority of Brothers you'd send here, binding them to the above described inconveniences, write me by telegraph, so that I'll know what to do.

I have yet to ask a sum of $150 or $200 for the first year and $50 or $75 for the following years, and to get classroom furniture as we see fit. This step would make us more independent of Mr. Bacon. If you approve or disapprove, write me by telegraph.

Brother Louis de Gonzague is still often sick. I bought him a bottle of Cholagogue ($1.50). Brother Basil has a bad cough, and I have a small one, but I'm better than the other two Brothers.

We're still in our boardinghouse provided with a nice old man and old woman. I paid at the rate of $3.25 per person yesterday for board, lodging, heat and light, with laundry. I haven't yet finished bargaining with Miss Murphy who hasn't yet taken the rent from Number 108. I wanted her not to take it before we'd finished our agreement with Mr. Bacon. But, that's a vain desire. Spending about $12 per week, I have trouble believing that the school in its state of vegetation can support us up to the end of the year. We need about $180 here the month of July for board and little expenses. We've got only three weeks advance right now. It'll soon be necessary perhaps to call on you. We owe about fifteen dollars at Dunigan's and we'll have to take yet about ten dollars at his place from now to the end of the year. We don't have summer habits nor enough personal items. We'll have expenses.

My love to everyone,

Brother Gatian

160. Brother Gatian (13) to Father Sorin

Brooklyn March 16, 1849

Reverend Father Superior,

I shall close my visit this evening and send you the result of my labors and the determinations which I have taken, after a mature consideration of three weeks. You will please approve or disapprove the decrees by the first mail, that I may not be left in the dark.

I have not received any letters yet from you, and by this time, however, I ought to have several and also some telegraphic despatches. The Brothers and myself are becoming very impatient in our terrestrial hell: they wish, with very good reasons, the downfall of the establishment, and interiorly I am of the same opinion. It appears evident to me that at present no Brother is able to teach at Brooklyn and still more plain that no Brother will consent to teach for any length of time at Father Bacon's church. Being fully persuaded of these truths and also that it would be no harm if you had no establishment in New York or Brooklyn for two or three years, during which it would be proper to have Brothers Aloysius, Anselm, Thomas and Lewis taught by some experienced professor or sent to a college, I have taken the determination of speaking right up and down with Mr. Bacon and to abandon the establishment and all expenses we have made, with the exception of such as we could recover by law. I shall probably propose one of three following agreements.

First, if Mr. Bacon wants a permanent establishment, he must at once free the Brothers from the Sunday School, give a gratuitous place sufficient for 200 pupils in the church, procure a room of 1496 foot square for the commencement of next scholastic year, furnish before the 22nd of next April 3 desks, 3 blackboards, a seat for Brother Basil, a partition in the schoolroom and curtains.

Second, the above will probably be rejected at once and then I will propose the following compromise, viz., we will agree to stay until the end of the year if he consent to keep our intended departure secret, to furnish the articles above mentioned for the 22nd of April, and to keep Brother Basil. This last article will be a hard pill to both Mr. Bacon and Brother Basil. In this second case, I would leave free to choose between paying the Brothers $60 per month in advance, freeing them from the trouble of collecting or letting us collect, and himself paying for boys admitted at an underprice.

Third, if he does not consent to the above, I will propose to leave on the 22nd of April, the end of the present quarter, allowing us to collect all that will then be due by the pupils or at once now if he consent to pay us our present due without minding what he has advanced.

Should you have too great an aversion for any one of these three proposals, you might let me know by telegraph. I shall try not to conclude anything before next Saturday, tho' the Brothers will scarcely suffer me to wait so long.

I spent yesterday and the previous day in visiting Brother Basil's class. I find less disorder than in the other, but it is still very imperfect, tho' only thro' Mr. Bacon's fault. For instance, his boys do additions and subtractions, tho' they are ignorant of numeration, and this because they have no blackboard. They write and yet have no writing tables.

Brother Basil on the whole appears much less indisposed, much more zealous and regular than Brother Aloysius who is slow and very sickly and who, as I said before I left the Lake, is not able to learn by the private lessons I give him, his mind being too much distracted. I told and foretold you everything, but you would not believe.

We have been doctoring our coughs, and our bodies, not our souls, are somewhat relieved. Next Saturday I shall buy another bottle of cholagogue for Brother Aloysius and a bottle of Dr. McNair's acoustic oil for my ears, having lost the sense of hearing of the left ear. I wish you would allow me to consult an optician with respect to my wonderfully decreasing sight. I have thought proper to employ a remedy for my ears at once as it will only cost one dollar, but the consultation might cost more. However, if I do not take the proper means, in a short time I will be unfit, not only for teaching as I am already, but for any kind of business. I have not yet recovered from the shock of the mad dog (Campau) which you set at me. He has taken full vengeance, but he may one day yet become as crazy as I ever was.

I am more uneasy than I ever was at the Lake. No longer restrained by my promises to J. Hays, my wild imagination runs over the whole earth. I am a desparado. It would seem at times that I ought to set the city of New York on fire and even destroy the whole world. Then if I were once alone in the world, no one would contradict me. But again, where would the friend be that would comfort my heart? Friends I have not. John Hays loves me not. I am intimately persuaded that he does not. I can't take it out of my head. Without him, I can't be happy. Why won't he love me? Oh, If I did but see him come to me with open heart, but he won't. And when I take the first step toward him, I always think, even if he says he loves me, I always think, I can't help thinking that he says so only to get rid of me. I do not think it proceeds from his heart as long as he does not make the first step and take me by surprise. O, how homesick I am! How I do love the Lake. How I do love the boys, especially the apprentices. How are the apprentices doing? My best love to them. I [MS torn] care of them. I would like very much to hear from them, to be with them and to press them to my heart. I would like to hear something of my old pupils, of Richard Ferris, John Connolly, Francis Wolke, etc.

What news from the Lake? Have you got the circulars? No news from here, excepting that I am as crazy as ever, yet no [?] takes place because no one contradicts or endeavors to correct me. Am I not a droll fellow? Pray for me. Make the apprentices pray for me. Pray for the [MS torn] that I may speedily settle everything or complete the downfall of the school, if it be God's will, as I think it is.

The Brothers here and myself will offer our prayers and communion for the prompt termination of the affair on St. Joseph's Day. On that day I shall treat the subject, if all my materials are ready. I have paid our debt of $11.81, and when we will have paid our board tomorrow, we will still have enough of money for nearly three weeks of board. We have received nearly $20 this week.

I enclose a few questions on the Constitutions which I have not commenced translating yet. Answer all my questions and you will oblige your obedient servant, respectfully yours,

Brother Gatian

I'm out of my mind. How is my Patrick Clemen? I am very crazy today, yet as reasonable as ever.

161. Brother Gatian (14) to Father Sorin

Brooklyn March 16, 1849

I, the undersigned, in virtue of a Letter of Obedience of Reverend E. Sorin, local superior of Notre Dame du Lac University, of the fourteenth day of the month of February, Anno Domini, one thousand eight hundred & forty nine, appointing me Visitor of the schools of Brooklyn, Fort Wayne, make known, by the present act, to all whom it may concern, that, in compliance with the obligations marked out in the Rule of Visitors, I read my letter of obedience to the Brothers of the School of Brooklyn on the twenty first day of February, Anno Domini, one thousand eight hundred & forty nine & ascertained:

1st. That the establishment of Brooklyn had on hand (as much as the disorderly state of accounts would permit) a balance of sixteen dollars; that an amount of sixty dollars was due by the pupils; that it had a debt of eleven dollars and eighty-one cents, with the immediate necessity of making another of about fifteen dollars for books, crosses, and good points;

2nd. That no agreement of any kind had been made with Reverend D. Bacon, the founder of the establishment, and that the Brothers and he were on that account a burden to each other and greatly indisposed against each other;

3rd. That the Brothers had not sufficient room for their children in the church on Sundays, nor in the schoolrooms, that the privy was disgustingly indecent, the classes not provided with tables, benches, pictures, seats for teachers, blackboards, window curtains, and a play yard as the Conduite requires. That the pupils and teachers were not encouraged by the priest, Reverend D. Bacon, and that, in a word, the school was in a state of destitution.

4th. That the Brothers were charged with the care of the Sunday School, to the great detriment of their own pupils and of the peace of their minds.

5th. That the reputation of the Brothers, and especially that of Brother Basil, was bad in Brooklyn.

6th. That the Brothers were homesick and solemnly protested that they would not teach any longer at Reverend D. Bacon's church.

7th. That the class of Brother Aloysius was a tower of Babel, without so much as the shadow of method, the pupils deficient in nearly every article mentioned in the Constitutions, especially in writing and grammar, the teacher not being sufficiently advanced to teach these branches properly. That catechism was not properly taught by Brother Aloysius, nor the prayers and arithmetic by Brother Basil. That the parents of the pupils created disturbance by their frequent visits during school hours, and that the number and variety of authors tolerated in the class of Brother Aloysius rendered teaching very difficult, if not absolutely impossible.

8th. That the Brothers did not perform their religious exercises regularly, omitting particular examination, spiritual reading, visit to the Blessed Sacrament, and the Chapter.

9th. And finally that the most of the above disorders were the natural results of Reverend Father Superior's unfortunate precipitency in sending Brothers to Brooklyn before having procured them the necessary instructions in science and in the method of conducting children, before having made any agreements or so much as procured lodging for them. And, in virtue of the power granted to me, I have decreed and decree as follows:

Art. I. An agreement shall be made with the least possible delay for the foundation of the school; such agreement shall secure the independence of the Brothers from Reverend D. Bacon so that the school may be entirely under their controul, and Reverend D. Bacon shall bind himself to furnish tables, benches, blackboards, stoves, a privy, clocks, and a gratuitious place in the church with the necessary schoolrooms as the Conduite requires, or he shall pay a sum of money to procure said articles.

Art. II. No agreement shall be made with Reverend D. Bacon if he does not consent to free the Brothers from the Sunday School, this school exposing the Brothers to the loss of their vocation.

Art. III. If no agreement can be made, a compromise shall, if possible, be made in compliance with Reverend Father Superior's instructions.

Art. IV. The sum of twenty-five dollars shall be paid to Mr. Twomy thro Mr. Bayer, as indemnity for the loss suffered by the former on account of the departure of the Brothers from his house.

Art. V. Brother Basil shall be sent home as soon as the agreement shall have been made out and his place shall be filled by some able Brother.

Art. VI. The necessity of giving more instruction to the Brothers and of teaching them how to keep their schools shall be urged upon Reverend Father Superior and the Administration of Notre Dame du Lac.

Art. VII. The necessity of making written agreements and of visiting new establishments before sending Brothers shall also be urged, the failure of the establishment of Brooklyn being justly attributed to the mismanagement of the Minor Chapter and the ignorance of the Brothers.

Art. VIII. The expenses of Father Superior's journey, the expenses of Brothers Basil and Aloysius for their journey and clothing, the travelling expenses of the Visitor both in going and returning and his expenses at Brooklyn from the twentieth day of February to the seventeenth of March shall be charged against the establishment of St. Mary's Church, Brooklyn; all other journeys of Father Drouelle, Brother Vincent, etc., shall not be charged against it, unless otherwise ordered by superior authorities.

Art.IX. The following ordinance shall be read in Chapter to the two Brothers of Brooklyn on Friday evening, which is to be considered as the close of the visit.

Ordinance

In virtue of a letter of obedience of the fourteenth of February, A.D., one thousand eight hundred & forty-nine, I have decreed and decree as follows:

Art. I. The Brothers of the Establishment of Brooklyn shall for the future perform their religious exercises regularly, viz. meditation at 1/2 past 5, particular examination before dinner, spiritual reading at 8 o'clock P.M., followed by beads at 1/2 past 8, and then night prayer. The Chapter shall take place on Friday and during the time of spiritual reading.

Art. II. If a permanent agreement be made with Reverend D. Bacon, the articles necessary for the use and ornament of the classrooms shall be bought, also the Christian Perfection and large English Grammar.

Art. III. The Brothers shall conform as far as will be in their power to the Conduite in the management of their schools, following the arrangements made by the Visitor.

Art. IV. The use of the Cow hide shall be tolerated, unless contrary orders should be given by the superiors. Good points shall be distributed weekly and premiums quarterly.

Art. V. The small geography, the definer, and the history of the United States, now used in the first class, shall be done away with, as soon as possible. The following authors shall be used in the first class until contrary orders be given, viz.: Reeve's Bible history, Mitchell's Geography and Atlas, Cobb's Second Reader, Davies' Arithmetic, Algier's Murray's Grammar, the Juvenile Spelling Book and Preston's Bookkeeping.

Art. VI. If a permanent agreement is made, means shall be taken to have the boys' confessions heard as often as the Conduite requires and to have the catechism regularly taught.

Art. VII. If a permanent agreement is made and the school kept by the Brothers on their own account, payments shall be required in advance and the parents will not be allowed to interrupt the classes.

Art. VIII. The Brothers shall endeavor to establish silence in their classes and they will require their pupils to keep it as far as the street. They are dispensed with the keeping of ranks in the streets, this year.

Art. IX. The chronicle and the accounts of the Establishments shall be set in order without delay.

Art. X. The Brothers of the Establishment of Brooklyn, in compliance with Reverend Father Superior's wishes, shall write to him once a month in future.

Decreed and read in Chapter, at the Establishment of St. Mary's Church, Brooklyn, on the sixteenth day of the month of March, Anno Domini, one thousand eight hundred and forty-nine.

Brother Gatian,
Visitor

162. Brother Joseph (52) to Father Sorin

Indianapolis March 18, 1849

Reverend and dear Father,

Tomorrow I shall celebrate, in union with Notre Dame du Lac, the festival of my glorious patron. I hope I will one time or other on this holy festival obtain a thourugh conversion of heart; it is now 22 years since I look for this change, and it is not come yet. On the contrary, it seems that my case is getting worse every day.

I have done nothing for my poor father and mother, unless a few little prayers in a hurry. I wish you would have two Masses said for them. I would be very thankful for it.

The pasture has been layd off this week past. I will not sell any lots for a week or two, for I do not know what turn things will take.

If the bishop insists upon having a part of the profit, he must get no interest, and let him take his part in land and do with [it] what he pleases.

I took two poor widdows. One has three small children. They were sick, could not pay their house rent and nearly starved with hunger. They dared not to beg and still could not get along without assistance. So when I made it out, I gave them a room with the little kitchen for nothing, and a few potatoes and such things as I raise myself. Beside their washing and sewing for other people for their living, they do my housework, as cooking, washing, mending, etc., so that I loose nothing. I could not give you notice before I took them because the necessity was urgent, and I thought I had a good many debts to pay towards divine justice, and that it would be good to pay a little of them in this way. I hope you will not be against it, and as I say, the Community looses nothing by it. Widdows and orphans have a great power with God.

With reply to some of your remarks, I answer, first, I send you no schollar, because I do not find any. The chance is to[o] good in and this town, in the Methodist schools, and the Catholics are all poor. Second, I send no postulant, because I find none that is fit for a religious community. I know that I am very far from having the spirit and the dispositions of a true religious man, and I have met with but very few men in my life whose dispositions are better than mine. I am certain I would be less gulty in the sight of God had I never been a religious, not that I repent for it, however.

I remain, dear Father, with respect and love, your most obedient but unworthy son,

Brother Joseph

I have received no news from George since some time. Is he doing well? Give him my love. Please give my respect to Father Granger and to all the other priests, and my love to all the Brothers, in particular to Brother Vincent. I am all the time so very busy that I have no time to write letters. Last night my two gates were broke down with the fence in one place, and my big sow has been taken out of my pasture, a loss of five dollars.

163. Brother Gatian (15) to Father Sorin
[Translated from French]

Brooklyn, 108 York Street March 20, 1849

My Father,

A month ago, minus a few hours, I arrived in Brooklyn, and I've accomplished, as I predicted to you, very little. There's no agreement made; the Brothers are more discouraged than ever; everybody is more indisposed against us and sees more clearly the folly of your enterprise and idiocy of your proceedings. In a word, everything formerly evil still exists and hidden evil, by my frankness, is brought to light, because you know I always speak frankly, I spare no one: thus when the occasion arises, I acknowledge your mistakes as well as those of somebody else. Nevertheless, I have a clear conscience, and I've done my best although against my better judgement, to make things better and sweeten spirits. And as proof, I defy Mr. Bacon as well as the Brothers to accuse me of a single harsh word: not even the appearance of discontent between the Brothers and me or between me and Mr. Bacon, although Mr. Bacon and the Brothers have much bitterness to put up with. In spite of my demands and the conditions of agreement proposed to Mr. Bacon and which the latter can't fulfill, in spite of my frank acknowledgment of the desire I had that the Brothers abandon the establishment if he doesn't meet our conditions, in spite of all these things, we are excellent friends and Mr. Bacon hasn't been irritated a single time, although it's rare that he doesn't become furious when others resist him less than I do.

The Brothers up to now have been fine with me, but they grow impatient that things aren't decided faster, and they begin to suspect me of wishing to keep the establishment, in spite of all the difficulties, although I've told them my opinion was that it must be abandoned, but that I couldn't do it without express orders from you. I have an infinitely bitter pain—Mr. Bacon, to be specific. They say that he's trying to prevail all the time, that he wants to do nothing for the Brothers, and that there's no trusting him. That's the opinion of the Brothers and other people. I'm of another opinion. I believe only the guile of a prudent man (of Father Gouesse's type) who acts and aims at prevailing and doing nothing for us, being sure that we won't abandon him and that we can furnish him with able men who'll enjoy putting up with the troublesome position he finds himself in and who'll let themselves be led by him. All the Brooklyn priests have the same opinion, and although it may be difficult to bargain with him, it would still be infinitely more difficult to bargain with the other priests. As a matter of fact, Mr. Bacon would have been able to bargain with you as Mr. Mc Donough and Mr. Schneller had. I well understand the reasons of these priests who fear bargaining with you, after you gave a similar proof of ineptness. They agree with me:

1) That we could have succeeded if you had acted with the prudence of an ordinary man, preparing places and persons before sending them.

2) That to succeed in Brooklyn, it's necessary that the men be more than ordinary and not resemble so many idiots like the Brothers you've sent.

3) That it would be necessary to do things in a big way and make all leave the establishments at the same time.

4) That it would be necessary that the Brothers be made to shape their rules to circumstances and follow up to a certain point the direction of the priest.

Mr. Bacon and I believe that the greatest difficulty at present is the lack of personnel. If you had two professed Brothers, very wise and disposed to suffer a lot, I would say let's keep the establishment, even without a contract; let's leave everything up to the good pleasure of Mr. Bacon. But knowing very well that you don't have adequate Brothers, and that our Brothers (me included, although, etc.), unless they are put without much ado under the following conditions, will certainly lose their vocation and won't persevere even as long as Brother Louis de Gonzague has, who is nevertheless very ill at ease. I've proposed three conditions to Mr. Bacon demanding a *yes* or a *no*, as follows:

Agree:

1) to excuse the Brothers from Sunday School starting next April 22.

2) to furnish for next semester a space of 1496 square feet to accommodate 200 students, $200 for classroom furnishings, so that a Brother has everything he needs. And then to give annually $50 for renovating furniture.

3) to furnish before April 22, three tables, a blackboard, a partition wall, curtains and a stool.

Mr. Bacon has only replied that he couldn't say yes. At which time I said to him that I'd send you a dispatch asking if the Brothers should keep the establishment, without a contract, leaving the rest to his good will, and that I'd hold to your yes or your no.

I'm in the greatest incertitude: I've gotten from you only the March 16 telegraph message although I wrote seven letters. Your dispatch made me change my plans a little. I believed it'd be enough to send a Brother to stay simply two months; that's why I sent you my telegraph message on March 17. Not seeing it unnatural to break off the establishment on April 22 or to do it right away, because of the departure for New Orleans, I'd have on my own broken off the establishment, but not being sure if you'd preferred to spend some hundreds of dollars and lose a half dozen Brothers sooner than abandon the establishment, I sent you yesterday (on the 21st) a dispatch insisting on a yes or a no. I said in my dispatch: Learned Saints can succeed, And in effect, if you had Brothers of a zeal equal to that of Brother (I don't know who has enough of it) disposed to suffer a lot and at the same time refined and wise, it would be better to continue the establishment, because it has begun. Once the thing starts, says Mr. Bacon, it has to go on or die. Then I said, "Will you, to preserve the establishment, give Brothers and risk losses without a contract," etc. Because if you wish to continue the establishment, it'll be necessary not to skip over these difficulties for many years and expose yourself continually to losses of vocations and to stiff travel expenses. I thus say "yes" may destroy many vocations, "no," future prosperity. I say "may" because especially for the "no" that I wish with all my heart to receive in a few hours, there's much doubt. Mr Bacon says it'd be impossible to reestablish ourselves, but fear heightens his imagination; the Brothers of the Christian Schools reestablished themselves. Nevertheless, your precipitation of last year could slow down for five to six years desired establishments. You bought experience, as Mr. Schnells, the pastor of St. Paul's, told me yesterday. As I see it, in effect, Father, you're paying 500 dollars for this unfortunate Brooklyn affair. This Mr. Schnells has spacious classrooms, 3200 square feet, and 1000 children in his parish. He'd take four wise and well formed Brothers (notice!) September 1, if you assured him of them by May 15. There's now a "free school" of 200 students and a "pay school" of 140 students. The Brothers at the "free school" could make $250 per year. The others would live off their school. [Letter incomplete]

164. Brother Gatian (16) to Father Sorin

Brooklyn March 24, 1849

Reverend Father Superior,

This is my ninth letter, and yet I have not received one from you: it will be my last.

The two Brothers have positively told me they would not teach after the 22nd of April, and you know that I cannot. I have written twice by telegraph, and you have not answered. I shall write once more next Monday, and if I don't receive a dispatch before next Saturday, on next Sunday week, I shall inform Mr. Bacon of our departure for the 22nd of April.

If you wish to keep the establishment, your Brothers will have to be the slaves of Reverend Bacon, and but few will be found willing to carry their obedience so far. If on account of the Council of Baltimore, you wish to keep establishment until the end of the year, you will have to send two Brothers, one of whom must be willing to take the Sunday School, and the other our 120 boys on Sundays. And besides you must let me know by telegraph before next Saturday. The Brothers must here [hear] before the 22nd of April. You will also have to send me $30 for Brother Aloysius's journey home.

Yours,

Brother Gatian

165. Brother Gatian (17) to Father Sorin [Telegram]

New York March 27, 1849

The Brothers wont teach after twenty second April. I cannot give telegraphic directions if you keep establishment. Send two able and zealous teachers immediately.

Brother Gatian

166. Brother Gatian (18) to Father Sorin
[Translated from French]

Brooklyn, 108 York Street March 29, 1849

My Father,

I just got your March 21 letter, the first since my arrival. I was almost in despair, and in three days I'd have told Mr. Bacon we would leave on April 22.

The slowness of your responses has unsettled the little hope I had left to make peace. The impatient Brothers won't wait for the arrival of other Brothers, and I wouldn't know how to take their place, being half deaf. I'll make Brother Basil leave at the end of the quarter for New Orleans, and I'll have to let Brother Louis de Gonzague leave—he doesn't want to continue at the school, and can't, given his ignorance and bad health.

Experience, as my letters of March 12, 16, 20 and 24 explain to you, demonstrates to me the impossibility of doing anything at present, even signing the contract such as it is, because the conditions couldn't be fulfilled, neither by us, nor by Mr. Bacon. The two great obstacles to the realization of the advantages I made clear to you are at present the loss of Brothers and the estrangement of the clergy. I deny nothing that I sketched in my first letters, but experience is proving to me that we can do nothing now. That's why I won't draw things to a conclusion before you've answered my last letters.

I sent you three telegraph messages, one on the 20th, the other on the 17th, and the other on the 26th of this month, and I don't understand why I get no response. All these delays throw me into a greater confusion. I've spent more than seventy dollars ($70.00) since my departure, which would not have been laid out if I had stayed at the Lake, and up to now I've accomplished nothing. I believe that the sooner we abandon this establishment, the better we'll be.

Let me know in writing, in English, if you've received my three telegraphic messages, so that if they didn't get to you, I can recover the seven dollars I spent for the messages.

Brother Victor is in no way suitable: he thinks highly of himself and knows less than Brother Louis de Gonzague. Do you think you're going to trap me saying that it's only bookkeeping? He's impossible. He seems the same as when he was here—he's not respected! the Brothers, the students, and Mr. Bacon didn't like him.

If you want to keep this establishment, you have to send two Brothers immediately to replace all three of us, and you don't have any who are superior to us, not even equal to us, not (in a word) who are competent. Abandon this establishment. The only one who could do as well as I (and I can do nothing, being deaf) is Brother Thomas, but you said he's not fit for this establishment. You should have said the establishment isn't fit for him because he'd lose his vocation here, as truly as I've lost my ears.

March 31

All my telegraph messages, it seems, came to you because of the response to my fourth telegram, which I just got. The New York operator, seeing himself threatened by a law suit (wrongly and by your fault) wanted to send one free of charge for me to the South Bend operator. That seems to reveal your receiving the three preceeding ones.

I can't send Brother Basil (who likes the idea) to New Orleans before having a replacement. There's much hostility for doing it, seeing that it'll be necessary that he furnish himself with board and bed, but his passage would be only six or eight dollars. The trip by first class cabin is $50; second class cabin is $25. In these two cases everything is furnished to the passengers. Added up, there's a difference of only five or six dollars; I'd make him travel second class. As soon as you've received this letter, which I'll post Monday (April 2nd), you'll write me by telegraph that you're sending a Brother and $55. If I don't receive a dispatch before April 10, I'll presume that you haven't received my letter and thus I'll carry the expense of a dispatch myself. The Brother has to be here around April 15 so that Brother Basil can return for the beginning of May. He'll need twelve to twenty days to return. Since you're obeying me, I'll temporize with Mr. Bacon next Monday, and I'll leave things in suspense without making a contract, so as to get as many concessions as possible. Before sending you this letter, I'll tell you if I've succeeded. I've just made Brother Louis agree to stay, and for that I'll have to take steps which could diminish our pecuniary resources. I'll demand all payments in advance, so as not to have to beg for payments and to free us from a heap of brats who infest our schools. I'll take charge also of the bookkeeping classes and algebra, etc., which I'll teach individually in my boardinghouse so that I can hear them. The reason I'm asking for a Brother immediately to replace Brother Basil is that being deaf, and up to now remedies being useless, I absolutely cannot teach when there are more than ten children. I've tried many times, and I've always been obliged to abandon the class, seeing that I can't maintain order nor understand anybody.

Besides the Brother you're sending now, it'll be necessary perhaps to send another if Brother Louis de Gonzague falls seriously ill (as I fear) and if I don't recover my hearing. The Brother you're going to send me now will have to take charge of the Sunday School and you'll have to put that in his obedience, burdening Brother Louis de Gonzague with all our students on Sundays. I now have the Sunday School, but I can't enjoy it, the children already being aware (although I've had it only four Sundays) of my infirmity. In burdening Brother Louis de Gonzague and the other Brothers with all the schoolboys and the Sunday School, you can make a last ditch effort at the possibility or impossibility of continuing the school on its current footing. At the same time, if you promptly answer the question I've made on the Constitutions, they will be promptly printed.

I saw Mr. Ryan this morning. He had almost lost hope of seeing me, your response having been silence. I hadn't been to see him because of the great distance there is between the house in Brooklyn and his in New York (4 miles). I was there the day before yesterday on the receipt of your letter, but darkness overtook me before I got to his address, which I found with difficulty, but he was absent. I came back in the darkness and made his wife promise to send him to me yesterday, but he was sick. I saw him today, but he doesn't want to finalize the agreement, despairing of being able to support and clothe his family with the little money you're offering him. He understands you can't give more, and he very much wants to go establish himself in the West. If there were a small farm to buy near the college, or if you wished to sell or rent him a part of your land, he'd very much like to go alone to the college the first year and then take measures to maintain himself in subsequent years. He now asks $400 per year (and then you'd have to furnish him neither board, nor lodging, nor anything whatsoever), and he'd teach six hours a day. Please respond if you'll take him, if you haven't found cheaper.

Such would be the contract, but I believe, as he told me, that he'd put his sons in school, either as day students or boarders, as well as his girls at Bertrand (and he'd gladly take your provisions), as his means would let him. He's an excellent mathematician and philosopher, but he's neither chemist nor researcher. That's why I believe the best for the university, the academic year being so advanced, will be to keep Mr. Hachett up to vacation and to leave the ad in the newspaper until July or until my departure. If we don't find better than Mr. Ryan, we can always take him. We are both in agreement on what I just told you. His intention being to go sooner or later out West, he's going to commit himself only by the month, so that if you need him, you can leave me let him know. Please answer: what is the price of cultivated land, of wilderness? How much would he have to pay to rent twenty acres of land and a house?

It's almost certain you won't find a professor who teaches mathematics, philosophy, chemistry and the uses of instruments, and especially one who wants to go to the West for $400, when they can make $1000 here, much less a Catholic and religious person like Mr. Ryan. After all, Mr. Ryan would have only $50 more than Mr. Hachett, because lodging, laundry, food are well worth $50.

I'm asking you for $55 because I anticipate not having any money for Mr. Twomy before tomorrow's over. We now have $46; that's to pay boarding for three people for five weeks, or up to May 7, if we have no debts; but we owe almost $25 for approved items. I even believe that instead of $55, you ought to send us $75, because it'll be good if you'd pay the $12 you spoke to me about for Freeman's and also $12.38 to Mr. Dunigan to finish off his old bill, as soon as Mr. Romey has paid his $50. Here's the bill:

Brother Basil's Trip	$30.00
Twomy	25.00
Freeman's	12.00
Dunigan	12.38
Truth Teller	3.00

Clothes, shirts, etc. pants
for Brother Louis and me 25.00
$107.38

It'd be good of you to send a summer levite for Brother Louis de Gonzague, and each of us summer pantaloons, for me and Brother Louis de Gonzague and Basil, and if you want to, shirts for Brother Louis de Gonzague. (I'll be 23 years old on April 3.)

In rereading my first two letters, you'll see what you have to respond to.

April 1

I was at the bank yesterday, and I see that I can't have any money, unless I have securities or else my draft on you would not clear. I'd also have to pay a deduction, bigger than you pay at South Bend. Thus it'd be better to send me money immediately for the Brothers who'll come, and when you'd like to send me some money another time, it'll be necessary to send me a draft payable to someone at our bank.

I've collected, as I wrote to you last week, about $50 on the $130 I spoke to you about. I still have to collect $80, but I would be proud if I get half of that.

Tomorrow I'll send you a telegram asking for a Brother who can be here in a fortnight. If my letter arrives before this Brother's departure, you could send me two of them if you find that less expensive, because it's almost certain that Brother Louis de Gonzague won't be able to continue his classes long. He still has a bad fever today. If you prefer to risk Brother Louis de Gonzague's health and to wait for the absolutely impossible, get ready to send me a second Brother when I ask for him. In any case, let me know by telegram how many Brothers you're sending me and how much money, so I can take appropriate measures for their reception and the departure of the others.

Brother Louis de Gonzague has already recanted and returned to his first decision not to stay after April 22 because he hates the students and Mr. Bacon and is always sick. So on April 22, if two Brothers aren't here, the school will be abandoned. I'll put the Brothers on their way and I'll wait for your orders about my fate (without teaching, being sickly). But you can send two Brothers, even when they have to return home for vacation (as it's more than probable they'll do), seeing that you'd sooner want to lose $500 than the establishment before vacation; because the two Brothers' trips will cost you only $100, Brother Louis's $25—their time will be worth scarcely $60 to you. That adds up to only $185. Their school will probably pay for their board.

The two Brothers you'll send will have to be told that you're sending them into an earthly hell—that they'll have to suffer especially from Mr. Bacon (who is a pain), from the students, from lack of a salary, rooms and furniture in church, and above all from Sunday School, which one of them will absolutely have to take charge of, while the other will supervise all the school children. Because remember I'm too sickly to get involved with these children! If I hadn't extraordinary or imprudent courage, the school would have already folded. Don't go cajoling these Brothers with nice promises and beautiful prospects of ease, as is your usual way; nothing gets people riled against you more than seeing you try to trap them.

My opinion, as well as those of the two Brothers, is that Brother Thomas is the most suitable and capable man you have. It would take a soldier like him to manage our brats and face off Mr. Bacon. If his vocation appeared shaky, you could call him back at vacation time; he'd scarcely have the time to lose it in one quarter and it'd be a great test of his talents. As for the second Brother, I don't know. The two Brothers here think Brother Michael would fit the bill. We all object to Brother Victor who is too deaf and too slow to supervise, as is necessary, a class as big and noisy as Brother Basil's.

April 2

I just saw Mr. Bacon. He'll do absolutely nothing to encourage or help out the school before having the assurance shown by experience that the Brothers will succeed and persevere at his place. I can't help having a good opinion of him and granting that he's right and that our Institution is the only cause of all that exists cross-wise. I believe he's well intentioned; he's our best friend among the Brooklyn clergy; but at the same time, he's selfish and sly, discreet and excessively lively. There is a wide field open for us—many schools and two orphanages, one in New York and the other in Brooklyn. In the New York one, the bishop wants Brothers of some kind; the bishop would prefer us if we had capable men. But for him to take us willingly, we first have to succeed at Mr. Bacon's, because he often consults the latter who up till now has hidden our difficulties. You'd therefore do well to send two zealous Brothers who are disposed to deal frankly with Mr. Bacon, both to take and continue the school with all these difficulties, at least during the final quarter, if not for all next year. These two Brothers would have to appear unhappy about nothing all this time and frankly make Mr. Bacon see all their needs; they would have to be disposed to suffer everything with a good heart, because they'd know that Mr. Bacon could help them and he will. I believe that in doing this, after two years or perhaps 18 months, when the Brooklyn orphanage could be ready, Mr. Bacon would have enough influence to win over Mr. Schneller and then they'll get the better of Mr. Mc Donogh, and we could make a huge establishment. He objects a lot to Brother Victor against whom, outside of the faults I've already spoken about, he charges a tendency of faint heartedness. It seems that the bishop also has a bad opinion of him. So I repeat, Brother Thomas (with a soldier's character) for the upper class and Brother Michael for the lower class would seem the least objectionable. Perhaps little Brother Louis would do better, putting Brother Thomas as director. I'm not positive about Brother Michael. But above all, tell them that they'll have big troubles and that for the love of the work, they'd have to endure them for a year at least, without a complaint and without showing any sign of discouragement. If they weren't able to come at all, I'd try to obtain Mr. Bacon's free school for them the following year, or another school, and I'd find it almost certainly. The priest from Williamsburgh, whom I met at Dunigan's last Saturday, invited me to go see him. I'm going there tomorrow.

Mr. Bacon told me he didn't write to you because he didn't know what to write. As I hadn't received your first letter in response to my first two letters, I wish you'd repeat it and especially give information on the value of our establishment, the dates for the Chronicles. Is it neccssary to have the Constitutions printed at Dunigan's prices? How many copies of each book should be bound? Can one give his Constitutions to priests?

Brother Gatian

167. Brother Gatian (19) to Father Moreau
[Translated from French]

Brooklyn March 30, 1849

My reverend Father,

For the first time since I entered the Community, I find myself alienated from the motherhouse. It's not without revulsion that I left the Lake to throw myself in the middle of a city of 150,000 inhabitants, across from New York, the [ ] of America. Father Superior gave a very difficult task to my bashfulness and inexperience, but with the grace of God, I'm pulling through it better than I had hoped. I now have as much freedom and courage as our Americans. I already know more than forty streets in the city of Brooklyn, and I don't fear venturing two or three leagues deep into the heart of the city of New York. Last night, darkness surprised me two and a half leagues from the river that separates the two cities. I was in the center of New York and made my way so well that in an hour and a half I got to one of the steamboats that perpetually crosses between the two cities and serves as a bridge. The river is crossed in five minutes, and it takes ten minutes to get from the ferry to Number 108 York Street where we're boarding. I was sent here to put in order the affairs of the school which was, as it were, put off, having no foundation. I'm also general agent here. I don't teach, but when I get finished with the school business, I'll be busy with the translation of the Constitutions. According to the plan given to me, that'll be a joke because up to now we still haven't received any Constitutions or complete Directories from France. They want me to have six books printed: three for the Brothers and three for the Sisters. The postulants' books (Brothers and Sisters) will include the Directory except for the prefaces and the introductions and the fourth and fifth part with the first twelve Constitutions to the end of the Directory. The novices' book (Brother and Sisters) will include the entire postulants' manual, with the first and second sections of the second part, leaving out what would have already been inserted in the postulants' manual. The book for the professed will include the novices' book, with the third section of the second part, leaving out what would have already been inserted, and also the rules for the Rector and superiors. They want me to make all the allowed changes expressly or tacitly and to make the books of the Brothers and Sisters alike as much as possible, leaving out numbers and phrases which could differ so as to save money in printing.

When Father Drouelle came to the Lake, Father Superior and he went to New York where they made their arrangements so well and examined things so well that, having sent five Brothers in November, three had to go home immediately, and the two that Mr. Bacon wanted to keep preferred Purgatory to being at his place. The establishments were not visited, no accord or agreement was concluded, and the Brothers were sent, without warning the three Brooklyn pastors, two months after the school year began, when these priests had already pledged founders for the year and consequently couldn't take any Brothers!! The result of this inconceivable imprudence, or rather this illegal enterprise to work miracles, which is pretty common with Father Superior, was the cause of useless expenses for trips, etc., and a loss at the time of 3000 francs, and he'll no doubt have to spend more than a thousand francs before the thing goes ahead or folds. I also have to add that this unfortunate affair will probably mean the loss of several good vocations. The Brothers here are really in Purgatory. They have no clothes, furniture, rooms, court for recreation. They have to heap up 200 students on Sunday where they can put only 125 in the church. On Sunday they have to take care of 100 brats who don't come to school during the week. They have no regular place to board, being exposed every day to being thrown from house to house, among unknown people or even perhaps into the middle of a public Protestant boarding house. They have to live on what they make from their school, and when they go to beg, so to speak, from house to house for their payments, they have only the Irish rabble in Brooklyn, their reputation for learning (and actually they don't know what they should, our American cities having extraordinary scholarships, and public primary schools, where there is no tuition, teach even algebra, geometry, etc.) not being sufficient to attract Catholic American students. I have to remark here on the disgrace of the Catholics: almost the entire rabble in our cities is Catholic and Irish. But if we had a good reputation and if our schools were free or non-paying, we would have all the Catholic children in the parish which amounts to more that 300 for Mr. Bacon's parish, 1000 for Mr. Schnell's, and as many for another. But all the schools ought to be free, like those of the Christian Brothers in New York, or many parents will prefer to send their children to public city schools, where the children don't learn any religion since no religion can be taught; they can have children from 30 to 40 different religions, and the teachers are more often pagan or Protestant than Catholic.

I've been here five weeks trying to mend everything, because it's my sole duty to unravel what superiors tangle here, but I don't believe it best to let the establishment sink and to think no longer about it until we have capable Brothers. If they had wanted to believe me last year and waited a year or eighteen months before making foundations in New York, so as to train a half dozen subjects and have them leave for the three Brooklyn parishes at the same time, we would have had a stable and lucrative establishment in two years. And now we'll have to wait perhaps four or five years before being able to do anything. Father Superior bought five or six thousand francs worth of experience by this affair. I don't see how Father Superior takes on a heap of impossibilities with such calm indifference. He must think he's capable of doing miracles. I'm really afraid his faith is presumptuous! But it doesn't matter much—if he gets himself in a mess, I'll help him with all my heart to pull himself out of it even at the risk of my life. It's possible that God blesses his presumptuous faith [with] my rash courage.

On my trip I suffered a lot, since I had to travel through Canada around the [Great] lakes, and I was afraid of losing an ear I had frozen. I no longer hear except in the right ear and that still faintly. I can no longer teach. I travelled in open sleds, and for several leagues I travelled on Lake Erie on the ice where there were from time to time crevices two feet wide, not frozen, so our driver made his horses leap with a couple of filthy oaths. I also endangered myself crossing the Niagra River near the waterfalls in a bad canoe amid waves and chunks of ice so as not to miss the cart waiting for us on the other side, although twenty of my travelling companions didn't dare do it. Only two or three braved the storm with me. Another time in the middle of a dark night, the carriage dumped us in a ditch, and my head went through the window of the carriage. I was under all the others and asleep at the time. If the horses hadn't been stopped abruptly, we would have all been killed and as for me, the car would have certainly decapitated me.

I'm feeling pretty good, except for my ears. My soul is, as usual, impatient and a little upset, but I'm holding to the ink of obedience. I'm not crazy, but I don't know why foolishness appeals to me so much.

I'm very happy here: our American cities are so peaceful, so open spirited and so friendly. There's less noise in New York than in a French borough of 1200 people, although the streets are so crowded that you can hardly cross. But nobody talks, and bargains are made in a low voice and with few words.

Brother Gatian

I'll probably stay here until August. When you send wine to St. Lawrence, don't send any more through New York because then you pay customs twice and the wine costs you three times the price.

Brother Gatian

168. Brother Joseph (53) to Father Sorin

Indianapolis April 1, 1849

Reverend and dear Father,

In answer to yours of the 29th March, I must acknoleged that I have not even looked what Smith or any other would give me because I had good reasons to abstain from such an inquiry; however, I will try to do my best to see what I can get at least for thc pasture. I wish with all my heart that all this would take an end, for I am, indeed, tired to live as I do. I sometimes would rather be in the bottom of the sea, if it was allowed me to wish it.

I will write to you again in the course of this week. Please send Brother Vincent if possible.

I remain, dear Father, with respect and love, your most obedient but unworthy son,

Brother Joseph

P.S. Mr. Phipps is very anxious to get his money. He wants to leave, and besides this he needs it very badly.

[As] For this poor family, I am obliged to keep them for a while until they will be able to make out for themselves. They get some alms from some charitable persons.

169. Brother Joseph (54) to Father Sorin [Telegram]

Indianapolis April 2, 1849

Reverend E. Sorin,

If I can trade sixteen acres of land, McKeinan in town for forty-four hundred dollars worth of dry goods, good article, and at New York prices. He will loan one thousand dollars cash, six percent. Five hundred more in about four months, same interest. Several other offers but prefers mine. Goods to be delivered at Logan's hotel.

Brother Joseph

170. Brother Joseph (55) to Father Sorin

Indianapolis April 2, 1849 [II]

Reverend and dear Father,

I am affreight that you are not sufficiently aware of the telegraphic despatch I send you. However, the proposition is a very good one, if you have use for or can dispose of the goods. These are all excellent articles at very low prices. If you sell them at a profit of 25 percent on an average, you will sell every particle of them in less than one year and so turn the whole into ready cash. You will never find a better bargain, if you will sell all in one lump, because capital to a large amount is not easily to be found in this westeren country. Father Granger knows that Mr. McKernan is an honest Catholic, and I am sure he would not impose upon me, but he wants to sell out and to go to some other business.

Of course, there are a few articles which will be of little service to you, as tobacco, a few ladies' hats, etc., but all such do amount to an inconsiderable sum. Most of the goods are: cloth, satinett, cashmere, and beautiful articles of summer stuff for men and ladies. If by this time you have not sent me a despatch, please do it immediatly because Mr. M. is about trading with a man from Noblesville, and he wants to conclude his bargain with that man if you do not like it.

I remain, dear Father, with respect and love, your obedient but unworthy son,

Brother Joseph

P.S. He will deliver the goods to Logansport. From thence we will have to haul them. I believe I can turn [them] into cash myself here in town.

2 P.S. I received your telegraphic despatch. I am sorry that you decline. You may depend that there is gain not loss in the goods. If you can dispose of the goods, the bargain is certainly advantageous, but I will not urge you, nor need you be affraied. I will do nothing without your consent.

Please send me another telegraphic despatch, only yes or no. It will cost you but 11 cents. I paid nothing to the telegraph office.

171. Brother Gatian (20) to Father Sorin

Brooklyn April 6, 1849

Reverend Father Superior,

Time rolls on, and to our great annoyance, nothing is done to deliver us from the chaos of uncertainty from which we cannot emerge without your assistance. You seem to have entirely forgotten us. Why do you not act? You have all necessary informations. You are perfectly aware of our dispositions, and we have repeatedly given you the broadest hints of the fatal consequences which must result from the dilatoriness of your conduct. Will you temporize until you have compelled Brothers Basil and Aloysius to leave the institution! Believe me, your policy is false. By it you may gain time, but you will certainly ensure a perfect discomfiture. I have neglected nothing on my part. I have written twice a week, i.e., *ten* letters since I have been here, and you have written *once*. I have sent you *five* telegraphic dispatches, and you have sent me but *two*. But you may rest assured that you will not overreach me, nor the two Brothers. If before the 22nd of April measures have not been taken by you to keep this establishment or to abandon it, and if we are not informed of these measures before the 15th, or if we find them impracticable, *we will take our own way*, that is, we will abandon the establishment, and perhaps some of us may do worse than that.

I am so harrassed that I would prefer *death* a thousand times to *life*, were I certain of escaping hell. I feel all the vicissitudes of old age: my hearing, my sight, the sense of smelling, my strength, and my whole corporal system is in a declining state. But the worst and the most incurable of my maladies is in my soul. I have no rest, no happiness, as long as I am away from him whom my heart loves. I am homesick, and I wish I were again at the Lake, were it but to enjoy his presence from time to time. I am in despair and would put an end to my life, if the fear of hell did not prevent me. It is high time for me to see my friend again, for impatience might well cause an outburst of folly, which would be very scandalous here, where I am now favorably known. I shall probably be able to keep my courage up, if I am busily employed at the Lake, not too far from him, having always some hopes of eventually recovering his friendship. But if all possibility of gaining his affection were taken from me, or if he died before having showed me this affection, I would be a broken heart. *I would pine away and quickly follow him to the grave*. But I have said enough of personal matters. *Now about business, my great remedy or rather solace.*

I become daily more convinced that we cannot take a footing in Brooklyn or in the neighborhood, unless we succeed at Father Bacon's. I have spoken to priests and others in Brooklyn, New York, and Williamsburgh, and after they have candidly told me that the system of the Brothers is not in good repute, that they have not the qualifications of learning necessary, they add: *However, if you succeed at Fr. Bacon's, your Brothers, being religious, will be preferred. Or, well! I will go down to Father Bacon to see how the new system works.* I also know that Father Bacon will not give favorable accounts, until he has had an experience of a year or six months, in the manner I indicated in my last letter. Do then what I have indicated, unless you would adopt the far better plan of abandoning the establishment entirely and of not making any foundations in Brooklyn, N.Y., for five or six years, during which you could prepare good teachers. I have been at Williamsburgh. There is nothing to be done there for at least 18 months.

Father Bacon is suspected of having an intention to dispense with the Brothers after this year. I do not know whether this rumor is grounded, but I know for certain (he has told me) *that he will not make the least advance this year, though he has the means and even the objects wanted.* It is also probable that in case the two Brothers would leave Father Bacon next year, they would have no choice but between Father Schneller's free or pay school. This choice must also be made before the end of May, and I know that he is so particular about learning that, at present, none of our Brothers are fit for him. *Once more, then, would it not be better to abandon the whole?*

If the two Brothers leave the Community, how much money shall [MS torn] to each? Brother Aloysius has the money under [MS torn] have direct me to pay some debts such as the Freem [MS torn] sing to send money instead of that, that I might have a pretext to get the money from him. He has about $50.

We are indeed very expensive, as we have so much to pay for medicine, postage, telegraph, etc. Last week we spent $15, tho our board was only $9.00. I think I will have to pay about $5 for Brother Aloysius and myself this week. Brother Basil is sick in bed today. He and I have horrid coughs. I will have the mortification of seeing Brother Basil's infirmity exposed to Miss Murphy, for the latter will take charge of us next Monday, and she has already moved to our number. We are now in Holy Week and have no school. In Father Bacon's church women sing the prophecies of Jeremiah and lead the choir and organ.

My love to Jo[hn] Hays, T. Glenmen, Wm. Hacy, and all the apprentices and boarders, and all your family, and rest assured, reverend Father, that with all my roughness, I shall do my best for the interests of the Institution here, while I breathe in my senses.

Brother Gatian

172. Brother Gatian (21) to Father Moreau
[Translated from French]

Brooklyn April 10, 1849

Reverend Father,

In sending on to you Father Superior's letter, I've decided to say a few words to you about our affairs here.

I'm very perplexed and in very great uncertitude. It takes twenty days in winter to get a response by mail from the Lake, although a traveller can make the trip in summer in six days. It's true one can have a dispatch sent in the blink of an eye by telegraph, but one has to pay twelve cents a word. If I don't receive news before the 15th, this establishment will sink with a bang because the two Brothers absolutely refuse to stay any longer, and I'm too deaf to teach. I'm coming up with remedies, but up to now they've done me no good. For how many of my misfortunes are just fruits of imprudence or improvidence of...Some weeks after this event, all the bishops in the Republic will hold a synod at Baltimore and will talk, no doubt, about our successes and our setbacks! I'm truly overburdened with sadness in seeing the useless confusion we're thrown into, confusion which will be able to ruin several good vocations.

I can't tell you anything more about it: I'm completely destroyed and in agony.

Brother Gatian

Nevertheless, one can't reproach me with having contributed to the discouragement of the two Brothers, because I had never lied so much before I came here. Against my nature and temperament, I appeared cheerful, happy and affable. Exteriorly I take pleasure in all news, and I listen to everything, even politics, in order to shock no one.

An American just invented a steamboat that'll travel in the atmosphere [?] with a speed triple (at least) that of the steamboats that travel by water. The first departure will take place in a month: it'll go to California. It is fifty feet high and will be able to accomodate as many passengers as the biggest steamboat. You'll have to pay only $50 or 250 francs.

There's an election today in New York and in the suburbs for mayors, members of the municipal council, etc., etc.

Brother Gatian

173. Brother Gatian (22) to Father Sorin

Brooklyn, 108 York St. April 11, 1849

Reverend Father Superior,

I received your letter of the 31st ultimo yesterday and dispatched the accompanying letters to France. You reproach me with my numerous letters. You should have praised me. For I obeyed you with a vengeance. You complained bitterly and wrongfully that the Brothers did not write to you. Well! I have written *for myself and the other two!*

You seem to reproach me with mismanagement, but you have only to blame yourself. Did I not tell you that I was unable, that my journey was more than useless? You would not believe, though you are perfectly aware that my worse prophecies always turn out true. If you had followed my advice then, if you had followed it last year, when you spoke of founding the establishment, *you would not have got yourself into all these scrapes and difficulties*. But after all, I have not done anything to compromise the institution so far. If you would only act in the direction of my letter of the 2nd inst., everything would come off pretty nicely. As to proving that the Brothers are able to teach, I will never do that for it would be defending an untruth. I will not defend heresy, though you should command me in the name of holy obedience.

We have been three days under the care of Miss Murphy (108 York, as before), and so far we are contented. It will be hard for us to find boarders to take our places, if we do not decide on leaving before May 1st / 49.

I will not pay Cooper, Storm and Smith 12.34 until I see how I am going to be paid back. I must watch my funds.

I received Reverend Father Rector's circular yesterday, and I will give the information required in the prescriptions numbers 1 and 2, which you will enclose in the common answer which you have to send.

1. My name is Monsimer.
2. Urbain Jean Baptiste Victor (my surnames)

3. I was born at Saulges. I don't know if it's Mayenne or Sarthe, but it's near Chemin-le-Roi (Mayenne).

4. I was born on April 3, 1826, at 7:35 AM.

5. My parents were farmers.

6. I was one also before entering the Community.

7. I entered August 13, 1839.

8. I took the habit in 1840 at retreat. I don't know the date.

9. My religious name is Brother Gatian.

10. The day of my profession has not yet come.

11. I spent my first year at Ste. Croix studying under Mr. de Marseuil with Brothers Valentin, Alexander, Ferdinand (defrocked), with Brother Anselm (died by drowning), with Brother Robert and a Brother Marin (defrocked thief: I've forgotten his name), with Brother Francis Xavier and Brother Sylvain. I worked for four weeks in the kitchen when I arrived in 1839. I believe I was also in class under Brother Euloge (defrocked) that year or the following. I believe I also had class for some time in the Brothers' second division that year or the following. But I'm too old to remember these events which are too mixed up in my head. The following year I was employed as second prefect in the small study hall with Brother Chrysostom and prefect in the dorm with Brother Hilaire and in the children's courtyard with the same Brother. I believe I also had the first division of arithmetic for some months. Brother Hilarion had another division, and another Brother had another. But all these things are now forgotten. I left on August 5, 1841, for America. I also was a brick layer for some time under Brother John of the Cross. Brother Hyppolite preceeded me, but I don't know who succeeded me nor how long I spent at it.

Brother Gatian

April 14

I received last night your unintelligible and nonsensical telegraphic dispatch. *Is Basil gone to New Orleans—Teach yourself.* Have I not already told you everything about these questions? How could I send Brother Basil since I have nobody to take his place? Do you want a *deaf* man to teach? or do you believe I would tell you that I cannot teach when I could do it? Besides where is the money that is going to take Brother Basil to New Orleans? You give me debts to pay as if I coined money. We have not too much money to pay our board, medicine, and school expenses, and behold, you want us to spend over $75 otherwise. *Truly a Brother must have an iron vocation to stand the trials you make him undergo.*

Brother Basil will leave on Monday or Thursday next [ ] I shall take the class, though deaf, till the end of next week which will be April 20th. If next Friday I find out that I can absolutely not teach with one ear, I shall give the boys vacation for one week and send you a telegraphic dispatch informing you of the same and asking for men and money. The quarter will finish at the end of next week, and I shall not begin another unless we are able to go through it. Brother Aloysius says he won't teach over half a quarter more. If this letter reached you before your departure and you wished to continue the establishment even for half a quarter, you should take a Brother along. You should try to be here if not next week at least three or four days before May.

Brother Gatian

P.S. If the letter is opened by another person at the Lake, you will only have to mind the French part and to keep Brother Thomas ready to start on receipt of first telegraphic despatch of Father Superior. If Father Superior had not taken money with him for us, you should send $75 by Brother Thomas.

Brother Gatian

174. Brother Vincent (20) to Father Sorin
[Translated from French]

Indianapolis April 15, 1849

Very dear Superior,

Father Granger didn't tell you what we had to suffer during our trip. Brother Théodule had fever here while the next day he left for Louisville, and since then I have [heard] nothing from him.

I'll tell you what I think about Brother Joseph's affairs. I don't have much faith in them. He's not discouraged about his vocation, but about his confusion, because he's as bad off as he can be. One must have as good a vocation as he possesses in order not to seem silly. Walking around many places in this town, I've seen lots of big tracts of land which will be easier to sell than ours, and all this time they remain unpurchased. It'll be necessary meanwhile to find $500 by the end of May for Mr. Phipps and 100 dollars for other debts. I'd like to have $6000 and the poor Brother free to return to the Lake.

Good Father Granger was our consolation as long as he was with us. Can he accompany us up to our last station? I can't tell you how much I, of course, miss Notre Dame du Lac; meanwhile faith makes me love my new assignment, and I'd prefer to die in the middle of the Mississippi than to live in some place of my own choosing. If you're looking for advice, try to arrange all our business with the bishop of New Orleans about the administrators.

Goodby, Father. You'll have no more news from us until we're settled in our new house.

Your very humble and obedient son in our Lord Jesus Christ,

Brother Vincent

175. Brother Théodule (5) to Father Moreau
[Translated from French]

St. Mary's College [Kentucky] April 16, 1849

Reverend Father,

I arrived here this morning at 6 o'clock where, thanks be to God, I found everybody. They can't be better disposed toward the Sisters' departure about which I was very anxious after my interview Saturday morning with Monsignor Spalding who, rest assured, knew why I came. Before anything, he begins by outlining his purpose in a way I wasn't expecting and to which I did him the honor of saying nothing. There was in his tone, his manners, and his words so much hatred against us I was surprised. We are a "Community of children and headless folks so as to make all the bishops reject us and send us packing." He's so tired of us that he can no longer stomach us. Nevertheless, he says that if the affair of the Sisters interests him, he'll sooner take you to court than let them go, because they are too difficult to replace. He compares you to one who renounces his signature. Finally he ended by telling me just who was involved in everything when the Sisters left. Everything Mr. Maguire did he approved of.

I left yesterday morning to come here. He himself comes tomorrow evening to sleep at St. Mary's. But, Father, if the bishop takes us the wrong way, everybody else doesn't. I don't know how to tell you all the trouble Mr. Hervinlle goes through for me and the interest he has in our Community. He's very much afraid that "I can't have Sisters because of their well-being, and that of our New Orleans establishment." He told me that on my return to Louisville I should tell him ahead of time so that he can find a boat to accommodate them and can introduce the Sisters to the captain. Very probably I'm going to be obliged to draw money on you. He'll do me a good turn for that. In Madison I didn't run errands for Mr. Cavana for lack of time. A new arrangement is being made between two steamers waiting there to take travellers from the railroad, the one to Cincinnati, the other to Louisville, so they can throw the trunks from the car into the boat. When you cross there in the front of the ship, you'll have a chance to see this.

The priests at St. Mary's bent over backwards to help the Sisters at their departure in recognition for the services they received from the Sisters. Mr. Maguire is very happy you were kind enough to leave them up to today because, he said, their leaving will mean less right now than when they're en route. He told us he certainly wouldn't have been president if they hadn't stayed last year. Oh, how I value all the kindness of all these priests at St. Mary's. I was temperate with them. I let things go since they had been kind to arrange them, although the Sisters were upset, and this morning too if all they say were true. Finally this evening a beautiful stagecoach just arrived which will carry us all off tomorrow morning. Sister

Mary of the Nativity is going to take the New Orleans road, I believe. Sister Mary of Calvary, however, just decided for herself to go to New Orleans. I felt very bad. She consulted these priests. Finally she just told me "I'll go." One good thing I'm telling you is: Sister Mary of the Five Wounds asked me this morning if she were the Sister who was coming along because you had written that to them. I said that in fact you had thought about Sister Mary of Providence. "Oh," she said to me, "what bad luck; I never could have decided to go there and live with her."

We'll leave Louisville as soon as possible because cholera is hitting everyone from time to time. Saturday at noon a priest from the bishop was called to a man dying of this disease.

Tell Mr. Shortis that everyone in this area thinks about him.

I'm finishing this because I don't have any time. I have to close the Sisters' trunks.

I am with profound respect, Father, your very humble and obedient servant and son in Jesus Christ,

Brother Théodule

A very good gardener here wants to be a Brother. He wants to put himself under your guidance in November.

176. Brother Joseph (56) to Father Sorin

Indianapolis April 29, 1849

Reverend and dear Father,

I expect Father Granger has told you that I am not able to sell anything because my power is not legal. I have written to the bishop to this effect, sending him a formula of power of attorney, but I am affraied he had left Madison before my letter reached that place.

There was a man with me from Jasper. He is a French Suisse; he came to Indianapolis in hope to find a place for his children, where they could learn the French and be raised in there religion. He lost his wife and has four children, two bois and two girls. The oldest is 11 years of age. The man is a carpenter and waggoner, a stout and healthy man. I told him that he migh[t] perhaps work for the board of his children, but that he would have to fournish them their clothes. I promised him that you would write to him to Jasper, du Bois county, and you might ask Mr. Condeck about him.

Please do for this man what you can. He is a good Catholic and a great friend of Mr. Condeck, and it will be a good way of silencing our enemies. Here is this man's address: Francois Rottat, Jasper, Du Bois Co., Ia.

If I cannot sell before six weeks, I will have to get $300 bon gré, mal gré [nilly willy], else I will get in difficulties with Phipps.

I remain, dear Father, with respect and love, your most obedient but unworthy son,

Brother Joseph

177. Brother Vincent (21) to Father Sorin
[Translated from French]

New Orleans May 17, 1849

Very dear Father Superior,

I think you've returned from Baltimore. Did your business go well? And how is our Brooklyn school? And at the Lake, how's everything? And are my trees green? There's undoubtedly been news with you during the six weeks I've been gone. Suppose we start to catch our breath although everything may not be in order.

The good Sisters are fine and give me much consolation. People have already made [ ] for them for our asylum, and they're doing and will do great good there. The name of the Sisters of Charity is respectable and respected all over, and I can speak for everyone. I'm almost sure that we'll have to augment the number.

Poor Brother Francis de Sales will return to the Lake at the moment you don't expect it. He is what he was. It's enough to tell you Brother Louis is fickle. He doesn't bother to follow the rules and almost never does spiritual exercises. Brother Basil and he beat the children too much. I hope that little by little they're reforming. Our establishment is important for the Society. Mr. Butteux wants two Brothers. Can you give them to him?

We had Holy Mass this morning for the first time in our establishment, and Mr. Rousselaus let us have the Holy Sacrament. We'll have Holy Mass on Sundays and once during the week. Our lines of power are set in order nicely, but we should have a director who can lead this big house. It'd be a great setback for the Society to lose it. I'm confident that you'll give us a priest and assure yourself thereby of success, not only for the Brothers and Sisters, but even for the well being of many children and people. To think that for two years our children haven't gone to confession! Priests are scarce sometimes. Mr. Percher told me he'd gladly take one of our priests into his house because he's overworked. We have 100 children. One died this morning of cholera after several hours of the disease. I can't send you any sugar right now. Many plantations are ruined by Mississippi River flooding which crested, and now the water is in the city, in some places four feet deep. Two to three thousand workers are working to rebuild the levee, but up to now they've had no success. The loss is great. The water is still a mile from us. They don't think it'll get to us. They're giving us very bland food, and I don't think that we can keep from sometimes buying something to make ourselves eat because here the taste buds aren't working. However they bought us a [ ] of red wine. We manage ever since!

Brother Théodule was sick this morning with fever. I don't think it's anything but bile. Answer me on the subject of the child I spoke about to Father Granger in my last letter. I have another of them before sending [MS ripped]. I'd like to send off both at the same time. I haven't had a word from the Lake [since] I left.

You'd do well to address my mail in care of Monsignor without which address they won't get to me.

Goodby, very dear Father Superior. Replace me as soon as possible. You'll do a favor to him who is with respect your very humble and obedient son in our Lord Jesus Christ,

Brother Vincent

Have you gotten [the bill] for 250 dollars that I sent to you in my last letter to Father Granger? It was payable to the City Bank of New York.

178. Brother Vincent (22) to Father Moreau
[Translated from French]

New Orleans May 18, 1849

Reverend Father,

In my last letter, I had told you that Father Visitor had named me to head the orphan asylum at New Orleans. I went there on April 25 and entered the asylum on May 1.

Our establishment is composed of five Brothers, two for the classes (Brothers Basil and Louis), one for the dormitories (Brother Francis de Sales), one kitchen director (Brother Théodule), and finally I, who am in charge of the house and am liaison with the administration of which the bishop is spiritual head, and the other members, all lay, are the temporal heads. The Brothers are paid 630 francs apiece, and the director 750. There are also three Sisters who are reimbursed 500 each. These prices will seem a little high to you; however, it's low for the area. You understand that with that we have board, but very simple food. The three Sisters are Sister Mary of the Five Wounds (Superior), Sister Mary of Calvary and Sister Mary of the Nativity. This last one is Irish and is in charge of the infirmary. We have 98 orphans. Cholera killed one of them the night between Wednesday and Thursday. In two months 16 to 17 children have died in the asylum. The good Sisters will do immense good here. They've already been given gifts for the asylum by ladies they don't even know.

Very odd: on Wednesday toward evening, Sister Mary of Calvary, coming back from confession at the Ursulines' (that's where we go to confess to the chaplain of those ladies), encountered several people fighting in the street. She heard a voice which said, "Sister of Charity, come to me, I have a broken arm." Someone else wanted to stop her, but the good Sister, listening only to her zeal, like the good Samaritan bound up the wound of the injured man and returned home entirely joyous to tell her superior what had happened.

Our administrators promised me that they're going to have a chapel built for us. While waiting, we've obtained a rather large room which will serve us provisionally as a chapel. Holy Mass was celebrated there for the first time on Ascension Day; we have the good fortune to have with us the very Blessed Sacrament. We need a priest of the Society here, whether he comes from the Lake or is sent to us from France. The problem is that we have to have a priest here who can speak English well because all our children, except one, can confess only in English. The need is urgent: for two years the children have not been to confession. Nevertheless, there's no need to rush: I have to see Monsignor when he returns from the Council in Baltimore. Otherwise Father Superior would have had to go there. I'm also ignoring the arrangements they've made. The New Orleans climate for many years has been unhealthy, especially for strangers. The water isn't good. We drink water only from the rainspout collected in immense tubs and saved. Everything is as it is in Algiers: oranges, lemons, pomegranates, etc., etc.

The Mississippi broke its dike, which we here call a levee. Water rushed in and is still rushing like a torrent in a large part of the city, from there into the sugar and cotton plantations. The inhabitants have to save themselves. The loss is immense. It is thought that the water won't reach us. It's still half a league away. Two or three thousand workers are employed to fix the levee, but in the evening they aren't any more ahead than in the morning. They made the [water] run into ditches. Although they were reinforced with stones and bricks, they haven't been any less carried away by the current. God sometimes shows men His power before which all ingenuity and knowledge can do nothing.

Every day near us there are slave auctions. Here's how it's done: men who make a business of it go to buy them, and then they dress them in beautiful blue cloth, and then they are exposed on the sidewalks from morning to night. Fathers are sometimes separated from their children. The same happens to women.

When you write to us, you have to address your letters in care of Monsignor Le Blanc to send to the Brothers or the Sisters of the Catholic Orphan Asylum, or address them to Father Sorin in an envelope. He'll send them to us. It's the surest way.

Goodby, reverend Father. I have the greatest wish to see you before I die.

Brother Vincent

If Father Superior can't replace me here with a director, I'd ask you to do the same yourself. It isn't necessary that the one who replaces me knows English, but he should have a sense of order and tact. I'll die happy, it seems to me, if I die without office.

If I had stayed at the Lake, I would have asked to make a trip to France, because I have many things to tell you for the good of the mission.

179. Brother Vincent (23) to Father Sorin
[Translated from French]

New Orleans May 27, [1849]

Very dear Father Superior,

Are you all dead at Notre Dame du Lac? This is the fourth letter I've sent without getting a word of response.

Poor Brother Théodule has been sick ten days. He has what is called intermittent fever. The doctor who visits him every day told me these fevers aren't dangerous, but he [Théodule] isn't less affected by it, and he told me yesterday evening to write you that he doesn't have the energy to stay in the kitchen, that he could never put up with the heat. I told him that I wanted him to try at least once more when he is cured. Don't change anything before another letter.

Brother Louis has a kind of sediment on his hand. He suffers a lot. The doctor opened his finger this morning. As you see, Providence sends us crosses that we weren't expecting. Brother Basil is doing well here. He seems to be happy. Please write him a few words. I'm pretty good in the midst of all this work. I have to go to the market every morning for the day's provisions. Brother Francis de Sales does his best in the dormitories. He runs them properly and orderly. Our administrators seem content. The good [Sisters] are doing wonders, and with the grace of God, I hope their numbers will increase.

Don't make any changes until my next letter.

Write to Brother Théodule also. He's shown good will. I'd be in despair if I lost him. In any case, if a change has to be made, here's how I'd do it in your place: Brother Théodule would run the dormitories, Brother Francis the lower class, and Brother Louis would return to the novitiate. He needs it. Have you received Mr. Percher's propagator? We got it free.

Monsignor ought to be here on June 7. I'll have several questions to submit to him.

Respect and good wishes to those deserving them.

I am with the most profound respect, very dear Father, your very humble and obedient son in our Saviour Jesus Christ,

Brother Vincent

Not being able to post my letter this morning, I have another day. The doctor fears that Brother Louis may lose his finger, and he [Louis] doesn't want to suffer through the operation that has to be done.

Yet another child carried off from us by cholera tonight. Pray for us, better for Brother Louis.

180. Brother Théodule (6) to Father Sorin

[Translated from French]

New Orleans June 6, 1849

Reverend Father,

I'm endeavoring today to pen some words to you. I think my energy allows my doing that because, as you know, I think Brother Vincent told you I'm recuperating from sickness. I'm never the last to succumb to a country's diseases. I think I'll have to drag along with them nearly my whole summer. The doctor, in whom Brother Vincent has the utmost confidence, has made me take quinine. I don't know when I'll get through it. I don't have any confidence in this doctor with all his medicines. But, dear Father, one always has to be ready to go. Cholera is in the asylum as elsewhere and carries off a person in less than 24 hours, and the big problem is not being able to have priests. You have to die that way. Truthfully, I was afraid. I can tell you that Mr. Seveque and several members of the asylum authorities said we need a priest from our Society, if it were possible. A request was to be made to you for one like the administrator of those who are heading the administration. Father Gouesse is not suitable at all. You see that I [ ]. I don't like the way the asylum is administered nor the methods of him who is at the top, an old German. [ ] and to dispute [ ] who sees all over and [ ] to everything. When he comes here, he meddles in everything, even doing the cooking. When I cook, he doesn't get tempted to do it, but he has to give me directions on how to peel potatoes. When I go to town on business to look for meat and do other errands, I have to go to his house. He wants to buy everything. Everything is spent too quickly. He is very quick to try everything himself. However he has a rather good heart, but has to order at the butcher's the quantity of meat; then enough or not, I have to make do with that. Always beef. No variety. We never have anything but fresh beef to eat and potatoes. Nothing else with our money.

Dear Father, now some words on my schedule. Every morning at 5 AM, I leave for the city three miles away. That's six miles in this little prison cart. The New Orleans streets are horrible, paved in stone but very badly. That's not good for my health. For dinner I have to cook by myself at my stove where you could cook for 300 people. It's as high as my shoulders. How can it be done, to work in a small kitchen paved in very beautiful stones, which from sunrise are heated until noon by the sun besides the heat of the stove? Do you yourself think I'm capable of being able to do it? I say it's impossible in a country so hot.

I didn't come down with fever at Notre Dame du Lac in hot weather. Certainly it's more hot here. To tell you the truth, before leaving, if I had known that I'd have to cook, I would have said that it wasn't possible for me to do it in a country so hot, but I never believed that they relied on live coals in the kitchen. There's an old black woman alone in the kitchen. She does what she can. Certainly she has enough to clean and wash. The doctor himself gives me advice in regard to the kitchen. I tried to satisfy them all. When I'm better, I'll begin again but by frequently falling, I'd fall one time for the last time. I'm not complaining to anyone about the position where I find myself, but Father Drouelle should get more information about it. You said only to do cooking. For me it's too much. We have lots of trouble keeping blacks. Brother Vincent says he believes I can do it. The doctor told him that. And Brother Vincent the other day for supper made a hundred things of corn.

Our position is very extraordinary. I'm beginning to catch on. We never have any exercise in common. Brother Francis de Sales thinks himself free of everything. Brother Louis the same thing. Each does as he pleases. That's the way it is. Thus since my sickness I've done my spiritual exercises in private. I'll try to continue more recreation together. Each does as he pleases. Brother Vincent himself goes off, and then everyone is free to do anything. There's no complaint to make to Brother Vincent because it has to be for the best. I don't see any way of dealing with certain people who don't want to do anything unless it pleases them. So it's too much. They are perfectly independent. In certain circumstances I almost took complaints to Brother Vincent. If two were sent back to Notre Dame du Lac, we'd have peace and less trouble here. It's useless to speak more about it. I just received a very nice letter from Mr. Lavialle in which he tells me that he received the bill I sent him in reimbursement for 40 dollars that he had lent me. I'm happy with this. His letter and wonderful testimony more [Letter incomplete]

181. Brother Joseph (57) to Father Sorin

Indianapolis June 10, 1849

Reverend and dear Father,

I will briefly state [to] you that the bishop has been here, and that he has done nothing. He told me that he wants to see you first. I have greatly calmed him down. I think he will make you the concession of the $3000 if we make an orphan assylum, but he prefers to have it at Indianapolis, and so would I for many reasons.

I am hemed up. I can do nothing. I wish these things would take a speedy end. I am sure I could have sold the half of the lots since I sold one last week. I took $5.00 on account until I can make a bond.

Write to the bishop.

The army worms destroyed me over 5000 cabbages and a great many other things.

Receive, dear Father, my respect and love, and believe me always your most obedient though unworthy son,

Brother Joseph

182. Brother Joseph (58) to Father Sorin

Indianapolis June 17, 1849

Reverend and dear Father,

My situation is not very desierable, from the fact that there is nothing about what I have to do. If there was some kind of an institution to be here, I would take a great satisfaction in exerting my zeal and efforts to this end. If I could and should sell, I would have the consolation soon to be freed from the burdensome and toilsome life I lead here, but in my tedious state of uncertainty, I am almost tempted to run away. I have applications for lots almost every day, but I can do nothing. I think it will be necessary for you to write urgingly to the bishop or to go yourself to see him.

Miss Josephine is determined to become [a] Sister. She wants to come in a week or two. She will do such a step reluctantly, but she begins to see that it is the finger of God that leads her. I think now that she will make a good Sister, if she is treated kindly. Everything can be obtained of her by charity and kind treatment, but she has a very lively feeling for the least harshness or unkindness. She is a very smart woman, and very ecomnonical. I am sorry to lose her. I don't get any more letter[s] from you. Answer to this. I received a letter from Brother Vincent. How is Auguste doing?

I remain, dear Father, with respect and love, your most obedient but unworthy son,

Brother Joseph

Tell Auguste about his sister's decision.

183. Brother Vincent (24) to Father Sorin
[Translated from French]

New Orleans June 22, 1849

My very dear Father,

Good Father Granger told me in his last letter that the thorn lives near the rose and the cross near consolations. I'm experiencing the same. Since May 15, poor Brother Théodule hasn't had two days of health; always new setbacks. He's better, however, once again. His dysentery is over, but he's confined to his bed or room. Sister Mary of Calvary is also paying for getting used to the climate. Brother Louis is now teaching his class. I can say that I'm the most productive of all, but perhaps not the most contented or the happiest; my greatest pain is seeing that we live without doing any exercises in common. When Father Visitor promised us we'd be able to follow the rules, he hadn't foreseen, no doubt, the obligations the asylum imposed on us. We can never all get together, not even for meals, since we always have to accompany and supervise close to one hundred children. I also believe that no one is happy. Brother Basil said yesterday: "If a priest doesn't come from the Lake, I won't stay here." I counselled Monsignor to ask you for a priest, and I asked the priest-director. Both are devoted to us. I have to tell you in all sincerity, to do the greatest good you should send us Father Granger, if only for six months. I know Monsignor and the administrators, and the needs of the Brothers and Sisters. New Orleans can be a resource for Notre Dame du Lac. His Grace spoke to me about an establishment for two or three Brothers at St Patrick's; other requests for Brothers and Sisters will be made to you if we succeed, but you have to come to our help on the spiritual matter, without which New Orleans will be a tomb for vocations.

On Sundays we go to a Low Mass. That's it for the whole day. The Sisters are happier than we are because they can follow their rules. I wish you'd give me permission to give back to the Sisters the $150 that I get for them every six months. They'll be more free to buy what they need; you understand that it's hard for a Sister superior to ask a Brother for a dress or a veil, etc. I'm sure they won't misuse it, and this mark of confidence you'll give them will do them good, as you can understand. After all, you'll lose nothing; they'll have to account to you for the use they'll have made of the money they hadn't sent you.

Unfortunately Sister Mary of Calvary and Mother Superior can't get along; it's a continual hassle because they stop at nothing. You'll have to be so kind as to write to Sister Mary of Calvary not to get unravelled, and to Sister Mary of the Five Wounds, who is, in my opinion, a little busy-body or at least too moody, pushing too far what is only sometimes necessary. You see, the devil understood how to ruin us in our beginning a work which will raise us up or achieve our ruin.

Once again, as soon as the greatest hot spells are over, you'll have to send us Father Granger to have each of us make a good retreat. You understand I desire you with all my heart, but you'd be able to stay here a month at most. That's not enough. Father Gouesse can no longer make the visit because I know from a good source that he's not suitable for all the Brothers, even for confession and direction. I'd first thought about Father Barrou, but he barely knows the Brothers, nor they him. Once we are well established here, I think he could work out, especially if you mold him for that. I'm not of the opinion that you'd ask too high a price if you're asked for a priest; he'll get, I think, something for his perquisites, and then I believe our souls are dearer to you than any good thing on earth. If we were taken one or another by a case of cholera or diseases which only afford a few hours of preparation, it could be very likely we'd all die without the last sacraments. I've had the saddest experience of that with a child 8 to 9 years old. The day before yesterday, I was searched out in the afternoon to go baptize a dying child. That brave man had travelled four hours without being able to find any priest. This poor child died two hours after he was baptized.

June 25

Things are becoming more certain, but at the same time more perplexing and sadder. Whom do you have to replace Brother Théodule in the kitchen? No one, I bet. I believe we have to give that up, but how are the administrators going to take it? I don't know.

The doctor thinks the sick Brother would be able to have another job in the house. Here's what I propose, supposing that Brother Théodule becomes capable in a month of taking care of the dormitories. I'd put Brother Francis de Sales in to teach the lower class, and I'd return to you Brother Louis who is otherwise unsuited here and may leave us. This would be still another change I'd like to avoid. Moreover if Brother Théodule leaves the asylum, there's no hope that I could return to the Lake, not even for the most urgent business.

The meeting of our directors took place yesterday. I don't know if they'll ask you for a priest right away. Their finances are too low at this moment. That doesn't prevent you from sending us Father Granger to restore in us the spirit of our vocation, unless you come yourself since vacation time is the time when you are most free. If you give Brother Théodule or Brother Louis permission to go home, you'd have to send 30 dollars for their trip, because we have no money, nor do I know where to get any. If the sick weren't ruining us, I thought I could send you 200 dollars on All Saints' Day, but please don't count on me. As soon as I reach the second semester, I'll send you everything I can.

Please send back to Brother Théodule his medical certificate so we can present it to the asylum directors to justify the change. How's the harvest? And the lime and everybody? My God, Father, there are things on earth troubling to the heart! May God be praised. Goodby, very dear Father, your very humble and obedient son,

Brother Vincent

A thought is going through my head and makes me unseal my letter. If the Visitor had to come soon, it would perhaps be better to wait to effect the change at the time of his visit. I think I have to ask for no recompense for Brother Théodule since he worked only fifteen days.

June 27

Your letter of yesterday evening made me open mine again. Don't send anyone here if you aren't asked to, except to replace Brother Théodule. Don't send us Brother Placidus. You'll ruin everything. You should do what you judge appropriate for Brother Théodule. A resolution was taken that I would have wished to put off, but it's over. The doctor has made a decision; the same doctor told me this morning that Brother would be able to work in the dormitories. Moreover, I think that Brother Louis will become congested. He already has a bad cough, another reason to call him back to the novitiate.

I'm sorry you weren't able to send us Father Granger for a visit because we can't sustain the religious spirit in the midst of such disorder. I still don't know when the box will come. Mr. Rousselon does what he can, but he hasn't yet succeeded.

Respect and good wishes to those deserving them.

You say in your last letter that "old Brother Vincent ought to know how to give orders." I have never been able to, not even to our blacks. You knew it before sending me here.

I hope with God's grace that I'll die in New Orleans through obedience, but with the regret of not having a single one of our priests to assist me in the final moment.

Brother Vincent

I beg Father Gouesse to forgive me if I'm unable to write him yet today.

184. Brother Vincent (25) to Father Sorin
[Translated from French]

New Orleans June 27, 1849

Dear Father Superior,

Brother August asked me to beg you to send him a new habit of the Brothers' style. A mantle for adoration. The quality of the cloth which now ought to service priests and Brothers. We should also have a hat called a cardinal in the circular letter of Reverend Father [Rector], Constitutions, directories, books for saying office in the novitiate.

The eight postulants I found here seem to me well disposed for religious life, but the novitiate can only begin when you come back. The labors of the Cross and the sick, who must be replaced, take up all their time. I find myself studying for the most part.

The New Orleans marketing showed a profit of $4500 clear. Last semester has been paid for. Father Cointet sent a check here for $600. The college seems to me to be going along well. Your children can't be happier to learn that you had arrived [in] France, but all ask when you will come back. Don't leave us here without you, except for the shortest time possible. Brother Francis Xavier is in charge of the apprentices. Will I dare, dear Father, to beg you to offer my regards to Reverend Father [Rector]? I've written to him three times in the last eight months. He hasn't written me for a long time, that is, since his return from Rome. This is the second note I'm sending you in France by means of good Father Granger's letters.

Goodby, dear Father. We're praying for you so your trip may be happy and your return prompt. That's the hope of your very humble and obedient son in Jesus, Mary, and Joseph,

Brother Vincent, Josephite

Reverend Father [Rector] will learn about the New Orleans marketing with pleasure.

185. Brother Vincent (26) to Father Granger
[Translated from French]

New Orleans July 8, 1849

Very dear Father Granger,

Our letters of June 26 and 27 must have confused you a lot, but there are critical moments in life. You have experienced them as I have. Brother Théodulc is better. He appears to want to return to Notre Dame du Lac. I'm sorry about that. He could have done service here.

Brother Louis is always fickle and changing. God knows what'll become of him. Brother Basil is fine and does wonders with the orphans. The two months I've spent here are giving me enough experiences to tell you what an asylum is. No possibility of following the rule. Father Visitor and the members of the Minor Chapter at Notre Dame du Lac, without wishing to do so, have put us in a style of living a little like seculars, sending us a dispensation so that before God and in the eyes of the Society we may be treated with mercy. The Sisters don't have the same disadvantage because they aren't in charge of children. I ordinarily get up at 4:30. I say my vocal prayer; then with my little horse and cart I go for provisions at least two and a half miles away. I never return before 7 AM, sometimes very worn out. The Brothers in charge of the children get up at 5 AM, and the children at 5:30. As you see, no prayer for them, no more than for me. Then one hundred children on their backs all day long. They can't leave them alone for a minute. No [particular] examen for the Brothers who teach class, and very often none for me either, because with Brother Théodule being incapable of doing his job, I have to replace him as much as I can. The two Brothers are very glad that I take part of the recreation [supervision], because they're tired of always being with the children and have their studies and classes to prepare. Brother Basil presides over the children's meals and takes his meal after us. I've persuaded the Brothers to make up in private what they can. I also have a dormitory to supervise. Thanks be to God I'm pretty healthy in body; you understand the reason for it. A religious without regular exercises can scarcely leave the heart satisfied. Twice our confessor has been able to hear us only after a fortnight. Moreover, I go to communion only on Sunday since I have to go to market every day. However, I'm not losing heart. I always hope that God will have me die at Notre Dame du Lac or Notre Dame de Ste. Croix.

Before the last assembly, I hoped to have a priest from the Lake, but the asylum funds seem drained at this time. They can't make new sacrifices. I hope, however, to see you on a visit, but don't come before September because of the terrible heat and yellow fever. I believe good Father Superior has left for Canada; if not, you can give my letter to him. Sister Mary of Calvary also seems to want to return to the Lake, but watch out about making too many changes. You'll hurt the establishment.

Have the kindness to send $30 for Brother Théodule's return. I have already said that, because I have no money and don't know how to get any for his trip.

The child in question has been growing a little cold. I wrote to the father who hasn't responded. It's impossible for me to send you provisions before receiving the second salary payment, and besides, sugar is expensive now, and moreover, they don't like to give credit here.

Greetings and good wishes to all the good Brothers. May they all pray for me who prays little; and you, good Father, remember me often in the holy Sacrifice [of the Mass].

Your very humble servant,

Brother Vincent

Poor Brother Francis de Sales is so up in arms against Father Superior that he told me not to send him a single word. What do you hope to expect from a religious who has such a hatred against his superior? His state of mind troubles me, and even more his language. Good grief, my good Father, if you know how much I suffer in the pit of my soul, you'd sympathize with my grief and send someone to take my place. If you don't have a man at the Lake, you can ask for one from the motherhouse or from Canada.

Here's how our asylum is run: the assembly of directors is composed of fifteen people. Monsignor is the president and pastor of the cathedral. All the other members are lay. The director whom I have to answer to every day is an old German, zealous for the asylum, but a little too meddlesome and sometimes too severe.

I hope Fathers Cointet and Gouesse will excuse me if I'm so lazy as not to write to them. Be good enough to give them my news, and may they please remember me in their holy exercises.

186. Brother Théodule (7) to Father Moreau

[New Orleans] July 31, 1849

[This letter has been misplaced in the archives of the Holy Cross Generalate in Rome.]

187. Brother Vincent (27) to Father Moreau
[Translated from French]

New Orleans August 1, 1849

Reverend Father,

If you wish to create another Ste. Croix, I think you should take advantage of what presents itself. Mr. Ome [Homer?] Mignard, a former Lazarist, left in Provence to Notre Dame des Lumières, Vaucluse, an estate with buildings said to be worth nearly 300,000 francs. There's room for 300 people. The Provence missionaries occupy it now, but with no title to the property. In order to know how things stand, you have to address yourself to the Archbishop of Avignon. This good old man [Mignard] fears that death will come before things are set in order, and all this good stuff will go to his family who won't follow through on what he proposes, and he puts as a condition that our Society will agree to raise in perpetuity in one of our houses two students for the priesthood. Five Lazarists bought this establishment before breaking up in 1827, and the contract stipulates that it would belong to the last of the survivors. The donator has welcomed the death of three of his associates, and there's hardly any doubt the fourth will die. This Mr. Mignard comes to say holy Mass for us twice a week. If the matter were to take a good turn, I think that would occasion me the good luck of seeing it so.

We have no sick people in our city now. Our asylum holds 110; if means and lodging weren't lacking, we would have three times as many. Asylums are like colleges: you don't find your rule always followed, especially by those who supervise the children, but I also don't follow the rule. Reverend Father, every morning after saying my vocal prayer, I have a little horse and a cart to go for provisions. I never arrive at the asylum until after 7 AM. I'm rather content with our children, but I'm troubled that no priest is to be had to hear their confession and have them make their communion. For the three months I've been here, I have yet been able to get only 20 of them to confession. Many others haven't confessed for more than two years and perhaps not at all. This good Mr. Mignard who comes to say holy Mass for us twice a week is very old. He is no longer confided with any [spiritual] direction.

I have a great fear, Reverend Father: to die as Director. If you wish to unburden me of this position, I promise to say a rosary for you as best I can.

Please believe me very sincerely, Reverend Father, your very humble and obedient son in our Saviour Jesus Christ,

Brother Vincent

188. Brother Vincent (28) to Father Sorin
[Translated from French]

New Orleans [August 1?] 1849

Very dear Father Superior,

If good things on Earth were a happy omen, I could say I've done one here for the Society. A good old man, a Lazarist, offered me an establishment worth close to three hundred thousand francs. It's Our Lady of Light, Vacluse Department in Provence, one and a half leagues from the beautiful fountain of the same name. This establishment is occupied by the mission priests, but they have no title or right since Mr. Mignard is the proprietor and since he himself wants us to take ownership on condition that our Society will take charge of raising in perpetuity in our houses of education two poor students for the ecclesiastical state. I sent to Father Rector all the information that I could. He'll make, I don't doubt, good if the thing succeeds. I think that I need to make a trip to France, but I'll try to do it in part for Notre Dame du Lac. Let's pray God will direct this affair to His great glory. As Mr. Mignard is very old and there's a fear he may be hit with paralysis, I'm going to ask him to make me a regular will.

If you haven't yet let a person leave to replace Brother Théodule, you'll do well to send no one before October 1 or least before September 15. Ordinarily yellow fever isn't over before All Saints Day. The month of July was so wet that we didn't have two good days. Brother Théodule wants to return to the Lake very much; there are still others, but believe me, changes will not do any good in the first year.

Everything is fine. We have no more sick; only I'm feeling extraordinarily weak the last few days.

Goodby, very dear Father. I am with all possible respect your son in Jesus Christ our Lord,

Brother Vincent

If Brother Basil doesn't get tired, classes will be fine. He has an exactitude and order which is out of the ordinary. Brother Francis [de Sales] is not always in good spirits. He promised me, however, that he wouldn't blab any more. As for me, that's what I wanted. He treated me once rather coarsely. I gladly forgive him. If the last advice I gave him can help him, all will be well. Make sure you write to him. Your news and good Father Granger's make him sit up. I'll give you an account next time.

Brother Vincent

I've learned that your health wasn't good. That concerns me more than you think. I'd love to be near you to care for you in your labors.

189. Brother Vincent (29) to Father Sorin

[Translated from French]

New Orleans August 3, 1849

Very Dear Father,

You're going to be surprised to see Brother Louis. I had to take a side immediately. Brother Basil would have sooner left than to have him for the second class. He's too indifferent, has nothing, not even perseverance in promises. However, keep him. He can work at teaching a small class at the college. There's more. He also wants to go to Canada if his parents meddle. Try to be firm with him. He doesn't have a bad heart.

I'd like the conditions that say we'd be paid every six months changed instead to three months. That would suit us better. We are apt to have trips to make, and we have no money.

Monsignor came to see us on receiving your letter. We'll try to make our particular examen and evening prayer together minus an overseer.

If you could [ ] that your visit here would do good in October, I wouldn't be far from having money to pay for the provisions that you could take.

Goodby, good Father, goodby,

Brother Vincent

I'll write more about Brother Louis. I don't know how the authorities will take not having a supervisor any longer for the kitchen.

Our box finally came into our hands. We found in it a picture of the Blessed Virgin, eight Constitutions, and a directory, with a good number of almanacs. We owe six dollars to Mr. Rousselon for that. He's promised to wait until All Saints' Day.

190. Brother Vincent (30) to Father Sorin
[Translated from French]

New Orleans August 6, 1849

My dear Father,

I've written you by post to tell you about Brother Louis's return. I'm giving Father Granger the details that I promised you in my last letter so you'll be able to understand it.

We've got $90 in debts. The sick have ruined us, and we still haven't paid the doctor or the pharmacy. We had to buy habits for the Sisters, and we'll have to reimburse on the first payment the $25 from the trip which weren't paid for the Brother who's leaving, plus 62 1/2 for the salary of Brother Théodule who worked only three weeks. The above totals $177 1/2. Then we'll need winter habits. I think we should change the point in the contract which says we get paid every six months to "get paid every three months" because it's too troublesome to go so long without money or not be able to do any business, and besides, I don't doubt there'll be some unexpected expenses. You'll lose nothing. In January, I'll send you what I can. I'm asking you as a favor to allow us this latitude. The custom of the country is to pay by the month. They made us pay more for what we bought because we had no money.

Will you be disposed to give us a priest in October? I don't think you have any place where he could do more good—one hundred children to train who haven't yet been to confession nor made first Communion. The bishop had sent a young Irish priest. He just started. Then his business called him back. We haven't seen him for weeks.

I spoke of this spiritual misfortune many times with the bishop. He told me the following: if only your Father were able to supply a priest. That was said to me many times, but nothing's done and the spiritual need increases. So I say if you wouldn't have a salary from the asylum, you'd do a kindness that the priest wouldn't otherwise do. The Brothers and the Sisters long for this moment. Yesterday, I had to send the Sisters up to the bishop's for confession because Mr. Percher was sick and also this priest. If he had a healthy priest, I don't doubt that His Grace would permit him to bring help to so many people who need it.

Yesterday Monsignor told me that he'd like a Sister for the kitchen, if she were prudent about managing and not doing it all herself. Perhaps she could resist that if she began early enough. You could consult Sister Mary of Calvary. Perhaps she'd weather that better than a sedentary life. She told me many times that the active life she had at St. Mary's was more in line with her stuffing. I'd like to do it as a way of romancing the authorities, but she'd have to be replaced by a good seamstress.

Goodby, good Father. Your very humble and obedient son in Jesus Christ,

Brother Vincent

Father Rector tells me Father Drouelle is doing great things in Guadeloupe.

Brother Théodule thinks, as I do, that Sister Mary of Calvary would be suitable for the kitchen. Mr. Rasch and all the administrators would be happy to have a Sister in the kitchen. I have to know definitely if we'll have two more Sisters or not. I repeat, if you were to come, there'd be advantageous arrangements to make. Today they asked me for a baker, but the little concord there is among the members of the management keeps me tied up. The assembly of directors will only take place in two or three months; there's no set plan unless Monsignor speaks up. He's writing to you himself on the same matter as I am. You know what he'll ask you.

They'd already told me that I'm not delivering good happy Sisters. That's true. The directors don't understand the needs of a convent's linen-room and all the order that Sisters would like to see there. It follows from that that I'm carrying the entire blame. Sister Mary of the Five Wounds begs you to give her permission to have a private conference herself with the first director for the good of her linen-room. That puts a chill between us, and the Sisters have many reasons to believe that I'm putting obstacles to good order in their business since their director allows everything for them when he wants. Two days later he changes his mind.

If you can't come here, there'll be the troubles I've foreseen. After some time, if there's no longer harmony between the Sisters and Brothers, everybody'll soon see it and then they'll grieve.

Be good enough to answer Sister Mary of the Five Wounds about what you want her to do on the subject because I promised her I'd make you a party to her reflections. You must consider, my good Father, that you have to replace me as soon as possible, or else you'll see this beautiful establishment decay little by little. I suffer more than anyone in not being able to manage this place and seeing that the great hopes they had for us are waning.

Brother Vincent

Mr. Le Frone offers you his respect and begs you to tell him via me if you'd received in [18] 44 from the Brother in Vincennes the 20 dollars he owed you when he left St. Peter's.

191. Brother Vincent (31) to Father Sorin
[Translated from French]

New Orleans August 8, 1849

Very dear Father,

The delay of Brother Louis's boat gave me time to see once again the director of the asylum. They're asking you only for a Sister to replace Brother Théodule in the kitchen for October. Monsignor is writing to you. I don't know if he'll talk to you about a priest. I'm telling you in my long letter that the Sisters are complaining about being under the direction of a Brother. Sister Mary of the Five Wounds told me that Father Drouelle couldn't have put them under such a rule. Although I told you in my letter yesterday they weren't happy under my direction, I understand they're bargaining with the directors. I'm almost sure they'll cause a disturbance for us, because they're too changeable, especially Sister Mary of the Five Wounds. She's already got me chewing my nails: she wants to do more work than the ways of the asylum permit, and then when it's necessary to pay her, I get good or evil, but more often the one than the other.

Please write to good Sister Mary of the Five Wounds about what she has to understand. Sister Mary of Calvary says that Monsignor is appointed by you as their superior. Please put me up to date on everything so that I don't do any evil. All the troubles I speak to you about in my letters ought not disturb you. I don't think that the [ ] has much [ ]. His Grace told me the directors had confidence in us. It seemed very clear to me that as long as there's no priest as director of the two other branches, there'll be suffering. I'd need only an hour with you to arrange everything. You won't refuse me that.

My Father, for the glory of God, your very humble servant,

Brother Vincent

192. Brother Théodule (8) to Father Sorin
[Translated from French]

New Orleans August 24, 1849

My Father,

Although I don't know what you want to do about the New Orleans establishment, you've responded with nothing. As you know, they've given me charge of the dorms in place of Brother Francis de Sales who took the lower class from Brother Louis who left to rejoin you. In the present circumstances, I'd prefer to take a job than to remain doing nothing at all, and Brother Louis one way or another couldn't stay here. Now I have yet to see my position. I'm resorting to writing you this letter which I would have done three months sooner if sickness hadn't taken hold of me.

It's hardly possible to live in the same house as Brother Francis de Sales. Ever since May I've told Brother Vincent that I wanted to leave the house. Perpetually his war with this man—not that I contributed nothing to this criticism. He makes fun of all who don't go along with him. Everything goes to his head. It's useless to go into all the details. You know his character.

In arriving at the asylum, Brother Vincent without good advice begged him to be his monitor and give him all the advice or information that he'd need apropos to the good direction of the asylum. After that, he almost believed himself to be the director. It was Brother Francis de Sales himself who told me that. Moreover he's almost like a perfect of discipline. In the job that he had, which I have charge of now, work almost all done for the orphans, he believes that I'm not capable of doing as well as he. He can't keep from [ ] and Brother Vincent, who never had great confidence in me for my work at a job, inspects and criticizes. The director says such a thing ought to be done in such time. The other forbids it. They tire me out. Having two masters in the house is too much.

My dear Father, these are the things going on here. I don't know if the bishop asked you for a priest. If there were one here, I'd have no reluctance to stay here. My [ ] is almost done, but to be here longer as it is at present, it's impossible for Brother Francis de Sales or me to change. You must make a visit here. Almost [ ] otherwise seen so many things which would be taken care of if you were there. Who hasn't seen the dispositions of the two Sisters [ ] who are [ ] to approve the direction of the asylum. I believe the first executive director is going because of age. If that one were retired, certainly almost the entire direction would be done by us. Then I'd say that Father Gouesse should come. He'll have work to do.

I beg you, my Father, if things are to remain as they are, have pity on me. Don't leave me here. I'm telling you I'm afraid of it. I wouldn't hide anything from you. If I'm obliged to be the force in this position, I'd write to Reverend Father [Rector]. I'd prefer to leave the house than to be in such a position. My Father, that's what I think. I don't know what you have in mind for the future. I tried to tell you before you left to come so that you could arrange everything when you're there for the [Letter incomplete]

193. Brother Vincent (32) to Father Sorin
[Translated from French]

New Orleans August 27, 1899

Very dear Father,

Mr. Butteux must have already written to you to ask you to give him three Brothers for Bay St. Louis. If such subjects exist, you'll do well to accept, but if they are not strong, especially the chief, I think you'd do well to put off the departure for several months. You still have to look more for virtue and a vocation than to great scions, because in our evil part of the country everyone talks about loosening up.

Be suspicious of vocations of writers and men with devotion. It's only in an established house that they reveal what they are. Don't make any change here until you come because you're expected by everyone for the month of October or the end of September. I can assure you that we are gladly making a short retreat. You should bring with you a Sister for the kitchen if you can find her among your good Sisters at the Lake. I spoke to you in my last letter about the qualities she ought to have.

Brother Louis must have given you a letter from Monsignor Le Blanc, two from me and many from the Sisters.

We're all, thanks be to God, rather well. They don't believe that yellow fever will be so terrible this year.

Do you think you'll be able to replace me soon? The thing is perhaps more urgent than you could believe. If you don't agree with me, you have letters which are coming [MS torn]. I have to tell you that my greatest pain is seeing that I [hurt] those who are obliged to live under me, and I say that many complaints are familiar if they are not [MS torn], and you know that when people [wear out], they have no confidence, and the [MS torn] lost to God the good works of [both] sides.

Another case, not less serious, [MS torn] which is less sensible, is that [the] Director, with whom I have to speak every day, reproached me face to face [MS torn] had no order in my [MS torn]. I don't think, however, that there's any defiance when one speaks thus to a director. It makes him listen rather than when one has no great respect for him. Nothing surprises me, and no longer surprises you. You know me better than anyone. All my talent is reduced into three parts, but nothing leads to its finale. I have a plan in mind that I'll communicate to you as soon as you're here. While waiting, please believe me your very humble servant,

Brother Vincent

Are you all sick? We get no news.

194. Brother Théodule (9) to the Chapter at Notre Dame du Lac
[Translated from French]

New Orleans September 9, 1849 JMJ

To the members of the Minor Chapter of Notre Dame du Lac,

My dear priests and my dear Brothers,

I thought it best to address you in this way so as to make you see the importance of a trip by Father Superior to New Orleans, lest this trip were nullified or definitely stopped, lest this trip not take place, since it had been formerly announced for the month of October. Monsignor and the administrators are all waiting for Father Superior. And I know the bishop is saving this time to put things in order. He said so in my presence to one of the head administrators who asked him if he had written to you about replacing me in the kitchen. He answered, "I'll arrange everything when the Superior gets here." The other day he asked Brother Vincent if we were expecting our superior soon. We always hoped for next month. Then here's my main reason for you to make the sacrifice of absenting Father Superior from your midst: so as not to make us pass as liars with the authorities at the asylum.

Things pertinent to us here certainly are, I believe, in good shape, but they'll be better after Father Superior gets here. There's no doubt about that, a beautiful future in this part of the country if we know how to keep them not only interested in members of the New Orleans family, but also interested in the entire Community in the United States. I'll return Father Superior to you without fail: there's only one case of sickness that could justify the contrary.

On the other hand, for the good of each of us, you well know that when one begins in a place, there's always something. Above all, not only are the Brothers in good order, but also the Sisters. I know everyone's sentiments. If you don't want to see some disagreeable things, consider Father Superior's trip necessary. I won't return to any details on this subject. Here then, my dear priests and my dear Brothers, is the whole point that I'm proposing to you, to make you see our need in having Father Superior's visit, another that makes no difference to him. It would be time and money lost to think so. Brother Vincent asked me to tell you all that, in the interest of the whole Society, because he believes that he can't keep it a secret as freely as I can. He knows he's not loved and approved by all of us here. Not that I'm saying he's wrong. He's right in many instances. I don't tell him that any more. He's beginning to get a little old too. Be so kind, my very dear friends, to send us Father Superior. I make this prayer in the name of everyone here, and I make it to you because I know that you'll give permission. We've received a letter from Father Superior in which he speaks as one not coming.

Last Sunday for the first time we had First Communion for seventeen of our orphans who received confirmation at the same time. Monsignor Blanc said the Mass and gave Communion and Confirmation. We have a chapel which, although small, is very beautiful and nicely decorated, the back of the chapel done in white and blue linen, arranged with pillars at the altar. At each end of the altar there are two small altars, one for the Blessed Virgin where we have a beautiful statue of the Immaculate Conception, and on the other side another altar which I destine to receive a St. Joseph statue, because as I'm sacristan, I spend money quietly to decorate the chapel. And Sister Mary of Calvary does everything as I want it.

A while ago we received much. Soon we'll have too much. Since Brother Louis left, I've spent half of my time on the chapel. Monsignor will permit Benediction of the Holy Sacrament as soon as we have everything necessary for it.

The head director just left for New York where he's going to get a censer, which you don't find in New Orleans.

The most serious matter is a priest. We don't know what you've been told about that. If you've been told something on the matter, don't make us wait. Didn't he touch on remuneration right now? It'd be better to give us one than not to.

As to the offer of Mr. Mignard for his estate, he could make it when we've received a response from Father Rector who ought to have seen what this property is like near the bishop of Avignon, but Father Superior can finish that up when he's here.

I don't believe I can do better than to add a few words from Brother Vincent who makes me pass them along because he's obliged to take the place of Brother Basil who fell sick last night. Brother

Vincent says the St.Louis route is the most direct. I myself believe the contrary: it's the longest and most expensive. I prefer Cincinnati via Indianapolis.

I wish you'd take all these things into consideration because, I repeat in finishing up, a great good will result, but as Brother Vincent says, we'll at least have satisfied our obligation in putting you up to date about everything.

I am with a profound respect, my dear priests and my dear Brothers, your totally devoted servant,

Brother Théodule

I'm in good health. Yellow fever is in town, but will be nothing, they think.

195. Brother Vincent (33) to Father Sorin
[Translated from French]

New Orleans September 18, 1849

Very dear Father,

Your nice little letter yesterday evening consoled us and at the same time grieved us; consoled in seeing that we're going to get a priest superior and grieved because we believe you're not coming yourself when each of us feels the need to open his heart to you. I know almost all the reasons made to get you here, and I believe they're all founded on good motives. So come, good Father, with Father Gouesse.

Monsignor told me this morning that he'd put him with Mr. Perché. He's a very good priest. He'll be fine there if he likes it. He'll have many confessions to hear. He'll have to know German. He'll be separated from us about the distance from the college to the lime yard. In the rainy season the roads are bad. Father, when we have a chapel, the priest can live with us. But the asylum can't do it this year. Be kind enough to tell Father Gouesse everything so he won't be disappointed. I wish he'd hold chapel services for us once a week. He won't preside over our other exercises because he won't be living with us.

Without being a theologian, I fear that Brother Francis de Sales may not be conscientious in our Society. He does no exercise with us, criticizes everything done. All is fine in other congregations, but at the Lake there's always something to criticize.

Your fine letter of August 30 just arrived and cheers us up with the hope that you'll soon visit us. I won't want the $100 that we lacked. We think it'd be better for you to come with Father Gouesse. You'd settle everything with Monsignor, both for the number of Sisters and for the position of Father Gouesse. If the New Orleans establishment is well directed, it'll encourage others. Mr. Rousselon already spoke to me about a home for widows. I'm convinced that when he knows us, he'll entrust it to your Sisters as soon as you have a priest. If you came, you could perhaps finish the business affair with Mr. Mignaud. I'll have at that time a reply from Reverend Father Rector, and if it hasn't arrived, it were still better to transfer the gift than to remain in danger of seeing this good old man go into the other world with just his good intentions.

Two priests just died in the bishopric. Mr. Operman and one you didn't know.

If Brother Basil doesn't see you, I have some fears. You know him. He told me, a week ago after a disagreement with Brother Francis, that he'd stay until your arrival, that he feared your being far away. He must have something to tell you. He was a great hit here with the children. He's never been so good as in this job. He's so good to the little children that he made them his troop. I also wish that Mr. Buteux's foundation would be made only after your trip, or that you yourself were bringing the Brothers. If they're skilled, arrange everything with Mr. Buteux. Try not to give its direction to an Irish Brother. They're too fickle. I beg the members of the Chapter not to be opposed to a trip which must produce for the whole Society an advantageous development.

Thanks, good Father, for the truly paternal advice you gave me in your letter of the 30th. I like when one thus talks to me without subterfuge. You'll have many other things to say to me when you've heard the sentiments of each here. I'll again repeat to you that I'm not designed to give orders. Brother Théodule does wonders now that his health is back. He has good taste and good judgement and has succeeded in everything he's attempted. You have to see our little chapel as he's nicely arranged it. We have statues of the Blessed Virgin and St. Joseph and your tableau in the middle. That catches the eye magnificently in a place so poor. Will you carry off your tableau?

Goodbye. Come to us quickly. Forgive me for all the disorder and confusion that I've given you since your last going away. You will oblige, good Father, he who is with respect your very humble servant,

Brother Vincent

We're all fine. There's no yellow fever this year in New Orleans except for some very isolated cases.

196. Brother Vincent (34) to Father Sorin
[Translated from French]

New Orleans October 2, 1849

Very dear Father Superior,

My last letter must have given you some inquietude on the subject of Brother Francis de Sales. He's better, and he's promised me he no longer wants to pick fights so often. His change becomes necessary. You should try to give us a capable man to supervise the children at their recreation and to prefect them in the dormitory. Brother Ignatius, for example, with all his good will, can't do it. I can tell you nothing on the subject of the Sisters you're talking about. Our directors are absent, and Monsignor told me he'd do nothing before they assemble again. You haven't told me if it's Father Gouesse whom you're going to send or not. Our asylum is coming along well. There are no sick among our children who number 120. The Brothers and the Sisters weren't as well at departure as they are at present—I am.

One can no longer be surprised that you haven't received letters from Mr. Butteux who waits impatiently for your answer. I saw Mr. Mignard again. He wants a response from Father Rector before [concluding] the affair. He'd do it—I'm sure of it—if you came; but you didn't say a word in your fine letter yesterday.

I'm very concerned how things are at the Lake: if the Brothers are giving you authentic facts; if they're happy, and where they are lodged; if those who are destined for the schools have teachers, and who is directing their spiritual exercises. Have you tried something with the Propagation of the Faith? or do you definitely hope for nothing—how has your harvest been, etc., etc. All that is interesting to me more than you think because I don't really know if I'm still at Notre Dame du Lac in spirit or in New Orleans.

Good Father Granger and all his anchorites would do well to pray to God for us. Father Cointet is undoubtedly always out on mission. I recommend myself also to his prayers. How's Brother Gatian: is his mind okay?

Goodbye, dear and good Father. Come see us. It's the wish of your very humble and obedient servant,

Brother Vincent

I can't tell you enough good about Brothers Théodule and Basil, and about your three Sisters.

197. Brother Vincent (35) to Father Sorin
[Translated from French]

New Orleans October 26, 1849

Very Dear Father,

I answered your telegram from Madison uselessly since it arrived on the 23rd and you wrote it on the 19th. If my response came to you at the same time, it surely wouldn't have found you at Madison. I'm ignorant now of where you are. If unfortunately you've given up visiting us, you're going to see Brother Basil leave. He told me he was sent here for the job and that I had to be satisfied with him. He teaches his class well, but he does what he wants. You know his character. It's a loss for our asylum if we lose him, I've put the whole affair in St. Joseph's hands. [MS covered by seal] all expired cases. Do you have a capable subject for the large class? I'll try by telegram if the matter is too pressing.

Brother Francis de Sales is fine. Encourage him if you judge it appropriate. I'm also enlisting you to write to Brother Basil. Your letter will do him good. I'm sure of it. If he doesn't leave before having thought about it. You see that the Lord sends us crosses of many sizes. Be kind enough to ask Him for the strength to carry them.

Read the letter from Mother Superior.

Father Gouesse hasn't arrived. I really need a priest to help me carry my burden. My somber and sometimes melancholy character must displease those who live with me. They also tell me they'd prefer to do business with Brother Théodule than with me. Brother Théodule can do more in a day than I can in a week. But above all, I have to obey.

Your very humble and obedient son in our Lord Jesus Christ.

Brother Vincent

No reply from Father Rector on Mr. Mignard's business. I have a letter from Mr. Groens; but I don't know where it is.

198. Brother John of the Cross (1) to Father Sorin

Indianapolis November 19, 1849

Reverend and dear Father Superior,

I have contracted a small debt when I was leaving you, the sum of one dollar which I got from a yong man named Mr. Newgent Edward. I thought my duty to direct the litter to you and give you sum a count of myself. It belongs children to give an a count of themselves to there perents, but I am not worthy of that title at present. As soon as I came to Indianapolis, I got work at my trade at 16 dollers a mounth and my bord and has got good health sence I com here. Dear Father, be not displesd with me for leaving the Community for sum time as I have always been oneasy to [k]now a bout father and sister that is in this contry and has never seen her sence I came to America. I exspect a litter from Ireland in a fue weeks. I can get work plenty here in different shops and it is my intention to remain here this winter onless you would insist on me to go home for I now I have been to disobedient to you which leavs me surrouned with many dangers and a lone and on nown [unknown]. However, it discourages me when I see that I can not get work at my trade in the Community, a trade which I am now well able to work at. I now also that sum Brothers' vocation is to mouch exsposed to worldly people in the Community. I now I have been sum times more exposed than I would wish, but I hope I have not lost all yet.

Father, remember me in your prayers, especialy when you are offering the sacrafice of the Mass and also to the prayers of the Community.

I remain yours,

Brother John of the Cross
At present Michael Callon

Please to give this doller to Mr. Edward Newgent for me.
Indianapolis

199. Brother Stephen (1) to Father Sorin

Chicago November 21, 1849

Dear and Reverend Father,

It's with pleasure we anounce to you on our fortunate success so far. When we arived at Niles and ascertained the time the cars would leave, we hastened to attend to supply the wants of the shoeshop, aware as we have been that the Brothers were not capable, also the demands of the storekeeper, yet they acted very kindly but demands money on Saturday, if possible.

We have obtained the signature and seal of the bishops and their kind approbation and dined with them on this day, but the Right Reverend Bishop de St. Pallias don't sign the deed until next Tuesday at the colege on his way to Plymoth.

The good bishop and priests of Chicago received me very kindly but have no money, but what none other ever got I have permission to collect when and where I please.

Dear Father, we request the prayers and all the Community until we return and remain, your most devoted and very humble servant and son in Jesus Christ,

Brother Stephen

200. Brother Stephen (2) to Father Sorin

Ottowa, Illinois December 20, 1849

Reverend and dear Father,

We are once more enabled to communicate our affairs to you and to ask the prayers of the community to return thanks to God thro the intercession of our holy patrons and beg for further lights of grace. We scarcely need say to you the many difficulties are to be met with in this wild region and the infamous language we must listen to on our travels amongst all sorts and sexes.

We are at present requested by the Reverend Mr. O'Donald to spend Christmas with him, and after he will assist me as far as his influence can prevail. Indeed, it's good for me to have such an oppertunity to celebrate this holy time for it is necessary to spend a little time in peace and recollection, after listening to such follies and wickedness.

Dear Father, not very aware of the manner by which collections may be made profitably, it is necessary to remain two or three days in one village and to be introduced by some person of influence both temporally and spiritually. Otherwise we may travil without only very small benefit. Indeed, as yet we cannot boast of much. There remains in my hands ninety-seven dollars and forty-two cents. We intend to remit $100 when able. We hope you have received the draft on New York for our $100 payable to the Order of Ed. Sorin. If you have not received it, write to A.B. Brand and Co., Chicago, Ill., Lake Street. N.B., Chicago, Ill., the Exchange Office of A.B. Brand and Clarke Street. A draft for the avails of one $100 on New York, payable to the order of E. Sorin, No. 6614, drawn on December 1, 1849, and mailed.

The Reverend Mr. John Englisher of Joliet has directed a man by the name Lamb as a postulant for the Brothers. There is another by the name of Ballard in Joliet who is worth about [ ] dollars, and we have left some instructions for him how he may proceed to Notre Dame du Lac, but he has purchased land and paid to the priests [ ] for it to an amount of $4.50. He has the remainder in cash, $5.50.

We are asked on what terms Sisters are received or how much is required. To this we cannot answer decidedly. Please to say if you see fit to do so. We are under promise to the right reverend bishop of Chicago to say that if the orphans are not kept very differently from what they have been, that they will injure the college very severly, and that both bishops were of the same oppinion. This were communicated to the bishop of Milwake in my presence. Yet some others say the apprentices are entitled to more than our rules permit, such as when 21 years old $100 and three suits of clothes by law.

Mr. Obrine remarked to me that the manner by which a draft drawn on the citizens of Chicago was executed has injured the colege and that there were much taulk about how business were done and that they came to the conclusion not to send children since the board of businessmen there are incapable of business transactions. This Mr. OBrine is acquainted with you and has been there, but as to the draft unless that drawn of Oscar Collett and not allowed to take the regular course.

Dear Father, we have many things to vindicate and prejudices to remove that has been lodged against us. Mr. [ ] Brackin showed very bad will. Mrs. Brackin said in Chicago that John has given up the desire to be [a] priest. Therefore he will return to Chicago next year, but Reverend Mr. Inglisber said he disputes his lawful birth and that it's a question if they ever were maried, but he intends to find out if so or not. There has a brother of one of our Sisters died in Chicago a few days before I arived there. All speak very well of him.

Dear Father and Brothers, I am well at present. Please to write as soon as this letter comes to hand. I wish to know if the bishop had delivered the deed in due order to you as he promised.

Please to give my love to all the Community and what advice you see necessary to give to me and how business goes on. Mr. McLinchy came to Chicago, but what or where he has gone I don't know. He said the only objection he had not to stay is Brother Dominic's conduct.

We remain your servant and son in Jesus Christ until death,

Brother Stephen

Direct your letter to Ottowa, Ill., in care Reverend Mr. O'Donnel.

Chronological Table

2-17-37	Death of James Dujarié, founder of Brothers of St. Joseph
3-01-37	Fundamental Pact signed joining Brothers of St. Joseph with Moreau's auxiliary priests
6-26-39	Moreau's circular letter proposing a single congregation of Josephites, auxiliary priests, and Sisters
5- -40	Moreau announces plans for a new church at Ste. Croix
8-15-40	Moreau and four auxiliary priests take religious vows
8-08-41	Brothers Vincent, Anselm, Gatian, Joachim, Francis Xavier, and Lawrence leave for America (first colony) with Sorin and Sister St. Francis Xavier
9-13-41	First colony arrives in New York City
9-26-41	First colony leaves New York City by steamboat up the Hudson River
10-01-41	First colony arrives at Fort Wayne
10-02-41	First colony arrives at Logansport
10-10-41	First colony arrives at Vincennes
10-14-41	First colony settles at St. Peter's (Montgomery), Indiana

8-21-42	Eight novices received at St. Peter's
11-12-42	Three novices received at St. Peter's
11-16-42	Two Brothers (Gatian, Francis Xavier) and two novices (Patrick, Basil) begin trip north with Sorin to Notre Dame site
11-27-42	Sorin group arrives at Notre Dame
12-06-42	Three more novices arrive at Notre Dame: William, Peter, Francis
2-13-43	Brothers Vincent, Lawrence, Joachim leave St. Peter's for Notre Dame with six novices and two postulants
2-27-43	Vincent group arrives at Notre Dame from St. Peter's
8-30-43	Second colony arrives from France
5-27-44	Death of Brother Paul, first to die at Notre Dame
6-09-44	Death of Brother Joachim at Notre Dame
9-10-44	Third colony arrives from France with Brother Vincent
12-08-44	First profession for Sisters at Notre Dame
7-12-45	Drowning of Brother Anselm at Madison, Indiana
5- -47	Colony from Ste. Croix arrives in Montreal

COLONIES

First Colony (9-13-41)

Brother Vincent (John Pieau), 44, d. 1890
Brother Joachim (Michael André), 32, d. 1844
Father Edward Sorin, 27, d. 1893
Brother Lawrence (John Ménage), 26, d. 1873
Brother Marie (Francis Xavier) (René Patoy), 21, d. 1896
Brother Anselm (Pierre Caillot), 16, d. 1845
Brother Gatian (Urbain Monsimer), 15, left 1850

Second Colony (6-30-43)

Father Francis Cointet, 25, d. 1854
Father Théophile de Lascoux-Marivault, 33, left 1847
Mr. Francis Gouesse (acolyte), 26, dismissed 1855
Five Marianite Sisters: Sister Mary of the Heart of Jesus
Sister Mary of Calvary
Sister Mary of Nazareth
Sister Mary of Bethlehem
Sister Mary of Providence (in Sept.)

Third Colony (9-10-44)

Brother Vincent (John Pieau), d. 1890
Father Alexis Granger, 27, d. 1893
Brother Augustus (Arsene Poignant), 20, d. 1900
Brother Justin (Louis Gautier), 43, d. 1870
Three Marianite Sisters

EARLY LOGISTICS

November, 1842

Leaving St. Peter's for Notre Dame:

Brother Marie (Francis Xavier), d. 1896
Brother Gatian, left 1850
Father Sorin, d. 1893
Five novices: Patrick (Michael Connelly), d. 1867
William (John O'Sullivan), left 1847
Basil (Timothy O'Neill), left 1850
Peter (James Tully), left 1847
Francis (Michael Disser), left 1846

Remaining at Vincennes:

Brother Vincent, d. 1890
Brother Anselm, d. 1845

Remaining at St. Peter's:

Brother Lawrence, d. 1873
Brother Joachim, d. 1844
Eight novices: Joseph (Charles Rother), left 1850
Thomas (James Donoghue), left 1852
Paul (John de la Hoyde), d. 1844
Ignatius (Thomas Everard), d. 1899
John (Frederick Steber?), left 1846
Celestine (Lawrence Kirwin), left 1843
Anthony (Francis Ress), left 1842

Stephen Chartier (Salvatorist?), left 1843
One postulant: Samuel O'Connell (Brother Mary Joseph), left 1846

February, 1843

Leaving St. Peter's for Notre Dame:

Brother Vincent, d. 1890
Brother Lawrence, d. 1873
Brother Joachim, d. 1844
Six novices: Joseph (Charles Rother), left 1850
John (Frederick Steber?), left 1846
Thomas (James W. Donoghoe), left 1852
Paul (John de la Hoyde), d. 1844
Ignatius (Thomas Everard), d. 1899
Celestine (Lawrence Kirwin), left 1843
Two postulants: Samuel O'Connell (Brother Mary Joseph), left 1846
Peter Berel (Brother Francis de Sales), d. 1862

Remaining in Vincennes:

Brother Anselm, d. 1845

NOVICES AT ST. PETER'S

12-28-41

Joseph (Charles Rother), 33

9-21-42 (First novitiate class)

Thomas (James William Donoghue), 18
Francis (Michael Disser), 17
Anthony (Francis Rees), 23
Peter (James Tully), 34
John (Federick Steber?), 22
Paul (John de la Hoyde), 26
Ignatius (Thomas Everard), 35
Patrick (Michael Connolly), 44

11-17-42

Celestine (Laurence Kirwin), 21
William (John O'Sullivan), 27
Basil (Timothy O'Neill), 32

12-04-42 (entered at St. Peter's, became novice at Notre Dame)

Mary Joseph (Samuel O'Connell), 23

8-   -43 (entered at St. Peter's, became novice at Notre Dame)

Francis de Sales (Peter Berel), 38

LETTERS LISTED BY WRITER

All letters are written to Father Edward Sorin, except where noted. All letters are held in the archives of the Indiana Province of the Congregation of Holy Cross, Notre Dame, Indiana, except for the letters to Father Basil Moreau, which are held in the archives of the Generalate of the Congregation of Holy Cross, Rome. The one letter to Mother Theodore is held in the archives of the Sisters of Providence, Terre Haute, Indiana.

HISTORICAL INDEX

(Data is given for pioneer Brothers and priests who figure in the early history of Notre Dame but who do not appear in the letters. Brother Vincent, Father Moreau, Father Sorin, and Bishop de la Hailandière are not referenced because they appear so frequently as to make citations of little help.)

Alexis, Brother (Patrick Day). Son of Maurice Day and Bridget Cudmore, he was born in 1819, at Ballinvence, County Limerick, Ireland. He entered the Community September 11, 1848, became a novice October 21, 1849, and was professed February 2, 1851. He died August 9, 1854, at Notre Dame.

Aloysius, Brother (James O'Hanlon). Born in County Clare, Ireland, in 1805, he entered the Community August 2, 1845, became a novice August 21, but left in August, 1846. He reentered the Community in 1855, taking the name Louis de Gonzague, the fourth Brother to be so named. Professed August 5, 1856, he worked in New Orleans as a teacher and shoemaker. He died at Notre Dame, July 4, 1860. *96 ff., 111, 235 ff., 244 ff., 256, 262 ff., 268 ff., 294, 296, 300.*

Ambrose, Brother (Edward McCartin). Born June 16, 1807, in Glasgow, Scotland, he entered the Community in 1847 at Notre Dame, but left in December, 1847.

André, Brother (Michael Walsh). Born in 1800 in Ireland, he entered the Community in the summer of 1843 and began his novitiate August 27, 1843, with Peter Berel (Brother Francis de Sales) and Francis Englishby (Brother Anthony). He left the Community June (or July) 1, 1844.

André, Brother (William Tiggert). Son of Michael Tiggert and Margaret O'Brien, he was born in 1824 at Gort, County Galway, Ireland. He entered the Community August 21, 1849, became a novice October 21, 1849, with Patrick Dea (Day) and Dennis Rogan, but left March 24, 1850.

Anselm, Brother (Pierre Caillot). Born March 19, 1825, in Gennes (Mayenne), he became a novice August 23, 1840, at Le Mans and went to America with the first colony in 1841 at the age of 16. He drowned in the Ohio River July 12, 1845. See Introduction. *3. 13. 16. 20, 75, 104, 112, 178.*

Anselm, Brother (John Staples). Born in 1810 in County Limerick, Ireland, he entered the novitiate August 38, 1847. He was professed on his death bed in 1852 and died April 22, 1852, in New Orleans and is buried there. He was the third Brother to be named Anselm. *264, 268.*

Anthony, Brother (Francis Ress). Born in 1812 in Grand Duchy of Baden, Germany, he entered the Community at St. Peter's on December 8, 1841, and became a novice August 21, 1842. He left the Community December 1, 1842, probably from St. Peter's, Indiana.

Anthony, Brother (Francis Englishby). Born in 1803 in Ireland, he entered the Community at Notre Dame in the summer of 1843 and began his novitiate August 27, 1843. He left in 1844. He was the seventh Brother to take the name Anthony.

Anthony, Brother (Thomas Dowling). Born in 1780 in Ireland, he entered the Community in the summer of 1843 and started his novitiate July 22, 1844. He took final vows on his death bed August 30, 1846, and died January 10, 1847, at Notre Dame. He was the eighth Brother to be named Anthony. *124, 153.*

Audran, Father Ernest. Ordained by Bishop de la Hailandière for the diocese of Vincennes. *186*

Augustine, Brother (Jeremy O'Leary). Born in Ireland in 1822, he entered the Community at Notre Dame May 30, 1843, and became a novice July 9, 1843. Accompanying Brother Vincent, he went to Le Mans to teach English in July, 1844. He returned to Notre Dame in September, 1845, to pursue studies for the priesthood, but left the Community. He was the second Brother to be given the name Augustine. His July 4, 1844, letter gives excellent details about hazardous ocean crossings. *37, 55, 59, 60, 70, 220.*

Augustine, Brother (Dennis Rogan). Son of Charles Rogan and Anne McSherry, he was born in 1793 at Bright, County Down, Ireland. He entered the Community September 20, 1848, became a novice October 21, 1849, and was professed August 29, 1851. He was a baker at Notre Dame and died October 12, 1876.

Augustus, Brother (Arsène-Victor Poignant). The son of René Poignant and Louise Berrie, he was born July 20, 1824, in La Quinte (Sarthe). He entered the Community April 8, 1839, became a novice August 22, and left for Indiana with Brother Vincent September 10, 1844. At Notre Dame he was a tailor and assistant master of novices and played the double bass in both the orchestra and brass band. He was professed on November 22, 1848. He died at Notre Dame July 10, 1900. He was the second Brother to be named Augustus. *72, 108, 176, 313, 317.*

Baquelin, Father Vincent. Ordained by Bishop Bruté in 1837, he was responsible in 1844 for St. Vincent's parish in Shelby County and parishes in Indianapolis and Columbus. *91, 146.*

Badin, Father Theodore Stephen. He was 60 when he first went to the South Bend area at the request of Chief Pokegan. He founded an orphanage and acquired the 524 acres known as St. Mary of the Lakes, the property later given to the Brothers of St. Joseph in 1842. *119, 120, 154, 155.*

Baroux, Father Louis Stephen Alexander. Born March 25, 1817, at St. Michel de Chavagnes (Sarthe), he entered the Community as

an ordained priest July 30, 1845, and came to America June 21, 1846. He returned to France, served in India, but returned to America to work with the Indians. He died September 14, 1897, at Silver Creek, Michigan, where he is buried. *92, 232, 315.*

Basil, Brother (Timothy O'Neil). Born in Ireland in 1810, he entered the Community in November, 1842, at St. Peter's, Indiana, and began his novitiate there November 17, 1842. He was a cooper. Moving to Notre Dame with Sorin in November, 1842, he took final vows March 19, 1847. He replaced John Steber at Ft. Wayne in 1846. In October, 1848, he was sent to teach in Brooklyn. On March 19, 1849, he was reassigned to New Orleans to teach at the orphanage with Brother Vincent but left the Community May 12, 1850. *153, 227, 232, 244 ff., 254, 255, 259 ff., 281 ff., 294, 296, 300, 305 ff., 314, 318 ff., 332 ff.*

Bazin, Father John. Born in Lyons, France, in 1796, he came to the United States in 1830 to Mobile, Alabama. He was appointed the third bishop of Vincennes in 1847. He died April 23, 1848. *182, 228.*

Benedict, Brother (Patrick Fitzpatrick). Born in Ireland in 1803, he entered the Community August 2, 1845, and took final vows October 22, 1848. He taught in Ft. Wayne in 1848 (after Brother Basil) with Brother Emmanual. Each had forty students and drew a salary of $100 for the year. He was assigned as the first Indiana missionary to Bengal in 1852. Leaving from Plymouth, England, the colony took seven months to sail around Africa and reach Bengal. The letters reprinted here show the ups and downs that he experienced teaching in Washington, Indiana. He died in Bengal July 18, 1855, and is buried in Chittagong. *165.*

Benoit, Brother (Michael Gillard). Born October 8, 1808, at Housse (Manche) to Guillaume Gillard and Jeanne Noel, he entered the Community September 19, 1842, in France, became a novice December 18, 1842, and was professed August 22, 1845. Sorin brought him to Notre Dame in 1846. He died there December 20, 1873, the sixth Brother in the Congregation to be named Benoit, the first of only two to be so named in the United States. For twenty years the chief prefect of the seniors at Notre Dame, he was best remembered as an accomplished disciplinarian. *125, 265.*

Bernard, Brother (Patrick Leo Foley). Born in Leitirm in 1820, he entered the Community of Holy Cross August 18, 1845, and was professed March 19, 1847. A teacher before entering, he was assigned to Ft. Wayne and southern Indiana for several years. He joined the Jesuits in July, 1848, but apparently returned to Holy Cross. Then he withdrew in May, 1861, but reentered in February, 1877, taking the name John de Matha. He died April 28, 1895. In the letter reprinted here in which he explains his reasons for leaving the Community (letter #4), we get some sense of the frustrations that a professional man had when joining the rudimentary group in its early years at Notre Dame. *106,137, 146, 153, 181, 201.*

Blanc, Anthony. Consecrated a bishop in November, 1835, he was named the first archbishop of New Orleans in July, 1850. He died June 20, 1860. *227.*

Bruté, Simon Gabriel. Born March 20, 1779, in Rennes, France, he was ordained in 1808 and was named first bishop of Vincennes in 1834. He died in 1839. *51, 181.*

Celestine, Brother (Lawrence Kirwin). Born in 1821 in Ireland, he entered the Community August 27, 1842, at St. Peter's and became a novice November 17, 1842. He probably went to Notre Dame with Brother Vincent February 13, 1843, but left the Community September 4, 1843, from Notre Dame. *28, 33.*

Charles, Brother (Charles Riley). Born in England in 1799, he entered the Community November 23, 1843, and began his novitiate March 19, 1844. He left the Community August 1, 1845, according to one matricule, an obvious impossibility because of his September 6, 1845, letter signed "Brother Charles." According to the General Matricule, he left in July of 1846. The two letters of his that remain are well written and attest to a bright mind which was nonetheless a source of trouble to his superiors.

Charles Borromeo, Brother (Charles Haemers). Born in Vinkel, Belgium, he received the habit on August 21, 1845. He left July 2, 1846. *153.*

Charles Borromeo, Brother (August Mary Thebaut). Born March 4, 1818, at Izé (Ille et Vilaine), he entered the Community at Le Mans December 24, 1846, and came to Notre Dame in 1847, where he was professed October 22, 1848. He was the first man to make the three vows all on one day for a year. He was recalled to France in 1858. In the fall of 1870 he passed through Montreal and left secretly for New Orleans November 12, 1870. He died November 29, 1893, at Notre Dame.

Chartier, Stephen. Born in 1809 at Montreal, he entered the Community at St. Peter's October 12, 1842, and became a novice October 15, 1842, possibly with the intention of being a priest (Salvatorist). He left the Community February 9, 1843, from St. Peter's. *17.*

Chassé, Father John Baptist. Ordained by Bishop de la Hailandière, he was responsible in 1844 for the parish in Queret's Prairie, Knox County. *176, 177, 213.*

Cointet, Father Francis Louis. Born February 26, 1816, in La Roë (Mayenne), he entered the Community May 13, 1843, as a priest (ordained in 1839). He became a novice August 19, 1843, at Notre Dame after bringing the second colony to America May 23, 1843. He was professed September 5, 1846, and died of yellow fever in New Orleans September 19, 1854. *48, 97, 120, 124, 174, 175, 190, 317,320, 336.*

de la Hailandière, Celestine. Ordained in 1825 in France, he was named bishop of Vincennes in 1839 to succeed Simon Bruté. A man of unpredictable hostility, he was a cross to the missionaries who worked in his diocese. He resigned in 1847, returned to France, and died there in 1882.

de Lascoux-Marivault, Father Théophile. Born October 28, 1810, at Le Blanc (Indre), he entered the Community as a priest in August, 1842, and began his novitiate on September 8, 1842. He left France for Notre Dame on May 31, 1843. He left the Community March 14, 1847, while substituting as a minister to the Indians at Pokagon, Michigan. *48, 66.*

de St. Palais, Father Maurice. Born in 1811 in La Salvetat, France, he came to Vincennes in 1836. He was consecrated the fourth bishop of the diocese in January, 1849. He died June 28, 1877. *111, 131, 139, 141, 168, 169, 178, 181, 187, 213, 223, 339.*

Delaune, Father Julian. Pastor of St. Michael's in Madison, Indiana, from August, 1842, until June, 1846, he opened the school there in September, 1843, first in the church, then in the basement of the church. He then directed St. Mary's College (Kentucky). He died in Paris May 4, 1846, at the age of 37. *25, 32, 41, 44, 61,78, 79, 102, 111 ff., 188 ff., 197, 198, 216.*

Dominic, Brother (Michael Wolf). Born August 28, 1821, in Ingenheim, Germany, he entered the Community in 1844, became a novice December 25, 1844, and was professed October 22, 1848. He died September 16, 1854, at Notre Dame. *153, 160, 341.*

Doyle, Father William. Ordained by Bishop de la Hailandière, he was pastor at Washington, Indiana, in 1848. *194, 201.*

Ducoudray, Father Louis. In 1844 he was responsible for St. Genevieve's parish in Faux-Chenal, Knox County. *203, 213.*

Dupontavice, Reverend Hippolite. Ordained by Bishop de la Hailandière in November, 1839, for the diocese of Vincennes. *180, 195, 196, 200, 209.*

Dusaulx, Emile Alexander Xavier. Born on December 11, 1820, in Lisieux, he entered the Community October 25, 1844, to be a priest, began his novitiate May 22, 1845, and came to Notre Dame

in 1846. He left the Community November 1, 1850, but probably returned in 1858. *188.*

Eloi, Brother (John Leray). He was born on April 23, 1818, in Autrain (Ille et Vilaine), became a novice on June 10, 1841, left for Notre Dame May 31, 1843. He was a mechanic/locksmith. He left the Community in 1845. He was the second Brother to be given the name Eloi.

Emmanual, Brother (Anthony Wopperman). Born in Germany in 1820, he received the habit at Notre Dame on December 25, 1844. Professed in August, 1845, he taught German pupils in Fort Wayne in 1847. He withdrew August 1, 1850. *265.*

Francis, Brother (Michael Disser). Born in Alsace in 1825, he entered the Community at St. Peter's, Indiana, December 6, 1841, and became a novice August 21, 1842. He went to Notre Dame with Sorin in November, 1842, one of the six original Brothers to set foot on the site. Sorin's chronicle notes that in in 1844 Father Delaune in Madison, Indiana, asked for a teaching Brother. Sorin sent Brother Anselm, but when Anselm drowned in July, 1845, Sorin replaced him with Brother Mary Joseph and Brother Francis. Unexpected difficulties, however, caused them both to quit the Community, Brother Francis in November, 1846. See Brother Mary Joseph's letter #9 for insight into the problems with clergy and parents in Madison. Brother Bernard Foley was then sent, but he quit to join the Jesuits in July, 1848. Brother Francis's letters show a man of very poor spelling: he spells "water" three different ways. It is little wonder that such pioneer teachers were often frustrated in the classroom. The tenor of the letters indicates a gentle man, dependent for survival upon tougher men like Brother Mary Joseph. *96, 102, 106, 111 ff., 135, 153, 225.*

Francis de Sales, Brother (Peter Berel). Born in Monthault (Ille et Vilaine) in 1805, he entered the Community in August, 1842, and became a novice August 27, 1843, at Notre Dame and was professed there October 22, 1848. In 1850 he taught in New Orleans, but by 1856 he was teaching in France at Vassy. He died January 15, 1862, in Le Mans. He was the second Brother in the Community to be

Guegnen, Father John. Ordained by Bishop de la Hailandière for the diocese of Vincennes. *157, 201, 223.*

Ignatius, Brother (Thomas Everard). Born in December, 1817, at Drogheda, County Meath, Ireland, he entered the Community at St. Peter's July 26, 1842, and became a novice August 21, 1842. He went to Notre Dame in March, 1843, and was professed August 30, 1846. He worked many years at St. Isidore's College, New Orleans, before he died at Notre Dame, April 28, 1899. Brother Bernard Gervais stayed with him several nights in his final illness. He was the fifth Brother to be named Ignatius in the Community. *21, 212, 249, 264, 335.*

Jerome, Brother (Felix Riley). Born in 1815 in County Meath, Ireland, he entered May 2, 1844, became a novice August 21, 1845, and was professed October 22, 1848. He died November 11, 1871. He was a manual laborer.

Joachim, Brother (William Michael André). He was born June 3, 1809, at St. Martin de Connée (Mayenne), entered the Community June 10, 1841, and was professed July 25, 1841. He came to America with the first colony in 1841 as a tailor, but he cooked at St. Peter's and Notre Dame. The first of the French pioneer Brothers to die (April 13, 1844), giving in to tuberculosis, he was the second Brother in the Community to be named Joachim. *21, 48, 50.*

John, Brother (Frederick Steber ?). Born at Trieste (Illyrie) in 1815, he entered the Community, it is believed, January 12, 1842. Sent to France in 1843 by Sorin to help bring back the second colony, he missed them as they had already left for America. After returning to Notre Dame with Sister Mary of Providence, he went back to France to study for the priesthood, but left the Community in August, 1846. He has been confused, perhaps irretrievably, in Holy Cross records with "Brother John (Jeremiah Cronin)," for whom no grave exists at Notre Dame. The latter may have been the Brother John who died October 4, 1858, in New Orleans and is mentioned by Moreau in the circular letter for January 2, 1859. The matricule in the Midwest Province Archives gives Dover, England, as a birthplace for Frederick Steber and the year 1820. He was the first Brother to teach in Fort Wayne (February, 1843). After he left the Community, he supposedly married a Protestant in Milwaukee. Mother Theodore Guerin's diary has two mentions of a Brother John, one for November 24, 1843, when he brought her letters from Ruillé, France, and another for January 7, 1844, when he brought her letters from the Sisters at St. Peter's, Indiana. This Brother John, however, may have been a member of the Eudist Community. Sorin, in a letter to Moreau (April 10, 1843), refers to Brother John as one of the first persons to greet Sorin in New York City when the first colony arrived in 1841. Sorin mentions that John joined the Community eight months later and refers to him as the greatest hope for the house and "my greatest predilection." Sorin continues: "Time illum ut mes viscera suscipe—si habes me socium, suscipe illum sicut me, for I have no one here who is closer to me and who understands me better. Neminere eum habeo tam unani mem." When Sorin would go out to preach on mission, he would say a few words in French, and then Brother John would explain Catholic doctrine at length in English to the assembled congregation. Apparently assigned to teach at St. Peter's or Vincennes, he was less than edifying, according to Anselm's letter #7. *32, 36 ff., 48, 63, 105, 220.*

John the Evangelist, Brother (John Thornton). Born in 1806 in Munster, Ireland, he entered the Community October 24, 1844, became a novice December 25, 1844, and was professed August 30, 1846. A manual laborer, he died June 19, 1878, at Notre Dame.

John Baptist, Brother (William Rodgers). Born in 1815 in County Kildare, Ireland, he entered October 15, 1844, became a novice August 21, 1845, and was professed August 30, 1846. He died October 13, 1846. *111, 124, 153.*

John of the Cross, Brother (Michael Callon). Son of Patrick Callon and Catherine Nee, he was born in County Monaghan, Ireland in 1819. He entered the Community October 13, 1847, and became a novice March 25, 1848, at Indianapolis, but left August 28, 1849.

Joseph, Brother (Charles Rother). Born at Riedesheim, Germany, in 1808, he was the first postulant to join the Community in America (October 2, 1841). He was already in charge of a school at St. Peter's, Indiana, when the first colony got there. He became a novice on December 28, 1841, and went to Notre Dame in March, 1843, where he was professed on August 27. In 1844 he was sent to Indianapolis to sell Catholic books for the bishop. He bought property without authorization and thus precipitated a series of events which forced Sorin to move the novitiate to Indianapolis in order to placate the bishop. He left the Community February 5, 1850, but kept the name Brother Joseph as he ran St. Vincent's Male Orphan Asylum in Vincennes until his incompetence forced the bishop to turn the place over to Mother Theodore Guerin. When the orphanage was moved to Highland, near Vincennes, Brother Joseph lived close by as a recluse and was eventually buried in the cemetery there with a gravestone inscribed "Brother Joseph." *21, 23, 120, 121, 125, 131, 151, 152, 156, 168, 179, 300.*

Justin, Brother (Louis Gautier). The son of Louis Gautier and Julienne Poirier, he was born February 2, 1801, at Vivoin (Sarthe). He entered the Community June 17, 1838, became a novice August 22, 1839, and was professed August 22, 1840. He left for Notre Dame with Brother Vincent's colony September 10, 1844. He died at Notre Dame December 20, 1870, the second Brother to be named Justin. *70, 72, 73, 125.*

Lawrence, Brother (John Menage). Born March 12, 1815, in Brécé (Mayenne), he entered the Community July 7, 1840, became a novice August 23, 1840, and was professed July 25, 1841. He came to America with the first colony in August, 1841, and died at Notre Dame April 4, 1873. See Introduction. *13, 20 ff., 43, 44, 97, 115, 119 ff., 124, 127, 190.*

Lefevere, Peter Paul. Consecrated coadjutor bishop of Detroit in November, 1841, he died March 4, 1869. *74.*

Letourneau, Moses Francis. Born May 13, 1822, at Detroit, he entered August 19, 1843, became a novice December 25, 1845, but left in August, 1846, according to one matricule, or in March, 1847, according to another.

Lewis, Brother (Louis Derouin). Born February 21, 1829, at St. Jean, Canada, he entered May 12, 1845, at Notre Dame, became a novice February 24, 1846, but left May 25, 1850. *134, 153.*

Liguori, Sister Mary. A Sister of Providence at St. Mary-of-the-Woods. Born August 11, 1818, she was professed August 19, 1842, and died January 29, 1847. *113.*

Louis de Gonzague, Brother (James O'Hanlon). See Aloysius, Brother.

Louis de Gonzague, Brother (Robert Sidley). Born in 1830 in County Limberick, Ireland, he entered November 7, 1847, and became a novice Mary 20, 1848, at Indianapolis. He left August 27, 1852. *253, 265 ff., 278, 281 ff., 306, 308, 311 ff., 322, 324, 327, 328, 330, 332.*

McDermott, Father Patrick. Ordained by Bishop de la Hailandière for the diocese of Vincennes. *194, 195, 213.*

Marie, Brother. See Francis Xavier, Brother.

Martin, Father August. He came to America from Rennes, France, where he was chaplain at the Royal College. In Vincennes he served as vicar general of St. Francis Xavier Cathedral until 1843. He greeted the Brothers when they arrived at Logansport October 2, 1841, where he was pastor of St. Vincent de Paul parish. He was later consecrated the first bishop of Natchitoches (Louisiana). *27 ff., 38, 42, 43, 47, 52, 75, 81 ff., 95 ff.*

Mary of Calvary, Sister (Marie Robineau). Born in France June 2, 1818, she was professed at Le Mans May 28, 1843, in preparation for departure two days later for America. She returned to France in 1865 and died at Le Mans January 24, 1884. *227, 232, 306, 313, 314, 319, 325 ff., 332.*

Mary of the Cenacle, Sister (Louise Naveau). Born in France August 10, 1810, she received the habit at Le Mans June 23, 1846. She was professed at Bertrand, Michigan, September 10, 1846, and died at Ft. Wayne April 28, 1848. She is buried at St. Mary's, Notre Dame. *117.*

Mary of the Five Wounds, Sister (Elizabeth Paillet). Born at Haut Mearn, France, November 5, 1816, she was professed December 8, 1844, in the Chapel of the Immaculate Heart of Mary on the Island at Notre Dame. She left the Congregation in New York City after 1856. *232, 303, 306, 314, 326, 327.*

Mary of the Heart of Jesus, Sister (Marie Savary). Born in Quelaine, France, March 25, 1824, she received the habit April 25, 1842, in Le Mans where she was professed May 28, 1843, in preparation for the American mission. She went to Canada in 1847 and left the Congregation August 16, 1865. *126.*

Mary of Providence, Sister (Marie Daget). Born in France March 22, 1806, she was professed at Bertrand, Michigan, January 22, 1847. She died at St. Mary's, Notre Dame, May 24, 1879. *303.*

Mary Joseph, Brother (Samuel O'Connell). Born in Ireland in 1819, he entered the Community December 4, 1842, and went to Notre Dame with Brother Vincent February 13, 1843, where he became a novice March 19, 1943, the first postulant to do so at Notre Dame. He taught in Vincennes 1844–45 and followed Anselm at Madison in 1845. Brother Francis joined him in 1846, but Sorin says difficulties caused them both to quit. Mary Joseph's letter #3 gives us a contemporary view of Father Weinzloephen's sufferings. Mary Joseph's eye for detail makes him a valuable letter writer, e.g. in the matter of nineteenth-century banking practices (letter #6). Letter #9 may solve finally the question of why Mary Joseph and Francis left the congregation. Sorin sent them to Madison in October, 1846, without authorization from the pastor, the vicar general St. Palais, who gave a cold reception to the two weary Brothers. The machinations of the doting parent Mr. Griffin did not help the situation in Madison. Finally Mary Joseph tells Sorin of his intention to leave for Kentucky with Father Delaune to open a college (St. Mary's). He left the Community November 12, 1846. *51, 52, 57, 65, 79 ff., 87, 93, 96, 98, 117, 135, 153, 177, 178, 181.*

Mathias, Brother (Leopold Kock). Born February 28, 1820, at Hunfeld-Kurhessen, Germany, he entered October 7, 1845, became a novice February 24, 1846, at Notre Dame, but left October 15, 1853.

Maximus, Brother (Thomas Shelly). Born in 1797 in Ireland, he entered July 12, 1845, but changed his name to Brother James in 1848. A gardener, he died October 6, 1870.

Michael, Brother (James Flynn). Born in County Connaught, Ireland, in 1810, he entered the Community May 5, 1845, became a novice August 21, 1845, and took final vows October 22, 1848. After teaching in Vincennes, he worked in the laundry at Notre Dame. In 1860 he was fire chief at Notre Dame and worked in the lime yard. Later he assisted in the steamhouse and served as night watchman. He died April 2, 1884. *165, 178, 286, 287.*

Moreau, Basil. By combining the Brothers of St. Joseph with his own auxiliary priests in 1837, he founded the Congregation of Holy Cross and served as its director until 1866. He founded a community of Marianite Sisters of Holy Cross in 1841. Under his leadership, missionaries were sent to Algeria, the United States, Canada, and Bengal. He died January 20, 1873.

Patrick, Brother (Michael Connelly). Born in 1797 or 1798, in County Meath, Ireland, he entered the Community at St. Peter's on August 13, 1842, and became a novice on August 21. He accompanied Sorin to Notre Dame in November, 1842. A farmer, he was professed August 30,1846, and died April 18, 1867 at Notre Dame. He was the second Brother in the Community to be given the name Patrick.

Paul, Brother (John Bray de la Hoyde). Born in 1816 in County Meath, Ireland, he entered the Community July 17, 1842, at St.

Peter's and was accepted as a novice August 21, 1842. He had lived in New Orleans for seven years, working as a clerk. He went to Notre Dame with Brother Vincent in February, 1843, but died May 27, 1844, the first pioneer Brother to die at Notre Dame. He is the first named in the act of incorporation for the Brothers of St. Joseph in South Bend, January 15, 1844, along with Brother Augustine (Jeremiah O'Leary), Brother Mary Joseph (Samuel O'Connell), and Brother André (Michael Walsh). *21, 23.*

Paul, Brother (Peter Keegan). Born in Ireland in 1810, he entered the Community October 17, 1843, and started his novitiate August 21, 1844. He left the Community September 15, 1845, the fifth Brother to be given the name Paul.

Peter, Brother (James Tully). Born in 1808 in County Meath, Ireland, he entered the Community at St. Peter's April 15, 1842, and became a novice August 21, 1842. A farmer, he went to Notre Dame with Sorin November 16, 1842. He left the Community May 10, 1847. *153, 155.*

Placidus, Brother (Urban Allard). Born February 2, 1812, in France, he entered the Community June 4, 1838, and came to America in July, 1846. In February, 1850, he was sent to look for gold in California, but he died there and is buried in Placerville. *125, 150, 316.*

Rector, Father. Title for Basil Moreau, founder of the Congregation of Holy Cross.

Refour, Father Francis. Born June 10, 1821, at Sarcé (Sarthe), he entered February 28, 1845, came to America with Sorin in 1846, but left May 2, 1851, from Canada.

St. Francis Xavier, Sister (Irma LeFer de la Motte), the intrepid Sister of Providence who came to St. Mary-of-the-Woods with the first colony in 1841. She was born April 15, 1816, and was professed July 18, 1841. She died January 31, 1856. *3.*

Saunier, Father Augustin. Born in France December 29, 1814, he entered the novitiate July 14, 1838. He left for Canada April 25, 1847, and came to the United States in 1848. He left the Community from St. Mary's College (Kentucky) July 18, 1848. *173 ff., 188 ff., 197, 198, 216.*

Shawe, Father Michael. Ordained by Bishop Bruté, he was assistant vicar general to Father August Martin at Vincennes in 1842. *9, 10, 26, 31, 51, 75, 86, 87, 139, 196, 251.*

Silvester, Brother (Patrick McCarthy). Born in 1811 in Ireland, he entered November 4, 1844, became a novice December 25, 1844, and left September 4, 1845.

Sorin, Father Edward. The son of Julien Sorin and Marie Anne Louise Gresland, he was born February 6, 1814, in La Roche (Mayenne). Ordained May 27, 1838, he entered the Community April 10, 1839, was professed August 15, 1840, and left for America August 5, 1841. He died at Notre Dame October 31, 1893.

Spalding, Martin John. Consecrated coadjutor bishop of Kentucky in September, 1848, he was transferred to Baltimore in May, 1864. He died February 7, 1872. *192, 301.*

Stephen, Brother (Finton Moore). Born in County Queens, Ireland, in 1811, he entered September 14, 1844, became a novice September 25, 1844, was professed August 30, 1846. After serving as porter and sacristan at Notre Dame, he was sent by Sorin to Illinois to solicit money for Notre Dame. In 1855 he directed the orphan asylum in New Orleans, and in 1857 he was assigned to supervise apprentices at Notre Dame. In his final years, he served as engineer at St. Mary's and was assistant postmaster at Notre Dame. He died February 2, 1869. *153, 243, 251, 257.*

Theodore, Mother (Guerin). Recognized as the American foundress of the Sisters of Providence at St. Mary-of-the-Woods. She was born October 2, 1798, and professed September 8, 1825. Her sufferings under Bishop de la Hailandière are well documented.

She died May 14, 1856, and was declared Venerable by the Catholic Church July 11, 1992. *10, 29, 47, 83, 102.*

Théodule, Brother (Francis Barbé). Born in Mayenne, France, in 1818, he entered the Community of Holy Cross July 2, 1838, and took final vows August 22, 1843. He came to America with Father Sorin in 1846 and was appointed steward at Notre Dame in 1847. His early letters from St. Mary's (Kentucky) give us useful insight into the troubles at that foundation. In March of 1849, he was sent to New Orleans where he was appointed director of St. Mary's Orphanage a year later. He caught yellow fever and died there June 25, 1853. Of all the letters, his are the most difficult to translate, not because his sentences are elegant like Brother Vincent's, but because his language is very colloquial. *125, 150, 156, 173, 175, 176, 227, 232, 300, 305 ff., 313 ff., 322, 325, 326, 335 ff.*

Thomas, Brother (James William Donoghoe). Born in New Orleans in 1824, he entered the Community November 3, 1841, and was accepted as a novice at St. Peter's August 21, 1842. He went to Notre Dame in February, 1843, with Brother Vincent. He left the Community September 1, 1852. *21, 129, 169, 178, 255, 257, 264, 268, 282, 287, 300.*

Timothy, Brother (William Coffey). Born in 1804, County Meath, Ireland, he entered in 1845, became a novice August 30, 1846, and was professed November 1, 1852. A manual laborer, he died May 29, 1873.

Victor, Brother (Thomas John Walsh). Born in County Dublin, Ireland, May 10, 1810, he entered the novitiate at Notre Dame in 1848, and was professed May 26, 1850. Sent to New Orleans, he was in charge of apprentices, but died there December 19, 1852.

Vincent, Brother (John Pieau). Born at Courbeville, in 1797, he entered the Josephites November 1, 1821, and became a novice in August, 1822, under Father Dujarié, founder of the Brothers of St. Joseph at Ruillé-sur-Loir. He left for America with the first colony in 1841 to be Master of Novices and died at Notre Dame, July 23, 1890, at age 93. See Introduction.

Weinzoepfel, Father Romain. A priest of the Evansville diocese, he was born April 13, 1813, in Soultz, Alsace. He entered the Community of Holy Cross as a priest in 1845, became a novice July 5, 1845, but left April 12, 1846, because his bishop required his return to the diocese. He died a Benedictine at St. Meinrad's Abbey. The sad case of his being unjustly convicted by an Evansville court on a rape charge is well documented. Details appear in letters of the pioneer Brothers. *13, 26, 41, 45, 49, 75, 86.*

William, Brother (John O'Sullivan). Born in 1815 in Ireland, he entered the Community at St. Peter's, Indiana, August 27, 1842, and was accepted as a novice November 17, 1842. He went immediately to Notre Dame with Sorin but left the Community August 25, 1847. *153.*

Zamion, Father. Priest of the Vincennes diocese and pastor at Ft. Wayne. He died in Logansport in May, 1843. *27.*

Top: Brother Vincent (John Pieau).

Bottom: Brother Lawrence (John Menage).

Top: Brother Francis Xavier (René Patoy).

Bottom: Brother Augustus (Arsène-Victor Poignant).

Top: Brother Benoit (Michael Gillard).

Bottom: Bishop Celestin de la Hailandière.

Top: Artist's sketch of the arrival at Notre Dame.

Bottom: Old College, first building constructed by the Brothers at Notre Dame.